Students Taking Charge in Grades K–5

Discover how to design innovative learning environments that increase student ownership so they can achieve at high levels and meet rigorous standards. *Students Taking Charge* shows you how to create student-driven classrooms that empower learners through problem-based learning and differentiation, where students pose questions and actively seek answers. Technology is then used seamlessly throughout the day for information, communication, collaboration, and product generation.

You'll find out how to:

♦ Design an *Authentic Learning Unit*, which is at the core of the *Learner-Active, Technology-Infused Classroom*, aimed at engaging students;

♦ Understand the structures needed to support its implementation and empower students;

♦ Build the facilitation strategies that will move students from engagement to empowerment to efficacy.

This new K–5 edition offers a more detailed look into elementary school implementation. With the book's practical examples and step-by-step guidelines, you'll be able to start designing your innovative classroom immediately!

Nancy Sulla is an author, national speaker, and thought leader in transforming learning environments to build student engagement, empowerment, and efficacy. As the creator of the *Learner-Active, Technology-Infused Classroom*™ and founder of IDE Corp. (Innovative Designs for Education), Dr. Sulla leads her educational consulting firm in the pursuit of equity-focused instructional design, positioning students to change the world. Learn more at nancysulla.com.

Also Available from Nancy Sulla
(www.routledge.com/eyeoneducation)

Building Executive Function:
The Missing Link to Student Achievement

It's Not What You Teach but How:
7 Insights to Making the CCSS Work for You

Students Taking Charge in Grades 6–12:
Inside the Learner-Active, Technology-Infused Classroom

Students Taking Charge:
Implementation Guide for Leaders
With Tanya Bosco and Julie Marks

Students Taking Charge in Grades K–5

Inside the Learner-Active, Technology-Infused Classroom

Nancy Sulla

Routledge
Taylor & Francis Group

NEW YORK AND LONDON

First published 2019
by Routledge
52 Vanderbilt Avenue, New York, NY 10017

and by Routledge
2 Park Square, Milton Park, Abingdon, Oxon, OX14 4RN

Routledge is an imprint of the Taylor & Francis Group, an informa business

First edition published by Eye On Education 2011

Library of Congress Cataloging-in-Publication Data
A catalog record for this book has been requested

ISBN: 978-1-138-29454-7 (hbk)
ISBN: 978-0-415-34923-9 (pbk)
ISBN: 978-1-315-22919-5 (ebk)

Typeset in Palatino
by Apex CoVantage, LLC

Portions of this book were previously published as *Students Taking Charge: Inside the Learner Active, Technology-Infused Classroom*, © 2011.

Visit the eResources: www.routledge.com/9780415349239

Printed in Canada

Dedication

To the three pillars in my work: God, who always has a great plan for my days; *Team IDE*—a dedicated group of people who push my thinking and innovate better than any team I know; and the amazing educators who take the words on these pages and put them into action in schools, giving me inspiration and fueling my continued work.

Dedication

Contents

Meet the Author

Nancy Sulla is an author, national speaker, and thought leader in transforming learning environments to build student engagement, empowerment, and efficacy. As the creator of the *Learner-Active, Technology-Infused Classroom*™ and founder of IDE Corp. (Innovative Designs for Education), Dr. Sulla leads her educational consulting firm in the pursuit of equity-focused instructional design, positioning students to change the world. She holds a B.A. in education from Fairleigh Dickinson University, an M.A. in computer science from Montclair State University, and an Ed.D. in educational administration from Fordham University. Her diverse background includes teaching at the elementary, middle school, high school, and college levels; working as a computer programmer and systems analyst; and leading teachers as a district administrator prior to launching IDE Corp. Learn more at nancysulla.com.

eResources

Keep an eye out for the eResources icon throughout this book, which indicates a resource is available online. Resources mentioned in this book can be downloaded, printed, used to copy/paste text, and/or manipulated to suit your individualized use. You can access these downloads by visiting the book product page on our website: www.routledge. com/products/9780415349239. Then click on the tab that reads "eResources" and then select the file(s) you need. The file(s) will download directly to your computer.

Introduction

I am pleased to offer this new edition of *Students Taking Charge*, focusing on K–5 classrooms, thus allowing me to provide you with even more examples and strategies. As always, my thinking continues to evolve, so this edition offers new insights into designing student-driven classrooms, building student engagement, empowerment, and efficacy. I am indebted to the many teachers who run *Learner-Active, Technology-Infused Classrooms*, tweet about them, and share their stories with me. Their experiences help educators collectively take school to the next level.

Passion lies at the intersection of a dream and success. Those who are passionate about their craft typically have a dream of what can be, and have had glimpses of that dream in small pockets of success along the way. That combination fuels a desire to keep moving forward, regardless of personal sacrifice, fully believing that this is the road on which they are meant to travel.

The field of education is graced with many passionate teachers—those who believe that all students can learn and are fueled by those moments when students perform beyond their expectations. The Greek philosopher Heraclitus said that you can never step in the same river twice, because the river is constantly changing. So it is with the classroom. Each day brings newness: students are constantly changing, growing, and learning; passionate teachers are continually honing their craft; society possesses a momentum that repeatedly presents new challenges for schools.

Passionate teachers see beyond the barriers; they know there is a better way to prepare young people for their future and to unleash in them all the potential they possess. They explore new ways of approaching teaching and learning, and, fueled by isolated and sometimes small encounters with success, they forge ahead. I have no doubt that the relentless pursuit of instructional innovation by the passionate few will overcome the barriers of resistance and create innovative, adaptive learning environments that will both serve and form society in ways beyond our current imagination.

My own passion for changing the world through education is fueled by the *Learner-Active, Technology-Infused Classroom* students who thank me and share their stories; their dedicated teachers who challenge themselves daily and work tirelessly to make their students' educational experiences more productive and meaningful; and their school and district leaders who courageously find ways to make it happen, battle the status quo, and take the risk to forge a new and innovative path for school. I am blessed to be joined by the amazing group of educators at IDE Corp. Their passion and dedication to the educators and students we serve is inspiring; they challenge my thinking and enhance the collective work we do.

My Journey

My vision for the *Learner-Active, Technology-Infused Classroom* was inspired by many moments throughout my life. When I was ten, I began running a summer school program for the neighborhood children; by the time I was twelve, I was charging fees and holding graduation ceremonies for parents. In some ways, it was a one-room schoolhouse; I had neighborhood children of all ages anxious to come to my school for the three days a week it was open, including those who were gifted, those with learning difficulties, and a teenager with cerebral palsy. To meet their needs, I assigned varying work and spent a lot of my time working in small groups and with individual students. I still look back in amazement that the neighborhood kids hated to miss a day of summer school, given that we truly worked the entire time! One bright and talented young man had been attending my school since age three. When his mom had her first parent–teacher conference, his teacher pointed out how far ahead of his peers he was, no doubt because of the private school he was attending. Today, the young man is a judge, and I like to think his early experiences in "school" helped to fuel his own passion for his craft.

An early experience in my teaching career inspired me to solidify my vision and articulate it so that others could join my quest for the ultimate learning environment. It was the late 1970s, my second year in teaching and first year teaching middle school. I was assigned the lower-level math students who had repeatedly failed the state tests. I remember starting class asking my eighth graders to take out their books, only to find that few had brought them. Paper? Pencil? My efforts to recreate the traditions experienced in my own schooling seemed futile. One day, I asked my students to simply show up for class the next day—no books, no paper, no pencils. They all complied. I had pushed back the desks and arranged the chairs in a circle. I explained that I wanted to keep my job and they needed to learn math, and I asked them for the solution to my dilemma. My students pointed out that math instruction was boring and they didn't see the point.

I suggested that perhaps I could design projects that would make the learning more meaningful; they agreed to give it a try.

I don't remember the first project I designed, nor the entire complement, but I do recall a few. We created scale drawings of birdhouses to build; we used paper plates to create polyhedral disco balls (it was, after all, the 1970s, and John Travolta's nephews were in my classes). In those days, teachers could take their students out to play kickball on a nice day. My students would head out with clipboards to track the progress of the game; once inside, they would run the statistics on the game and analyze it in light of previous games. When the state tests arrived, my students did quite well, with almost all of them passing. I remember my principal asking me what I did; I didn't know. He persisted and pointed out that my students performed particularly well on percentages, but I simply shrugged my shoulders and admitted I hadn't gotten to that chapter yet.

Years later, I realized what had happened. I had designed higher-order problems for my students to solve and then provided them with the resources and support they needed to learn. I realized, too, that the problems did not encompass only the skills in a single chapter of the textbook; they spanned many chapters. I would venture to say we worked with percentages, for example, in most of the problems. I saw the power of students learning from a *felt need* in an authentic context, and that year and the successes my teaching style yielded never left me. The personal computer had not even been invented yet.

It was the invention of the desktop computer and its arrival in schools that further fueled my vision for the classroom. Teachers are faced with a classroom of students with varying needs and interests; computers provide them with a wealth of opportunities to help students learn. In the early 1980s, I was a district-level administrator when I decided to make "an offer to innovate" to a couple of teachers. Alysse Daches and Cyndie Bach taught fourth and fifth grade, respectively. They were both among the daring few who purchased desktop computers for their homes. I asked how they would like to have five desktop computers for their classrooms, and they jumped at the chance. Over the course of the next few months, I saw a new vision for the classroom spring to life. On one visit, they told me they felt guilty that the computers sat vacant while they were teaching lessons; I suggested that perhaps they could reduce the number of whole-class lessons in favor of other means of providing instruction. On another visit they told me how challenging it was for the children to push together desks of all different sizes and attempt to work collaboratively. I replaced the desks with forty-two-inch round tables. Structure by structure, strategy by strategy, my vision for instruction took shape. More than twenty years later, with myriad classroom teachers implementing the *Learner-Active, Technology-Infused Classroom* across the grade levels, I wrote the first edition of this book to capture the essence of this instructional framework to share with passionate teachers everywhere. This second edition is split into two books to offer a more detailed look into K–5 implementation and 6–12 implementation, allowing me to provide even more detail and examples for you to understand the framework and implementation strategies.

Your Journey

This book is intended to be a three-fold guide to:

♦ Designing an *Authentic Learning Unit*, which is the foundation of the *Learner-Active, Technology-Infused Classroom*, aimed at engaging students;

♦ Understanding the structures needed to support its implementation and empower students;

♦ Building the facilitation strategies that will move students from engagement to empowerment to efficacy.

Therefore, it's best if you pause after each chapter and spend some time designing the various components of the unit. Every six months, reread the book and you'll learn even more! The early chapters delve into designing an appropriate core problem for students to solve and the analytic rubric to provide them with clearly articulated expectations. Chapter 4 addresses differentiation techniques to further engage students in grappling with content. Chapter 5 focuses on the many structures of the *Learner-Active, Technology-Infused Classroom* that empower students to take charge of their own learning. Chapter 6 drives home the importance of teacher facilitation— a new role for teachers—in this environment. Chapter 7 addresses physical classroom design, which will prove to be more useful for those who have more control over their physical classroom space than for those who do not. The ten principles of the *Learner-Active, Technology-Infused Classroom* are woven throughout and then addressed more fully in Chapter 8. Chapter 9 closes the book with special considerations, such as a priming plan and designing a *Learner-Active, Technology-Infused School*; it also offers thoughts on how the *Learner-Active, Technology-Infused Classroom* addresses many of the instructional needs and programs present in schools today.

I hope this book helps to fuel your passion and provide you with many ideas for innovatively designing your classroom.

1

The Why for Your Instructional Design Journey

Change the World!

"Since we've been doing so many real-world problems, I feel like even though I'm in fourth grade I can change the world." This student's words sum up the "why?" of the *Learner-Active, Technology-Infused Classroom*: positioning students to change the world. Students deserve an education that positions them to tackle any challenge, pursue any goal, and be outfitted with the skills to meet with success. Before schools can consider what that should look like, they need to identify the why, their purpose. Why should we put all this energy, thought, money, and time into teaching children? My answer to that question is: efficacy!

Efficacious people can identify a goal, build a plan, and put it in motion; and if they don't achieve that goal, they can reflect on why and make adjustments for the next attempt. Efficacious people are driven by their passion to make a difference in their own lives and the lives of others; they make life happen rather than letting life just happen to them. Efficacious people can take steps to lead a happy life, be a productive citizen, and, moving beyond themselves, change the world! What would it take to create classrooms and schools that produce efficacious human beings and world citizens?

Imagine a learning environment in which students pose questions and actively seek answers, pursuing solutions to problems they want to solve. They decide how they will use their time, take charge of setting and achieving goals, and work individually to build skills and collaboratively develop solutions to real-world problems. Technology is used throughout the day, seamlessly, as students and teachers need it—from handheld devices to tablets to laptops to virtual-reality headsets. Students walk to a flat-screen monitor on the wall and talk to students in another part of the world. Teachers move around the room, sitting with students, who share their accomplishments, asking probing questions and gathering assessment data that will shape tomorrow's instructional plans. You hear students talking about content; their vocabulary is sophisticated for their grade level; their thinking processes are evident through their discussions and reflections. They are intent on the task at hand, yet not everyone is working on the same thing at the same time. No one is off task. Every now and then you hear a cheer or a student exclaim, "I got it!" as they excitedly dive into the next phase of a project. Students shift from current activities to others without the prompting of the teacher. No one watches the clock; no one wants to leave. This is a snapshot of the *Learner-Active, Technology-Infused Classroom*. Students in this classroom take learning seriously and pursue it vigorously. Teachers in this classroom masterfully craft and co-create learning experiences with their students that emanate from real-world situations; they facilitate learning, ensuring that each student achieves at the highest level. Parents are partners in the learning process, often via the Internet, working with teachers and students as one cohesive unit to ensure that the students are given the best foundation possible for the rest of their lives.

You may recognize aspects of your own classroom or those of your colleagues. Pockets of innovation exist in schools; it's time to stop celebrating pockets of change, incremental improvements, and isolated innovative teachers. It's time to take bold steps to secure the future of our students and the world.

School and Society

Schools both serve and form society. They serve society by building in their students the skills, concepts, and information needed to thrive in today's world. When the sundial gave way to the analog clock, people needed new skills. When the slide rule gave way to the calculator, school curriculum changed. The school community must continually consider changes in society, particularly technological changes, scientific breakthroughs, and historical events, and ensure that the curriculum is designed to shape successful world citizens.

In addition to critical subject-area content mastery, students need to build skills in creativity, innovation, critical thinking, problem solving, communication, collaboration, information literacy, technological literacy, initiative, self-direction, socializing, cross-cultural engagement, productivity, leadership, flexibility, adaptability, accountability, and responsibility. How do you build "ility"? Most of these skills cannot be approached as a subject. A student cannot take a class in flexibility and adaptability. These skills that fall outside of subject-area content are acquired based on *how* teachers teach more than *what* they teach.

> **"If schools serve society by *what* they teach, then they form society by *how* they teach."**

If schools serve society by *what* they teach, then they form society by *how* they teach. Schools that place a great emphasis on individual competition develop citizens who are well suited for that but may not be as able or willing to work collaboratively. Schools that place a great emphasis on project management, time management, and resourcefulness develop citizens who are better prepared to lead self-reliant, productive lives. This is a connection that schools often fail to realize, and it is why teachers and administrators must very carefully develop an ongoing, purposeful, instructional design plan that not only considers the written curriculum—the what—but also shapes the teaching and learning process in the classroom—the how. Both should connect to a powerful purpose, in the case of this book, positioning students to change the world.

In today's society, an event in one part of the world affects others around the world. Countries around the world comprise a global, interdependent system. Our economies, commerce, health, environment, and more are interconnected, which presents both opportunities and challenges. Beyond the realm of Earth, countries are engaged in a new space race to colonize Mars.

> In order for schools to meet the needs of a global society, they must prepare students to be problem-finders, innovators, and entrepreneurs. . . . Today's students are ready to make the leap from passive recipients of information to active participants in a classroom that will prepare them for their future.
>
> (Sulla, 2015, p. 5)

Moving Beyond "It's Always Been That Way"

Consider this anecdote I once heard. A mother is cooking a ham dinner. She cuts off the end of the ham, places the larger piece in the pan, and begins to roast it. Her young daughter says, "Mommy, why do you cut off the end of the ham?" Mom responds, "You know, I'm not sure, but my mother always did that. Go ask Grandma." The young girl goes into the living room and asks her grandmother the same question. The response is, "I don't know; my mom did that so I did too," and the girl turned to her great-grandmother and asked why. The elderly woman responded, "Well, otherwise it wouldn't fit in my roasting pan!"

What a wonderful anecdote for the ills of perpetuating the dominant paradigm of schooling. Teachers always stood in the front of the room when I was in school, so that must be where you stand. We always had textbooks, so they must be a necessary part of school. We've always had students write and solve problems on the board, so that must be a necessary component of mathematics instruction. It's time to think through what schooling looks like and make some significant adjustments to past practices. That's not to say you discard everything you currently do. Rather, you keep what works and make some adjustments. The important thing is to keep your mind continually open to change and be willing to shift some of your beliefs as to what the teaching and learning process could look like.

Shifting your belief system is not an easy process; it requires unlearning some of what you've learned in the past. Authors Ron Heifetz and Marty Linksy (2002) distinguished between technical and adaptive change. Technical change focuses on implementing known solutions to problems. For example, if students are not performing up to your desired level, use a rubric to offer them clearly articulated expectations. You learn how to use a rubric, implement its use, and teach others. That's technical change, and it is the focus of most professional development and college courses today in the field of education. It is a transaction of knowledge. Adaptive change, on the other hand, focuses on developing solutions to problems for which none yet exists. It represents an underlying transformation of thought and action. Designing classrooms to meet a new, emerging generation of learners is a problem for which there can be no available solution, given that students and society are continually changing. Adaptive change requires a change in one's belief system.

From a Compliance Model to an Efficacy Model

When you walk into a *Learner-Active, Technology-Infused Classroom*, you immediately notice how engaged students are. You look around the room and note that all students are on task and look very focused on whatever they are doing. Conventional classrooms are based on a compliance model of education: the teacher has rules, goals, and assignments and wants students to comply with those. The understanding is that through compliance, by following the teacher's lead, students will learn; and while that approach might produce temporary test score results, it will, in and of itself, fall short of producing long-term retention of learning and will do little to produce efficacious learners. Thus, a different model of education is needed to produce efficacious citizens who can change the world.

The first step toward an efficacy model is positioning students to engage with content at deep levels. This is one of the key goals for instructional design, as you'll read about in the next section. As students build the ability to engage in activities and with content, they will be better positioned to be empowered to take charge of their own learning. In the *Learner-Active, Technology-Infused Classroom*, many structures and strategies are put in place to empower students. With engagement and empowerment as the foundation, shifting focus from being empowered by others to empowering yourself leads to efficacy. The *Learner-Active, Technology-Infused Classroom* is an efficacy model of education.

Achieving Instructional Equity

A wonderfully diverse world means diverse learners with diverse needs. The equity discussion has schools challenged to provide not an equal but an equitable education for all by giving each student what he or she needs to succeed. At the core of equity is opportunity and access. Imagine classrooms in which students have myriad opportunities to thrive academically and access to the instructional approach they need and desire.

In his book, *For White Folks Who Teach in the Hood . . . And the Rest of Y'All Too*, Christopher Emdin (2016) defines reality pedagogy as:

> An approach to teaching and learning that has a primary goal of meeting each student on his or her own cultural and emotional turf. It focuses on making the local experiences of the student visible and creating contexts where there is a role reversal of sorts that positions the student as the expert in his or her own teaching and learning, and the teacher as the learner. It posits that while the teacher is the person charged with delivering the content, the student is the person who shapes how best to teach that content. Together, the teacher and students co-construct the classroom space.
>
> (p. 27)

In the *Learner-Active, Technology-Infused Classroom*, student voice and choice are at the forefront. Students work with teachers to identify problems they wish to solve and ways in which to learn what they need to achieve their goals. Teachers facilitate through small-group and one-on-one conversations with students to gain a better understanding of students' abilities, successes, challenges, and needs so they can be a powerful resource in their students' learning journey. It is a classroom in which all students thrive. The *Learner-Active, Technology-Infused Classroom* is an instructional equity model for education.

Three Critical Goals for Instructional Design

At the core of the *Learner-Active Technology-Infused Classroom* lie three critical goals for instructional design: engage students in learning, build greater responsibility for student learning, and ensure academic rigor.

Engaged Learners

Busy students are not necessarily engaged students, nor are seemingly happy students who are working in groups. Although "hands-on" activities are wonderful, what you truly want are "minds-on" activities. If you assume students are engaged in learning, take a closer look to see if what they are doing is directly related to academically rigorous content and if they are understanding and thinking deeply about that content. Suppose third-grade students are learning about the food chain. Consider the following scenarios as we peek into three classrooms:

- Students are locating information on the food chain from books and the Internet and creating charts to illustrate the food chains of various animals.

- Students are designing a computer presentation on the food chain and are working on adding sounds and transitions to make it more exciting.

- A group of students is developing a "what if" presentation, as they were interested in determining what would happen if a member of the food chain were to become extinct, under what conditions that might happen, how that would affect the rest of the food chain, and is there anything we can and should do about it?

Although all three scenarios cover the content of the food chain, it is important to consider how students spend the bulk of their time. In the first scenario, students are most likely engaged in finding and reporting information. Doing so will lead them to some level of knowledge of the food chain, but the work is primarily "regurgitation" of content: copying and pasting, taking data in one form and presenting it in another. This is a prevalent activity in the compliance model of education. The second scenario assumes students have already found their information and are reporting it using a digital presentation, sharing "known" information with others. Their engagement, however, is now in the digital presentation software. Again, although the students are focusing on important skills, as the teacher, you must consider what content is the *goal* of instruction. In this case, students are engaged in the use of software, not understanding the food chain. The third scenario has students "grappling" (Sulla, 2015) with the content itself—understanding the cause-and-effect relationships that exist and using higher-order thinking to consider future situations; they are identifying problems and posing solutions for them based on personal interest and curiosity. All three of these scenarios might occur when learning about the food chain; the key is the *amount* of time allocated to each and which is the end goal. In the case of the third scenario, students will absolutely have to search for "known" information, and they will have to develop a mode of presentation. That presentation, however, will focus on convincing others of the merit of their solution to the problem, the "unknown" that students have created as the goal of the unit of study.

Current standards demand a higher level of understanding and application of content than ever before.

> The word "understand" means to know how something works and to grasp the meaning of it. The definition intimates personal, often long-term, experience with the subject. . . . Achieving understanding involves deconstructing information, making connections to existing knowledge, making and testing predictions, and constructing new meaning—in short, grappling.
>
> (Sulla, 2015, p. 30)

The bulk of students' time should be spent on grappling with "known" content to provide an "unknown" solution to a problem. Engaged learners need to be grappling with curricular content in significant ways much of the time, no matter what their ages.

Student Responsibility for Learning

Student responsibility for learning is a concept that most educators embrace but few foster. Teachers are often frustrated that students don't come to class prepared, haven't done their homework, and so forth. If you take a closer look at most classrooms, students enter the room and wait for the teacher to tell them what to do; or they follow a "do now" written on the board, that the teacher created. You'll hear teachers saying phrases like, "clear your desks," "take out a pen and paper," "line up at the door," "quiet down," "speak up," and more. Teachers will call on students to speak; distribute materials; give, collect, grade, and return assignments; and tell students what their grades are. In this type of environment, students are asked to follow along compliantly; the teacher decides what, when, and how students are learning. This model typically does not actually produce learning; it might produce a short-term bump in test scores relying on short-term memory, but the goal of schooling must be long-term retention of learning. Many of us who succeeded in spite of the compliance model of education had other things going for us: parents who served as models and mentors, a national respect for education as the way out of poverty post–World War II, the ability to construct meaning from information, and so forth.

Imagine a classroom in which fourth-grade students walk through the door; pick up a folder or log onto a website, that includes their current work and a schedule that they developed the prior day; read through comments from the teacher; and start working on activities they decided upon. Students determine what resources they'll need to accomplish their tasks, and they sign-up for them, including *small-group mini-lessons* offered by the teacher. They use *analytic rubrics* to guide their work and assess their own progress; they share with the teacher how they're progressing and what they need to be more successful. The teacher facilitates learning through a carefully structured environment that allows students to take responsibility for the classroom. Student responsibility for learning requires clearly articulated expectations and consequences, structures that students use to meet with success, and guidance and feedback from the teacher.

Imagine a classroom in which kindergarten students walk through the door, move a magnetic nameplate into the "present" area for attendance, pick up a folder, and find a seat to get started working. They look in their folder for a paper with a set of choices that they selected yesterday, cutting out and pasting pictures that represent specific learning activities. They get started on the first activity. Some students get together in pairs for buddy reading; others scan QR codes on the wall to access videos on a tablet PC. Some students move to a math table to work with manipulatives. A student who needs help walks over to the *help board* and moves a picture of himself with his name on it to the *help board* area. Soon, the teacher joins him to help him with his work. About twenty minutes into the day, the teacher calls the students to join her in the carpeted area for the morning meeting.

Academic Rigor

If students are engaged in learning and taking greater responsibility for their own learning, then ensuring academic rigor is easy. The battle cry of most schools is to increase test scores, even if scores are already relatively high; but you can't force students to learn. In 1998, William Glasser determined that students choose to learn based on a sense of belonging, freedom, power, and fun. Sousa (2017) found that for information to move into long-term memory, it must have sense and meaning. Presenting content followed by practice, absent of these conditions, will not necessarily increase understanding and will, most likely, not lead to long-term retention. It may bring about a small, temporary bump in test scores, but weeks later, the students will have little to show for their work and little foundation to build upon the following year, which leaves the next year's teacher reteaching that which was forgotten.

I met with a group of teachers representing second grade through twelfth grade to discuss rethinking instruction. During the discussion, an eleventh-grade teacher commented, "Well not only do I have to concentrate on history, but I have to teach them how to write. I don't know what your curriculum is in middle school, but many of my eleventh graders can't write in paragraphs!" A middle school language arts teacher quickly defended her curriculum with, "I spend a lot of time on paragraph construction because they come to me with no knowledge; but they leave my classroom with strong writing skills. Our district needs to teach paragraph writing in the elementary grades." A second-grade teacher who happened to have a stack of student stories with her pulled them out and said, "I don't know what you're talking about. My second graders write great paragraphs." We passed around the student writing samples, and the upper-grade teachers were incredulous. The first teacher to speak exclaimed, "If they write this well in second grade, what happens to them between then and high school?!"

Many students can memorize content for the moment; if you engage students' minds in grappling with content through meaningful, authentic problems, they will build knowledge and understanding for the long term.

If you increase students' responsibility for learning, offering them freedom and power, they will be able to accomplish more, not remaining dependent on others to continue moving forward; they will strengthen their executive-function skills to enable them to take increasingly greater responsibility for their learning. You can then increase academic rigor through well-crafted assignments, questions, differentiation, collaboration, and more.

"if you engage students' minds in grappling with content through meaningful, authentic problems, they will build knowledge and understanding for the long term."

A Synergy

When the goals of engagement with content, responsibility for learning, and academic rigor are working in concert, the outcome is powerful and lasting learning (see Figure 1.1). This synergy is critical to the success of the *Learner-Active, Technology-Infused Classroom*.

Figure 1.1. Three Critical Goals

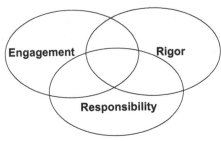

The Students We Teach

The Internet has significantly changed how people communicate, work, collaborate, engage in commerce, and think. Educators need to understand how our technologically advanced world has affected today's students and design classrooms that better suit their learning modalities.

As early as 1998, Don Tapscott described the ten themes of the then-emerging digital (or 'net) generation. They possess a *strong independence and autonomy*, considering they can easily access and challenge information. They reveal an *emotional and intellectual openness* based on their willingness to post their thoughts and opinions on websites. They are *inclusive*, using technology as a means through which to develop a community of diverse individuals with whom they interact. They believe in *free expression and strong views*, having unparalleled access to information and forums. They are *innovative*, continually looking for ways to improve the world around them. They are *preoccupied with maturity*, seeking to meld into groups of people who are older than they. They engage in *investigations*, willing to surf the Internet in search of the answers they seek. They thrive on *immediacy*, spurred on by the instantaneous connection offered by modern cellular phones and the Internet. They are *sensitive to corporate interest*, skeptical that media messages are designed to serve corporate needs. They are mindful of *authentication and trust*, given that, with the open architecture of the Internet, they must continually question what they see and hear. Tapscott (2009) later reinforced this, pointing out how these characteristics have been solidified in these students' adult lives. These adults are now parents of children in school, and yet their digital experiences were nowhere near as sophisticated as those of their children. This and future generations of students deserve formal learning environments that honor their unique characteristics.

Consider a few effects of technology on the digital generation. In a technologically advanced world, you:

♦ Can post opinions through blogs, share videos, upload podcasts, create personal social networking pages, and more. The result is that your students *thrive on expressing themselves in a variety of ways*.

♦ Go to websites and they welcome you, know what you're interested in, and refer to you by name. You create digital avatars that represent you online. The result is that your students *expect personalization*.

♦ Send instant digital messages to whom you want, engage in online environments with whom you want, control your tablet's screen layout, customize your cell phones, and wear technology on your wrist. The result is that your students *demand freedom*.

- Engage in online, interactive environments with others around the world, socializing, creating, and gaming. The result is that your students *thrive on social interaction*.

- "Google" people, use the Internet to learn to pronounce a word, watch a YouTube video to learn a skill, go to the UN website to learn about world hunger, check the weather, and get the news. The result is that your students *demand immediate information—* what they want, when they want it.

- Digitally message several people while searching the Web, engaging in an online discussion, streaming a television program, and posting to social media. The result is that your students *want to be everywhere at once*.

- Grieve the loss of others through social networking pages, raise money for starving people in third-world countries, raise money to support taking a stand against genocide in other parts of the world, and organize political events. The result is that your students are *socially aware and active*.

In our students' lives, the digital world is ever present and melded with the real world. "Very few adults have had any real long-term exposure to the digitally infused life experiences of the students who populate our schools" (Jukes, Schaaf, & Mohan, 2017, p. 31). The digital nature of our students speaks to the need to design classrooms that are engaging, authentic, differentiated, resource rich, collaborative, and that foster greater student responsibility for learning. In short, these are classrooms that support efficacy.

Stories From the Field

Whatever your grade level or subject, you'll want to gain insights as to what learning looks like for your students before and after they enter your classroom. As you read the stories in this book, if your grade level is below the story level, consider what students would need to learn at your level as a prerequisite. If your level is above the story level, consider how the students in the story would thrive in your classroom. Consider how you could interact with the students and teachers in the stories that are at your grade level but in a different subject area. That is, avoid glossing over those stories that are not on your level.

A fifth-grade teacher uses problem-based tasks to drive students into the curriculum through motivating, real-world problems. She has created structures that allow students to learn from her in small-group and independent settings, through written direction sheets, from one another, and through websites and apps. She made a radical decision to spend only fifteen minutes a day in the front of the room offering the daily "lesson." Even prior to redesigning her classroom, she was a popular teacher. She presented great lessons that were very interesting to her students, merging humor with content. Still, she decided to heed the brain research and limit her amount of time in the front of the room. One day a student approached her and asked, on behalf of the class, if she would present a lesson on equivalent fractions from 11:10 to 11:25, because the students really needed more information on this topic and were all stuck. She gladly complied. As she moved into her lesson, she was happily surprised by how attentive everyone was. She presented; the students took notes; they responded to her questions and asked their own. She admits she was so excited by how engaged her students were that she failed to end at 11:25 and just kept going. Soon students started looking at the clock and fidgeting. Finally, a student said, "This was a great lesson, but we only had until 11:25, and we've got to get back to our work schedules." Imagine a classroom in which students take charge and manage their own time to complete assignments by designing their own schedules. Imagine a classroom in which students take charge and ask the teacher to present lessons that will aid them in problem solving. Welcome to the *Learner-Active, Technology-Infused Classroom.*

I visited a third-grade classroom marked by the buzz of productive discussions. One group of students was working on ways to help their local ecosystem thrive by studying its producers, consumers, and decomposers. Another was working on plans for "A Local Party" in which they have to plan a class party serving only food items produced locally in their state. They were writing math equations to divide up the food items and creating a budget. A pair of students was reading *Stellaluna* (Cannon, 2007). They shared that they are creating a class tapestry of how people are all different and have different backgrounds but are also all the same; the tapestry will journey from hanging in the local library to that of another state to that of another country until it returns to the classroom. One student explained to me that everything they are doing has to do with their theme, which is posted on a classroom wall, "Being Part of a Greater Whole." This is their transdisciplinary theme that ties together the content across the curriculum.

When I visited a kindergarten classroom, I found students in various locations: five in a carpeted meeting area, on the floor with the teacher, engaging with math manipulatives; some at desks creating ladybugs from construction paper; some reading picture books; and some at interactive whiteboards with peers, matching words to pictures. I sat down next to a student who was constructing his ladybug. The conversation went like this:

Me: Hi, what are you working on here?
Student: I'm making a ladybug.

Me: And why are you making a ladybug?

Student: Uh . . . the teacher is reading us a book about a ladybug.

Me: I see your classmates are working on some other things. Are you doing those, too?

Student: I wanted to do this first, then I have to go to the carpet.

Me: And how do you know when to do these things?

Student (pointing to the board): See the list? I can do them in any order.

Me: Ah, I see. I like your ladybug. I see you so far have five spots on the left side and three on the right. Do ladybugs have the same number of spots on both sides?

Student: Oh no, butterflies are symmetrical; ladybugs are not.

My conversations around the room were similar. Students had three markers with their name and numbers that they posted next to activities on the board to indicate to the teacher their activity choice. The teacher was spending quality time with students on the carpet introducing a new math concept. Students who needed help went to one another with success. Even kindergarten students can take charge of managing their time. Welcome to the *Learner-Active, Technology-Infused Classroom.*

The wall of a fourth-grade classroom holds the statement, "Ways In Which We Are Changing The World" with a monthly timeline across the bottom. As students work on various problem-based tasks across the year, they write them on a paper plate and post them on the wall-sized chart. Students animatedly tell me about the current problem they're tackling. The quote at the start of the chapter came from this classroom.

A third-grade teacher was attending a professional-development session and, on a break, went to her classroom to check in on her students. She entered the room to find them engaged in learning as usual, working individually, in pairs, or in clusters around the room. The substitute teacher approached her and said that she'd expected to lead the class as a whole group as she usually did. She began to do so at one point in the day. Soon a student raised her hand and cautiously said, "I'm sorry to interrupt, but we all have things we need to get done. Do you think you could offer this as a small-group mini-lesson for those of us who need it, and the rest of us can work from our schedule?" The substitute teacher was amazed; the classroom teacher beamed. Welcome to another *Learner-Active, Technology-Infused Classroom.*

A Philosophy, Framework, and Solution

It is important to view the *Learner-Active, Technology-Infused Classroom* as a comprehensive framework for teaching and learning, not as one possible method among many that you may use. One cannot be *Learner-Active* in the morning but not in the afternoon. One cannot use this method for some students and something else for others. The *Learner-Active, Technology-Infused Classroom* is a complex framework of interdependent structures and strategies that, together, provide the best possible learning environment for all students, thus being differentiated in and of itself. Mastering the art of designing a *Learner-Active, Technology-Infused Classroom* requires certain paradigm shifts that will change your view of teaching and learning forever.

There is room for almost any method you may run across in the *Learner-Active, Technology-Infused Classroom*. As you read other books and articles, attend workshops and conferences, and complete coursework on various educational topics, consider how they align with this framework and how they can fit. Unless you're advocating for a totally lecture-based, teacher-centered classroom, most likely you'll find that most of the popular strategies for fostering learning will fit nicely into the *Learner-Active, Technology-Infused Classroom*. Just stay focused on the extent to which you are providing engagement, responsibility for learning, and academic rigor. Remember, though, that a lot of popular teaching strategies and programs today still presume the teacher is the information deliverer. So as you shift your paradigm, consider how these strategies and programs could be modified to work in your student-driven classroom.

This is not a framework that is meant to stand alone; it is meant to be a solution to many of the challenges facing schools today. The *Learner-Active, Technology-Infused Classroom* is the perfect solution for designing classrooms that offer Multi-Tiered System of Supports (MTSS), such as Response to Intervention (RTI). Relatedly, it is the perfect venue for implementing *Universal Design for Learning* (UDL). Schools are pursuing learning environments that provide a 1:1 ratio of student to computing device. The *Learner-Active, Technology-Infused Classroom* provides key structures for shifting from a more teacher-directed learning environment to one in which students engage in learning with significant access to a computer. Schools are looking to provide students with a STEM (science, technology, engineering, and math) or STEAM (add arts) focus. Design process is a natural component of the *Learner-Active, Technology-Infused Classroom* as students identify and solve real-world problems. Schools are looking to build twenty-first-century skills in students. The structures of the *Learner-Active, Technology-Infused Classroom* build all of the targeted skills and more. Schools are considering how to provide virtual learning experiences for students so that they may enroll in a course that they attend via computer. The principles of the *Learner-Active, Technology-Infused Classroom* apply in this venue, as well as in the more conventional physical classroom. Schools are challenged to design effective co-teaching (inclusion) classrooms to provide instruction for all students, including special-needs students, in one inclusive learning environment. The *Learner-Active, Technology-Infused Classroom* is the solution to this challenge, providing a perfect venue for two adults to share a learning environment without one taking precedence over the other.

Ultimately, consider how the framework and related structures and strategies presented in this book address the needs of your students and of the world of education today. Apply the principles as you make decisions about instruction in the classroom.

What to Expect

Designing a *Learner-Active, Technology-Infused Classroom* requires adaptive change, and adaptive change takes time and mental energy. Embarking on this instructional design journey will take you through three distinct levels in the change process. The first is "dynamic disequilibrium." This occurs when you are implementing new strategies and structures for the first time. One moment you are excited and celebratory, and in the next you find yourself disappointed and in despair. One day you're thrilled that you found this book; the next day you're ready to toss it in the trash. (But please don't.) This is a really important time to keep a journal (written or digital) to track your experiences, successes, and challenges. The act of writing allows you to reflect on events and learn from them. A year from now, the journal will be a wonderful documentation of an amazing journey in instructional design. One teacher kept a journal in her first year of transformation. In her second year, she complained that her students were just not as good at the *Learner-Active, Technology-Infused Classroom* as her last year's class. Then one day she sat down and read her journal from the prior year. She realized that she spent much more time in the fall teaching them the structures. In fact, last year's students weren't all that good at this learning environment either, but she helped them understand it. This year, she just assumed she was going to have students who were starting the year as if they were last year's students at the end of the year. Keeping a journal can provide you with important insights, particularly in your first few years of designing a *Learner-Active, Technology-Infused Classroom*. This first phase of the change process typically lasts a year or less. Once you begin to repeat the instructional design process with a new set of students, you tend to move to the next phase.

Human beings, by nature, seek stability. The early stages of the change process are often unnerving, so a natural inclination is to find those structures or strategies that appear to work the best and adopt them as the definitive solution. This causes you to enter the second phase: "contrived equilibrium." You'll design a rubric template, for example, to which students respond well; and you'll decide that all rubrics should always be written in this exact same way. This is a dangerous phase, because you meet with exciting, successful moments, but, to be honest, you don't know what you still don't know. Often teachers are asked to provide turnkey training and walk others down the exact path they have taken to designing the *Learner-Active, Technology-Infused Classroom*. I advise against any turnkey training until you've experienced your fourth year of implementing this framework. While you may enjoy the successful achievement of your goals, the journey is truly just beginning, and you have a lot more learning ahead of you. This phase can last a year, a few years, or, in some cases, the length of your career. The key is to push on to the third phase through continual reflective practice.

The third and destination phase of the change process in designing *Learner-Active, Technology-Infused Classrooms* is that of "reflective practitioner." Arriving at this phase means you are continually questioning the structures and strategies you employ and making adjustments along the way. Times change, society changes, students change; and masterful teachers adapt their classroom practices accordingly. Returning to the earlier example, you may find that different styles of rubrics work for different students under different circumstances. You may modify your rubrics based on the time of year, the type of problem students are solving, and so forth. Each time, you question whether or not this is the best possible implementation.

I met with a teacher to review her *Authentic Learning Unit (ALU)* and offered several suggestions for improving it. She exclaimed, "You know, *you* wrote this with me three years ago." I smiled and shouted, "I've evolved!" What was acceptable to me three years prior was no longer good enough. Reflective practitioners eagerly open their practice to their own critique and that of others.

Although you may think you can begin at phase three, the instructional design work that lies ahead takes time and is like learning any new skill. Let's face it, if you take up diving, you don't expect to enter the Olympics the following year. Only time will produce improved results. Malcolm Gladwell (2011) claims it takes 10,000 hours of practice to achieve mastery. Use a journal or other means to continually reflect on strategies and structures you are trying and how they worked out. When something does not appear to work, avoid the temptation to revert to former methods. Probe more deeply to consider what structure or strategy you could change to make it work. If you reflect on the situation, you will push yourself to find the key to success.

The Change Process in Action

If something is not working in your *Learner-Active, Technology-Infused Classroom*, it typically means that a structure or strategy is missing. I worked with a very talented first-grade teacher, schooled with innovative methods from Columbia University and the Bank Street College. I visited her classroom one day while her students were working on math activities related to place value. She had a collection of activity boxes and regularly introduced new ones to the students during their morning meeting time. During math time, pairs of students would select a box and work on the activity. I noticed two girls opening a box and looking perplexed; neither of them could remember what to do with this particular activity. I pointed out two boys who had just completed the activity and suggested they ask them. The girls looked at the boys, then looked back at me and said, in unison, "nah" and proceeded to select another box. I thought this was very funny and shared the story with the teacher, who was, to my surprise, horrified. "I should have been there for them. I should have helped them through it." I pointed out that with twelve pairs of students working on these math tasks, it would be impossible to be present to facilitate every student at the point of needing help. Regardless of your grade level, you no doubt have encountered similar situations. I used this opportunity to introduce the idea of students scheduling their own time. Some activities are what I refer to as "teacher intensive," where students benefit from the oversight and probing questions from teachers. Engaging in a math activity through which students are just learning about place value would be "teacher intensive," as would students conducting and analyzing results from experiments, following a recipe for the first time, and applying a mathematical formula for the first time. Other activities are "non–teacher intensive," where students can work independent of the teacher with success. I asked her what types of activities her students would be engaged in during the day that did not require her to be overly attentive to them. She mentioned buddy reading and journal writing, where students typically engaged in these activities with little participation from her. I suggested that she tell the students that they had to spend a certain amount of time on each of these three activities (math boxes, buddy reading, and journal writing) but they could choose any order they wished.

At first, the teacher was skeptical her students could succeed at this, as she kept fairly tight control over the classroom activities. Over lunch, she pondered the idea and decided to try it. I walked into the classroom in the afternoon, and there were her students with their schedules in which they ordered the activities, all going about their work. Sure enough, only a handful of students were working on their math boxes at any given time, allowing her to spend much more quality time with them ensuring they were building the right understanding of place value.

At one point, the teacher pointed out to me a student who seemed to be rather disoriented, walking around the room with no apparent purpose. Her response was, "See, this really doesn't work for special education students. He's supposed to be buddy reading now." It would be easy for her to have dismissed the idea of students scheduling their own time. In reality, she just needed to add a structure. I talked about how primary students, at first, do not know how to line up for, say, art class. So the teacher deliberately walks them through one step at a time: clear your desks, sit quietly, table one get on line, nice and straight, and so forth. By the next month, the teacher is simply saying, "line up for art class." So together, we developed a checklist for buddy reading: find a book, find a buddy, find an open spot on the floor, sit down cross-legged facing one another, and so forth (Figure 1.2). The teacher introduced the checklist to the students who needed guidance. They learned the steps to follow the checklist, and it worked! So as you reflect upon your challenges, always consider that you might just need to add another structure or strategy.

Figure 1.2. Buddy Reading Checklist

☐   Get your reading book.

☐   Find your buddy.

☐   Find a quiet, empty spot to read.

☐   Sit down knee to knee.

☐   Open your books.

☐   Decide who will read first.

☐   Read one page while the buddy follows along.

☐   Switch roles.

☐   Read for at least ten minutes.

Imagine, Consider, Create

As you work to design your *Learner-Active, Technology-Infused Classroom*, take time to *imagine* the possibilities, *consider* the research and experience of others, and then *create* your classroom. When you reach the *create* sections, I encourage you to stop and spend some time designing the materials being described. This book is not intended to be read straight through in one sitting. It is meant to guide you through rethinking your classroom and instructional design. You'll note that there will be some structures and strategies that you already use, some that you can easily envision adding to your repertoire, and some that you feel will absolutely not work in your classroom. Start by adding those that make the most sense to you; but never lose track of those seemingly impossible ideas. Keep them in your journal and return to them down the road.

Efficacy for your students is a worthy goal; outfitting them with the knowledge, structures, and strategies they need to accomplish their goals will help establish the trajectory of their lives. Several years from now, you'll look back on your classroom and find it hard to believe what you've accomplished. The key is to keep on innovating and reflecting. Enjoy the journey!

REFERENCES

Cannon, J. (2007). *Stellaluna*. New York, NY: Houghton Mifflin Harcourt.

Emdin, C. (2016). *For white folks who teach in the hood . . . and the rest of y'all too: Reality pedagogy and urban education*. Boston, MA: Beacon Press.

Gladwell, M. (2011). *Outliers: The story of success*. Boston, MA: Little Brown and Company.

Glasser, W. (1998). *Choice theory: A new psychology of personal freedom*. New York, NY: HarperCollins.

Heifetz, R. A., & Linsky, M. (2002). *Leadership on the line: Staying alive through the dangers of leading*. Boston, MA: Harvard Business School.

Jukes, I., Schaaf, R. L., & Mohan, N. (2017). *Reinventing learning for the always-on generation: Strategies and apps that work*. Bloomington, IN: Solution Tree.

Sousa, D. (2017). *How the brain learns* (5th ed.). Thousand Oaks, CA: Corwin.

Sulla, N. (2015). *It's not what you teach but how: 7 insights to making the CCSS work for you*. New York, NY: Routledge.

Tapscott, D. (2009). *Grown up digital: How the net generation is changing your world*. New York, NY: McGraw-Hill.

2

Engaging Students Through a Core Problem to Solve

It's Tuesday and a third-grade teacher is presenting her students with a lesson on using text features and search tools to locate specific information when reading informational text. Why? Because this is where it falls in the curriculum. She's a dynamic teacher who presents the material well. She involves the class in the lesson, demonstrating how to locate headings, boldface words, sidebars, and hyperlinks to find information. She gives them a page of text, has them read through it to find information, and then goes over it with the class. As you watch, you wonder what her students are thinking, how interested they are in the topic, and whether they see the need for this skill in their lives. Are they truly engaged in the meaning of the content, or are they merely being compliant?

Next door, her colleague has just presented her students with an opportunity to prepare for a kite festival to celebrate the invention of the kite and learn about the physics of flight. Students will engage in a design challenge to build a kite. Some decide they want to have their kites promote books they enjoy. Final kite photos will be shared with authors, libraries, organizations, and others who should know about these books. Other groups decide to use their kites to promote other messages. Given a set of parameters and goals for the instructional setting, students are to work in pairs to explore kites, read and discuss both fiction and nonfiction books on kites, and engage in a design process in which they will design and build the kite and then write about that which they are promoting. This interdisciplinary challenge will require students to assemble different kite kits and explore the physics behind flight and read about kites in order to eventually develop their own unique design. Excitedly, students begin working, mapping out how they will use their time to learn what they need. They generate ideas for learning and refer to a list of possibilities provided by their teacher. Some begin selecting and reading fiction books they want to promote; others begin filling out a graphic organizer of facts that they will glean from nonfiction books; others assemble a kite from a kit. Suddenly, you see the power of engagement. At the point at which the students need to locate information for the graphic organizer on the history and physics of kites, they will need the skills related to efficiently locating information. The students will now have a need to learn about using text features and search tools to locate information; the teacher will provide a variety of ways for each student to learn, including a *small-group mini-lesson* with her.

The first teacher relies on her charismatic personality and interesting delivery to engage her students. It's hard to tell if students are driven by the subject matter or by her. In contrast, the second teacher develops an activity that will allow students to take charge of their learning, producing a need for her students to learn the desired skills—not just a need she presents intellectually but a need that her students *feel* because they cannot complete the task without these skills. People learn best from a *felt need*.

The first step to engaging students' minds and getting them grappling with content is to ensure they have a *felt need* to learn. *Problem-based learning* provides an excellent venue for creating *felt need*. The more authentic the problem, and the more voice students have in deciding on a problem to solve, the more likely students will be to want to tackle it, learn, and then work tirelessly toward their goal.[1]

> "The more authentic the problem, and the more voice students have in deciding on a problem to solve, the more likely students will be to want to tackle it, learn, and then work tirelessly toward their goal."

At the start of designing your *Learner-Active, Technology-Infused Classroom*, you will design the problems for students to solve so that you build your own understanding of a powerful *problem-based task* and accompanying

---

1 The phrases "project-based" and "problem-based" are often used interchangeably. For the purposes of this book, project-based learning could involve closed-ended problems, such as designing a clay map of the state. *Problem-based learning* involves solving open-ended problems, such as developing a campaign to convince people to move to your city or town. In this way, *problem-based learning* is a subset of project-based learning. Here, you will focus on *problem-based learning* to truly engage students in the process of grappling with content.

structures. As your comfort level increases, you can have students identify problems they wish to solve within a content topic. Eventually, consider allowing students to present problems they want to solve while you determine how you can weave the curriculum into their interests. For now, we'll address teacher-designed *problem-based tasks*.

Three Pillars

The *Learner-Active, Technology-Infused Classroom* is a framework that includes problem-based, *Authentic Learning Units (ALUs)*, a collection of structures that put students in charge of their own learning, and powerful teacher facilitation of learning. The *ALU* engages students in learning; the structures empower students to take responsibility for their own learning; and the teacher's facilitation strategies build students' ability to put a plan into action to achieve success, thus building efficacy. Essentially, you can't have one or two without the others, or you don't have a *Learner-Active, Technology-Infused Classroom*. All three pillars are needed to support your classroom and the eventual achievement of student efficacy.

You might find that all of the structures work well in empowering your students; however, without the *ALU*, students only compliantly work through lists of activities. You might like introducing each unit with a new *ALU*, but without the empowerment structures, your students will still be dependent on you for their next steps. You might find that, armed with an *ALU* and empowerment structures, your classroom can run without you; but it can't. Your students don't know what they don't know; they need you to push their academic thinking and help them learn to take control of their learning. Three pillars: that's what you need!

First, you (and eventually you and your students) will design the *ALU*; then you'll delve into the related structures and facilitation strategies to make it work. Think of it as a three-legged stool: you won't have stability unless all three legs are present (see Figure 2.1).

Figure 2.1. Three-Legged Stool

Learning From a Felt Need

Think about all that you have learned in school and all that you remember. Can you name the six noble gases? Can you state the cause of the French and Indian War? Can you explain the relationship between the length of the hypotenuse and the length of the legs of a right triangle? Can you define a chromatic scale? Can you factor a polynomial? Can you identify the number of lines and rhyming scheme of an English sonnet? Can you name three artists from the Renaissance period? Most likely, you learned *all* of that in school; yet for many, it is difficult to recall the answers to all of these questions.

Can you offer directions for how to get from your house to your place of work or school? Can you tell someone how to succeed at your favorite hobby? Can you explain how to make an appointment for a haircut? Can you recite the lyrics to a favorite song? Can you explain how to brush your teeth? Chances are, these questions are slightly less challenging than the previous. Why? In the case of this set of questions, you most likely, at some point, were motivated, compelled, driven, or inspired to learn this information; you built this knowledge in an authentic context: you had a *felt need* to learn. You may have learned the information in the former set of questions well enough to succeed on a test, but how much of that knowledge did you retain?

The fact that many teachers offer review before tests speaks to the reality that they don't believe their students can learn and retain information. As a teacher, it is sad to think that your students will never remember much of what you will teach them. That's a lot of time and energy on your part to reap little return on investment. Clearly, part of schooling is mastering the art and science of learning, so it may not be so important to remember some of the content. However, given that people learn best when they have a *felt need* to learn, teachers could improve students' retention if they positioned content to be presented within an authentic context.

My first memorable experience related to learning from a *felt need* was at age twelve, when I decided to build a tree house. I started nailing boards to trees, and my father stopped me, pointing out that I really should start with a blueprint. Together, we created a scale drawing of the proposed tree house. I had a *felt need* to learn ratio and proportion. We then framed out the house with studs, sixteen inches on center, as they say in the building industry; we were doing this the right way! This tree house wouldn't have any ordinary ladder; we designed a staircase. I had a *felt need* to learn how to use a protractor. What an exciting project it was! I later became a math teacher.

Frank Smith, in *The Book of Learning and Forgetting* (1998), distinguishes between classic learning, which develops "inconspicuously and effortlessly" from a *felt need* in our everyday lives, and official learning, which is intended to develop from hard work and a structured, controlled teaching approach. He pointed out that by the time they enter school, children have learned about 10,000 words without any formal education, and that was before the advent of today's technology! Teachers complain the students can't learn the twenty vocabulary words on the weekly list; but Smith's research showed that, on average, young children are learning in excess of 2,000 words a year without formal training. Perhaps one of the differentiating factors is *felt need*. Note that this research was prior to the availability of digital devices and apps that provide independent learning experiences. I was in an airport listening to a young boy in a stroller recite his ABCs. He was two years old. I commended his mother, and she said, "Don't give me credit; it's his iPad." Combine *felt need* and access and you have a powerful equation for success.

From Skills First to Application First

It's time to consider a necessary paradigm shift for your classroom (Figure 2.2). The conventional approach to instruction has been to teach lower-order skills first and then to provide a scenario through which students can apply those skills, often known as the culminating project.

For example, the teacher presents lessons on addition of fractions with unlike denominators. Near the end of the unit, the students who have completed their work are presented with a project: create a plan for a local pizzeria to sell individual slices in a variety of fractional sizes that can then be added together to determine the final price.

While this may seem like an interesting challenge to pursue, the problem lies in the teacher's approach. Students are expected to learn addition of fractions absent of a meaningful reason why. The danger here is that

Figure 2.2. Paradigm Shift

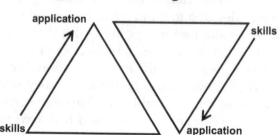

students may not see the need for isolated skills and therefore not fully engage themselves in the learning process, such that some students may never, in the teacher's mind, excel to the point of the problem-solving phase and thus remain at the bottom of Bloom's taxonomy indefinitely!

Instead, in the *Learner-Active, Technology-Infused Classroom*, instruction begins with an authentic, open-ended problem that presents a context for learning. Opening a unit of study on addition of fractions with the "Designer Pizza" problem (Appendix A), thus placing students in the position of menu designer with a potential pitch to a local restaurant, creates "buy in," as students know this enhancement for pizza lovers could actually occur. In this case, they may actually succeed in having a local pizzeria modify its menu. Two of our client teachers had this happen for their students! The open-endedness inspires students to create and therefore engage with the subject matter. Once students possess a *felt need* for skills, teachers can provide opportunities through which students can learn. Learning becomes meaningful and interesting. This requires shifting an age-old paradigm of the teaching–learning process: from teacher as information deliverer to teacher as learning facilitator. This shift is made easier by the advent of computer technology in classrooms. Computer technology and Internet access provide educators with exceptional resources for both setting the context and building the skills.

Let's see how this might play out in the classroom. (Some of the vocabulary here may be new to you, but all of the terms will be introduced in subsequent chapters.) A teacher is about to start the unit on life cycles, beginning with the butterfly. We all learned the stages of a butterfly, from egg to caterpillar to chrysalis to adult; we probably drew diagrams and watched butterflies emerge from the chrysalis that the teacher purchased. Consider how this teacher might build a scenario to set the context for learning:

Butterflies are beautiful to look at and helpful to the world around them, but they demand some very special host plants in order to live. With increasing habitat loss, butterflies are finding fewer and fewer places with the plants they need to thrive. This is resulting in the quasi-extinction of butterflies. You can help! Design a butterfly garden that someone in the community could plant and that we could plant at the school to attract butterflies and help them thrive.

The teacher has set the stage for learning about butterflies and life cycles (Appendix B). She is attempting to create a *felt need* for the subject-area content. First, the teacher will "launch" the unit by presenting the scenario through facts, videos, pictures, and more. The intent is to energize the students around solving the problem. Next, she will share an age-appropriate *analytic rubric* with the class, asking students to carefully read the Practitioner, or grade-level, column with their group and make a list of what they're going to need to learn. Then she will lead a class discussion on the task, what they will need to learn, and how they're going to find the information they need. From there, she will provide students with an activity list for the first day or two that provides them with a variety of ways through which to learn. She will refer to the *scaffold for learning* she designed during unit planning in order to develop subsequent *activity lists* from which students will plan out their learning paths. This scaffold includes certain whole-class, *benchmark lessons*, such as the concept of life cycles, the usefulness of insects, the importance of time and sequence in researching scientific events, and so forth. It includes some *small-group mini-lessons* for those students who need help in certain concepts or skills, such as identifying and drawing cycles, identifying your point of view as it relates to the author's, noting and graphing temperature, and so forth. For some skills, such as reading a thermometer, a *how-to sheet* of instructions or a screencast will provide the direct instruction needed. *Peer experts*, various related assignments, quizzes, tests, websites, computer software, terrariums set up with butterfly eggs, and more will complete the *scaffold for learning*. The teacher will ask the groups to determine how they will tackle the problem. She'll be looking for a mix between individual and collaborative work. Individuals will be expected to observe, conduct information searches, keep a scientist's log, draw diagrams, and suggest plants and insects for the habitat. Group members will come together to share information, discuss similarities and differences in their findings, and develop the final plan.

Many of the activities that will take place in the class will be the kind of activities that take place in most good classrooms today, with four major exceptions:

1. The *problem-based task* is presented at the start of the unit to build a *felt need* for learning.

2. The *analytic rubric* is used to guide instruction, not assess a final project.

3. Not all students are doing the same thing at the same time. Students plan how they will use their time, thus providing for seamless differentiation, maximizing classroom resources, and building the kinds of project-management skills needed in 21st-century society.

4. The teacher actively facilitates learning by moving around the room and meeting with individuals and groups, with minimal time spent addressing the entire class.

Designing your instructional units to present students with the problem or challenge at the start of the unit will increase the likelihood that students will be driven by a *felt need* to learn. This engagement will increase the likelihood that students will retain their learning. Teachers are always surprised when they realize that students coming to them from well-run *Learner-Active, Technology-Infused Classrooms* do not experience "summer slide," but rather retain what they learned the prior year.

What Makes a Problem?

The word "problem" can sound intimidating, as though there is something wrong that must be fixed. In the *Learner-Active, Technology-Infused Classroom*, a problem is an open-ended challenge, meaning that there is no one right answer. For years, students have been focusing on being able to raise their hands and have the one right answer, focusing heavily on convergent thinking. Today's global citizens must be both divergent and convergent thinkers: able to generate questions and ideas, thinking widely, thus divergently, and able to synthesize information and test out ideas against known facts and data to determine the best idea or plan, thinking narrowly, thus convergently.

> **"Today's global citizens must be both divergent and convergent thinkers: able to generate questions and ideas, thinking widely, thus divergently, and able to synthesize information and test out ideas against known facts and data to determine the best idea or plan, thinking narrowly, thus convergently."**

Years ago I was granted funding for a study to offer insights as to whether learning in a *Learner-Active, Technology-Infused Classroom* improved critical and creative thinking. (The results indicated that there is merit to that notion.) I conducted the study across two fourth-grade classrooms. One class (control group) studied in the more conventional ways of schooling. The other (experimental group) studied through a *Learner-Active, Technology-Infused Classroom* approach. Both groups studied their state, part of the social studies curriculum. At the end of the initial learning period, the two classes were presented with a related problem to solve in forty-five minutes in groups of four. The problem was to consider where to construct another airport in the state. For each group of four students, I read and handed out the problem, pointed out that they had a wealth of resources in the classroom, including Internet access, and told them they had forty-five minutes to develop their recommendation. I then asked if there were any questions. Consistently, the experimental group students asked questions about process, resources, and expectations. Consistently, the control group students raised their hands to call out a geographic location as the answer; I had to remind them that they had forty-five minutes to research and discuss a solution. Throughout the period, I was not in the room, but the researcher observing the groups said that the experimental groups were engaged and focused. After I returned to give them the ten-minute warning, they were even more focused to complete the solution in the time allotted; whereas the control groups decided on an answer within the first few minutes and then became behavior problems. Ten minutes later, I returned to the room to hear each group's decision.

Again, consistently, the experimental groups offered thoughtful responses with evidence as to why their chosen location would be the best; consistently, the control groups presented an answer with few supporting reasons, even when prompted for more. This small, beginning study into the topic was profound for me. By fourth grade, and no doubt earlier, students have learned that school means there is one right answer and you should identify it quickly. Still, in what was probably less than a half year of learning in a different way, the students in the *Learner-Active, Technology-Infused Classroom* broke through that mold and became thoughtful, purposeful solution finders. Engaging students in solving open-ended challenges makes the difference.

In the case of this airport problem, the challenge wasn't as much of a problem (there was nothing wrong with the existing airports) as a scenario: what if the state were to build another airport? The scenario has no one right answer, no teacher's-edition answer; it only has to satisfy a collection of criteria, such as being large enough, avoiding wetlands, and so forth.

Designing an original poem, story, piece of art, or performance are also open-ended problems with no one right answer, but, rather, criteria that must be satisfied. So don't let the word "problem" make you think something has to be wrong. Of course, there are a plethora of real-world situations with problems to solve that should be included in your collection as well; but every *problem-based task* does not have to be a problem to be fixed. Sometimes, the problem could be developing a new creation, work of art, recreational idea, or plan to enhance one's life.

The key is to ensure that, to address the *problem-based task*, it is not enough for students to simply learn information and present it in a new format. They must "grapple" with content to develop something new related to the content itself, as opposed to the presentation of content. More on this later. For now, just know that a problem is any open-ended situation in which students must create something original based on applying their understanding of the curricular content. In the *Learner-Active, Technology-Infused Classroom*, the problem is further enhanced by reflecting authentic, real-world situations or possibilities.

The best problems have a balance between collaborative problem solving and individual content mastery. The *problem-based task* is intended to be a small-group problem with two to four students engaged in offering a feasible solution. While the planning, brainstorming, solution discussion, and evaluation are best addressed as a team, activities related to building content mastery are largely accomplished individually. This ensures that students build individual content mastery but also build the skills of collaborative problem solving.

How Many Problem-Based Tasks?

In the *Learner-Active, Technology-Infused Classroom*, a unit of study begins with an authentic *problem-based task* and includes myriad rich and differentiated opportunities to learn. The *ALU*, therefore, with a *problem-based task* at the core, serves as the cornerstone of the learning experience. Armed with a well-crafted *ALU*, students can identify what they know and what they need to learn, make decisions about activities in which they will engage, monitor their own progress, and take responsibility for their own learning. Therefore, all content should be addressed through an *ALU*.

Given that students learn best from a *felt need*, every curricular unit should be designed as a problem-based *ALU*, which means you'll need to design back-to-back *ALUs* across the year. A typical *ALU* in kindergarten and first grade lasts two to four weeks; in second and third grades, three to four weeks; and in fourth and fifth grades, four to five weeks. The intent is to allow students enough time to engage with the problem and grapple with the content in order to build understanding and the ability to apply it to solve the problem. Younger students, however, may not remain engaged in solving a problem over a long period of time. A lot depends on the problem itself. As the teacher, it takes time and mental energy to design an *ALU* with all of the support materials, so you would not want to have to design them on a weekly basis.

From a student perspective, it can be challenging to engage in many problems across the course of a day, so consider how curricular content connects and work to design interdisciplinary *ALUs* such that students may only be engaged in two or three over the course of a day. This may be more difficult in a departmentalized situation, but it is worth meeting and brainstorming to see how curricular content fits. Be careful not to attempt to constrain those connections, for example, always pairing math and science or the humanities. Each *ALU* may lend itself to different combinations. Also, refrain from attempting to develop just one *ALU* to address all subjects. This often leads to curricular compromises that could mean you won't adequately address all content areas. For the student, it means being involved in one challenge all day long, which could prove to be boring.

If designing multiple, back-to-back *ALUs* sounds daunting, take heart. Although learning to craft an exceptional *ALU* at first takes time and patience, the results in the classroom will make the investment worthwhile. The first *ALU* is the hardest to design. You'll find each successive design experience to be faster and easier. If you have other grade-level or subject-area colleagues with whom to design, you can divide and conquer!

CREATE

Optimally, students will become problem finders and identify the problems they wish to solve. However, when getting started in designing your *Learner-Active, Technology-Infused Classroom*, it is important for you and your students to benefit from a careful application of the basics of unit design. As you become more familiar with problem design, you can involve your students in cocreating problems with you and, eventually, allow students to decide on problems they wish to solve independently or in groups. Students in *Learner-Active, Technology-Infused Classrooms* routinely generate lists of problems that need to be addressed in the school, community, state, nation, and world. They then decide on those they wish to solve. Move at your own pace, though: first learn to design a well-crafted *ALU*, and then you can move to increasing student voice in problem generation.

For starters, design the *problem-based task statement* of the *ALU* for an upcoming unit of study. Remember that the purpose of the *problem-based task* is to motivate students, giving them a purpose for their learning. Given that, think about your classroom and the content you need to teach. Your goal is to develop an authentic, open-ended task that will create a *felt need* for your students to learn the curricular content.

Here are some guiding steps to developing your task. If you find yourself having difficulty with any of the steps, return to the previous step and rethink your decisions:

Step 1: Keep the Standards in Mind

A well-crafted *ALU* addresses curricular standards and, even though it is focused on specific subject-area content, often addresses standards from across the year and across subject areas. The best design approach would be to simply consider your overall curriculum for the year; ask yourself what kind of problems or challenges students could address if they understood the year's content; brainstorm *problem-based task* ideas, and then, using scope and sequence charts, check off all of the concepts and skills that would be addressed by the *task*. After brainstorming a few different *problem-based tasks*, you will start to see the gaps and focus on designing additional *problem-based tasks* to address those gaps. However, in an effort to monitor teaching toward student achievement, some schools have put in place pacing guides that require specific curricula to be taught at specific times, which does not allow for a lot of flexibility in *ALU* design. If that is your situation, start with the curricular standards for the time period you need to address and brainstorm a *problem-based task* around that specific content.

Consider your curriculum and identify the general content, skills, and concepts you plan to teach over a reasonable period of time. Again, if you teach kindergarten or first grade, consider a two- to three-week period; second or third grade, consider a three- to four-week period; fourth or fifth grade, consider a four- to five-week period. Remember, units that run for longer than five weeks tend to become too complex, and students can lose focus on important content. Units that run for fewer than two weeks tend to be too labor intensive to design and don't allow students to explore content with much depth. If you teach multiple subjects, consider how you can address curricular content across two or three subjects in one *problem-based task*. In "Using Numbers and Words to Feed Others" (Appendix C), students launch a campaign to collect food for the needy, involving the use of English language arts (ELA) and math skills along with health (nutrition) content.

As you begin the process, make a list of the concepts and skills you plan to teach over the specified period of time. It's important that your unit not exceed the amount of time you would normally allocate for the content. If your content focus is too limited—for example, reading a map scale—it may be difficult to identify an authentic problem to solve, and you will not cover enough content in the time period. If your focus is too broad—such as geography—it may be difficult to identify an authentic problem to solve that covers all of the curricular skills.

You may also find that as you map out your concepts and skills, several that may have been originally slated for different times of the year will intertwine. For example, in "Designer Pizza" (Appendix A), the focal content is adding and subtracting fractions with different denominators. However, a natural extension is to calculate the cost of the pizza, which involves addition, subtraction, and multiplication of money. While those skills may not be slated for this particular time, students will have a *felt need* to learn those skills and may, in fact, learn a lot in advance of that content-focused unit. Developing the pizza menus produces a *felt need* for calculating costs, which is not typically taught in conjunction with fractions but is a perfect fit here. Additionally, the pizza problem includes writing a letter to pitch the menu approach to a local pizzeria, thus addressing English language arts skills. You could even build health into the unit by having students develop the nutritional charts and suggest healthy pizza choices. Be open to cross-unit content connections when generating authentic problems. Sometimes, however, a *problem-based task* can seem so interesting that it takes on a life of its own, but veers off the grade-level standards. Just be sure that you focus on standards your students need to master in the time allotted in the curriculum to cover it.

Step 2: Think Application

Suppose your students did, in fact, master all of that content. What could they do with it? What problems could they solve? What challenges could they address? What could they create? Why do students need the information? With what audience could they share their ideas and solutions? If you have trouble identifying a *problem-based task*, you might be looking at too narrow a topic. Try combining topics. In the earlier example of "Designer Pizza" (Appendix A), you would be hard-pressed to come up with a task for learning about denominators; it's much easier to design a task around the broader topic of calculating with fractions. That challenge will build a *felt need* for students to learn the more basic skills related to computation with fractions.

Start by asking yourself, "When would someone use this knowledge?" After you respond, once again, ask yourself, "So what?" That will drive you to consider how important that application of the knowledge is. Once you defend your answer, ask, "But why?" As you continually apply the "Why?" and "So what?" questions, you will home in on an interesting problem. Below is an internal dialog from those who have developed *ALU*s.

> Young readers need to identify the parts of a story, such as character, setting, and plot.
>
> *Why?* Because books and the stories in them have these critical components.
>
> *So what?* It's important to consider these three and the interplay that exists in the story.
>
> *Why?* Because it offers the student a better understanding of the story and how the author constructed it.
>
> *So what?* Well, authors need to create a believable plot that depends upon characters and setting.
>
> Ahhh, so perhaps students could write a letter to a favorite author, suggesting that the author write a next book about the student's city or town, thus requiring the student to reference character, setting, and plot to make a strong argument.

This problem-based challenge covers myriad concepts and skills in the areas of reading, letter writing, and opinion writing. Teachers could have students send their letters to the authors, thus adding relevance to the task.

Another strategy for identifying a strong problem is to use "The Tree of Whys." You can access a video on IDE Corp.'s YouTube Channel (www.youtube.com/user/LATIClassroom). You begin by brainstorming three reasons the content is important. From each of those, you draw three lines

Figure 2.3. Tree of Whys

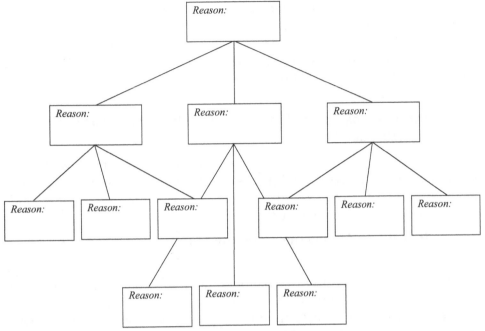

and develop three reasons why that reason is important. You then find the ones that are really compelling, and then, from each of those you begin to draw three lines and develop further reasons, although at some point in the process you will hone in on a strong problem. (See Figure 2.3.)

Given that today's Internet-savvy students are aware of and interested in the real world, problems derived from reality are often very motivating. A great source of real-world problems is the news. Peruse newspapers, news shows, and the Internet, and you are likely to find a wealth of ideas from which to write your authentic problems.

Your objective is to arrive at an authentic, open-ended problem that will intrigue and motivate students and build a *felt need* to learn the content. Most *problem-based tasks* should be addressed by a group of students so that they are collaborative in nature. (Note, however: individual content mastery and responsibility are the keys to success. Your *ALU* should never set up a situation in which one student does all the work or, conversely, a student fails to learn the necessary content.) As you brainstorm, generate as many different ideas as you can before you commit to one. It is often tempting to take the first idea that comes to mind; but the best idea generally emerges a little farther into the brainstorming process.

Step 3: Think Authenticity and Relevance

Remember, brain research (Sousa, 2017) tells us that for information to settle into long-term memory, it must make sense and have meaning. Consider this exercise from James Adams's book, *Conceptual Blockbusting* (1990). For best results, cover the rest of the page and only uncover the text as you read it. Take a look at the list of words below for about eight seconds and try to memorize them.

saw, when, panicked, Jim, ripped, haystack, the, relaxed, when, cloth, the, but, he

Chances are, you can remember about seven of the thirteen words, the typical number of disconnected pieces of information the human brain can remember at once. Now look at the same words below for a few seconds to see if it's easier to remember them.

Jim panicked when the cloth ripped but relaxed when he saw the haystack.

Most people find it easier to remember the words once they are presented in a sentence, because arranged into the known grammatical structure of a sentence, *they make sense.* Can you remember the sentence? Most people still have difficulty. What if I told you that Jim was jumping out of a plane using a parachute? Look at the sentence one more time. Now the sentence is even easier to remember. The context provides *meaning.* When you present content to your students in the absence of sense and meaning, it appears like those thirteen disconnected words.

Ensuring that content is presented with sense and meaning can be accomplished by providing students with authentic contexts for learning the content. Authenticity means that a problem is realistic, could happen, or could fall into the realm of science fiction. For primary-grades students, authenticity extends to the type of fantasy that is appropriate for the grade level. After all, in the life of a primary-grade student, animals *do* talk.

Relevance means that the problem could actually occur in a student's life at that time. Thus, relevant tasks are a subset of authentic tasks. For example, when you ask a student to consider where the governor might construct a new airport, you have posed an authentic but not relevant problem. Airports are constructed; government officials do weigh in on their location; the problem is authentic. Few if any fourth graders are actually going to be on a committee to help the governor decide where to construct an airport; consequently, the problem is not very relevant. Analyzing the nutritional aspect of the cafeteria food and making recommendations for additions and deletions of food items would be both authentic and relevant. Developing a plan to clean up a local river as part of a grant opportunity is both authentic and relevant. To those students who have pets, developing a plan to take responsibility for a pet is both authentic and relevant.

Elementary school students typically thrive on authentic tasks, with or without relevance. However, where possible, make the *problem-based task* both authentic and relevant. The following is a chart of inauthentic tasks along with possible revisions to make each more authentic, and, in some cases, relevant.

Inauthentic Tasks	Possible Revision to Make It Authentic
Create a model of an ecosystem and describe the life cycle and food-chain relations of it.	Identify an endangered species you want to save. Develop a plan for how people can help prevent that extinction, including exploring the species' place in the food chain and the other living things that would be affected by its extinction.
Using graph paper, draw as many ways as you can to create a 100-square-foot area using various shapes.	Let's convince our school administrators to allow us to plant a 100-square-foot garden in the courtyard to be a habitat for butterflies. Develop a series of designs for the garden, proving mathematically that each provides exactly 100 square feet of space.
Count objects up to twenty.	Organize the reading corner and create posters to let students know what's available. Count and share the number of books we have with authors' last names that begin with each letter of the alphabet; count and share the number of books we have on different topics.
Underline the adjectives in the story and draw an arrow to the nouns they describe.	Pick a favorite snack you like to eat and design a kid-friendly ad campaign to share with the company, convincing kids, parents, and school cafeterias everywhere to try this snack.

In the *Learner-Active, Technology-Infused Classroom,* learning is driven by a real-world, authentic, open-ended, application-oriented problem to solve. The learning activities in which students will engage along the way will most likely include the activities listed in the first column, but they become a means to an end. The *problem-based task* for your *ALU* must be authentic. If the problem is also relevant, then that's a bonus. It is most likely not feasible to develop a curriculum of entirely relevant problems; but some of the *ALUs* you present to students should be relevant. All should be authentic. In the second example above, you can move from authentic (people do create gardens) to relevant by creating an audience. Now the students are designing a garden that may actually come to fruition on the school property.

Step 4: Think Open-Endedness

In the world of content, there is the known and the unknown. In 1940s America, people worked largely in factories, on farms, or in service areas. Their success rested upon following specific rules and protocols. In today's creative economy (Howkins, 2013), the most successful workers solve problems, generate ideas, and create. All of the latter require being immersed in the unknown and its possibilities. School curricula today still focuses on mastering the *known*, with some expectation that applying that content to the unknown will magically follow.

An *ALU* should focus students both on the known and the unknown. It is in the realm of the *unknown* that the best open-ended, authentic problems emerge. If students are to learn about the topography of a geographic area, they could certainly create a clay map. Such a project exists in the realm of the known. The student researches an area and references maps in order to create a replica. It may be a fun and interesting project, but it is not open-ended, thus, it's not a problem.

Asking a student to paint an original picture representing a message to be displayed in the library focusing on a book they like is an open-ended problem that exists in the realms of both the known and unknown. Students read the book and must understand the underlying message the author is conveying. They must then determine how to artistically depict that message while including a reference to the book to promote the book for others to read. No one right answer exists, as the "right" answer is yet unknown. Open-ended problems do not have one right answer. At best, students can propose a plausible answer. In their quest for this answer, however, they grapple with content; that is, they think deeply about it, question it, and think about it through various perspectives. Open-ended problems produce a *felt need* to learn and allow students to grapple with content.

A typical assignment found in elementary classrooms today is to write a book or report on dinosaurs. This simply requires students to locate and report back information with no open-ended aspect related to the content and very little to the product. A teacher might assign a project in which students will create a dinosaur exhibit for a local museum with information on the various dinosaurs that once walked the earth. While this may sound like an engaging project, it is only slightly more open-ended than the first, with the open-endedness related more to the museum exhibit than the content. A more open-ended problem would be to ask students to consider that scientists may be able to clone a dinosaur from DNA and wish to create a habitat in today's world in which it can live. The students would have to learn about the dinosaur and make plans to accommodate its needs, thus providing a more open-ended challenge than the other two. To further increase the open-endedness of the task, ask students to research why the dinosaur may have become extinct and explore the possibility that other species may share the same fate.

Engagement in learning is less about what students are doing with their bodies and more about what students are doing with their minds. Some tend to think that if students are working in groups, talking with one another, using computers, and exploring content through hands-on situations, they are engaged. They may be engaging their bodies but not necessarily their minds.

As you brainstorm task ideas, continue to refine them to make them sufficiently open-ended, thus promoting engagement in curricular content. Decide how they might apply all of the *known* content to propose a solution to a problem for which the solution is yet *unknown*.

Step 5: Think Audience

Once the students arrive at their solutions, with whom will they share that information? As David Geurin (2017) says, "avoid the trash can finish" (p. 89). Audience is important as it connects students to a more authentic reason to solve the problem than handing in an assignment to the teacher for approval. Audience could include school-based personnel, as in the case of pitching to the food services director options for new menu items. It could be a local business or organization, a friend or family member, a government official, an author, a newspaper or magazine, a company, or a national or international organization! Might the task have global implications, promoting global citizenship? Might it have national or local implications? How can students feel like they are really making a difference by developing this solution? How can you use audience to expand students' thinking about their place in the world? "The sense of audience is an opportunity to practice empathy, to picture the project through the end user's eyes" (Geurin, 2017, p. 89).

Step 6: Think Product

What will students *do* to present their solution to the problem? What will the final product look like? Avoid thinking along the lines of a project, with "glue and glitter flying." A product could be a poem, persuasive letter, webpage, poster, song, prototype, storyboard, series of graphs, infographic, skit, work of art, or multimedia presentation.

Consider offering choices based on learning styles and multiple intelligences. If the presentation of the content is not the curricular goal of the *ALU*, might you give students options for presentation? Clearly, if your curricular goal is letter writing, then a letter it is! However, if your curricular goal is preventing the extinction of a species, does it matter whether students create a video, an infographic, or a letter? Universal Design for

Learning (UDL—www.cast.org), presents guidelines for ensuring that all students have access to quality instruction, thus maximizing their learning potential. One of the three tenets is to "Provide Multiple Means of Action and Expression." To what extent can you allow students to choose the product?

You must first decide what you are looking for students to demonstrate in terms of content. Then you can decide what options to offer students in terms of their delivery of that demonstration of knowledge. Students will appreciate the choice of final product. Students may even suggest viable products other than those you have in mind.

Design your *ALU* as a collaborative problem-solving experience for pairs, triads, or a group of four. Think about how many students should be involved in tackling the task, and design the task statement so that all students have a powerful learning experience. Even in fifth grade, where you may have students working in groups of four, you may want to create the problem such that they tackle it in pairs. You could also design a collaborative task in which there are parts that you want each student to tackle individually. For example, students might engage in problem-solving and brainstorming as a group but then individually write letters if letter writing is a skill you are teaching.

Step 7: Think Content

It is important to engage learners in grappling with targeted content that aligns with curricular standards. One common pitfall of employing a more authentic, open-ended approach to learning is to allow the product and/or media to overwhelm the content. Students who are asked to create a multimedia presentation on encouraging people to vote may spend a significant amount of time searching the Web for pictures and sound bites; they may work hard to learn new slide transitions and interesting ways to present the information. All of these are worthy skills, but they have little to do with civics. This is not to say that you should not have students make multimedia presentations; rather, you should have them use class time engaging with critical subject-area content and develop the multimedia aspects on one particular class period or for homework.

When designing an authentic, open-ended, *problem-based task* statement, continually assess how much of students' time will be spent focusing on the primary content of the unit. Figure 2.4 represents a graphic organizer that can be used to assess content focus in a task statement. The center bull's-eye represents the concepts and skills included in solving the authentic, open-ended tasks that are most closely aligned to the curricular content. Concepts and skills that are related to the content or other grade-level skills, perhaps covered in other units or subject areas across the school year, reside in the second ring from the center. Finally, concepts and skills that have little to

Figure 2.4. Bull's-Eye Graphic Organizer

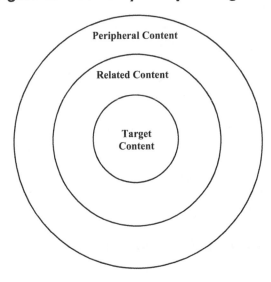

do with the course content or related content, no matter how worthy they might be, reside in the outermost ring, representing peripheral content.

In "A Place for Robots" (Appendix G), students are designing a robot that could help NASA in its quest for exploring Europa, one of Saturn's icy moons. While it might prove interesting for students to research other planets and moons that might have evidence of water, and it might be helpful for building students' science knowledge, if science is not your target content, you'll want to minimize the amount of class time spent on this in favor of the targeted content, which in this case is robotics. You could allow students to research alternate sites for NASA to explore outside of class as an optional activity. You could connect with the science teacher to see if there could be a connection between science class and robotics class for this unit.

When designing an *ALU*, strive for the bulk of the content and the bulk of the students' in-class time to be focused on targeted content, with some time spent on related content and little or no class time spent on peripheral content. Peripheral content may be tolerated based on other school goals. For example, if using a design process is a goal of a STEM/STEAM school, it would make sense to engage students in applying design process strategies even when writing an original poem.

Students will need to develop a final product that demonstrates their mastery of the content, and, in some cases, the skills involved in that physical product development are neither in the center nor the second ring of Figure 2.3. For example, developing an argument might be the content; however, creating a multimedia presentation to portray it may not be course content.

To ensure that the product does not overwhelm the content, establish clear timelines as to when your students can work on the product. For example, have them gather up the information they plan to present and then give them one block of time to develop the presentation.

Another pitfall is to design an authentic, open-ended problem around a real-world event that is exciting, such as the Olympics or a presidential election, where the content isn't in the curriculum. Students are engaged and excited, but they are not grappling with the content of the course or grade level. It is often possible, however, to creatively connect your content to a critical news event by focusing on one aspect of the event or from the perspective of the subject area.

Take a moment to reconsider and refine your task ideas to ensure that your students will focus most of their time on the target content of your curriculum standards.

A Look at a Sample Task Statement

Read through the following *problem-based task* statement, designed for students in grades three or four (see Appendix B for the *problem-based task* and *analytic rubric*):

Have you ever seen butterflies in person or on video? Have you ever been to a butterfly garden? Butterflies are beautiful to look at, adding wonderful color to our world. They are also helpful to the plants and animals around them, and they help pollinate plants that produce food for us. Butterflies, however, require some very special plants to lay eggs and to eat during the different stages of their life cycle, and those plants are on the decline. With increasing habitat loss, butterflies are finding fewer and fewer places with the plants they need to thrive. This is resulting in the quasi-extinction of butterflies. You can help! Design a butterfly garden that someone in the community could plant and that we could plant at the school to attract butterflies and help them thrive.

Let's take a look at how the task designer purposely and deliberately designed this task:

1. The task statement immediately connects the students' personal experience to the content, asking if they have seen butterflies or visited a butterfly garden.

2. The task statement deepens the students' understanding of the needs of living things in their life cycle by referencing the need for special plants on which to lay eggs and which to eat during different stages of the life cycle.

3. Presenting the reality that butterflies are losing their habitat is intended to elicit an emotional response of concern.

4. Presenting the opportunity to plant butterfly gardens that will attract butterflies and help them thrive is intended to elicit an emotional response of excitement and anticipation.

5. Planning and growing gardens to attract and help butterflies is an authentic situation. If the students are then able to actually plant the garden, it also becomes relevant.

The students will have some choice as to how they will present their proposal for the garden. It could be a written proposal, hyperlinked document, poster, or multimedia presentation. Regardless of the presentation choice, the content remains the same. *Problem-based task* statements should be written with great thought and intent aimed at building in students an excitement and *felt need* to learn and offering them some choices in the solution.

Slow Start, Quick Finish

When designing *ALUs*, you'll most likely spend a significant amount of time designing the *problem-based task* statement. This might make you anxious at first. After all, if you spend too much time on the task statement, how will you finish designing the unit? The reality is that unit design is not an incremental process. *ALU* design is heavily front loaded, requiring a significant amount of time to arrive at a worthy task statement. The *problem-based task* is so crucial to the success of the *ALU* that it is worth the time invested. The remaining support pieces will flow from this and take considerably less time to complete. The up-front investment in time and energy to develop a strong task will pay off in the end.

RECAP

At this point, you should have at least one task statement that you think is your best. See how it matches up to the key points covered in this chapter. Use this list to ensure that your task statement:

♦ Is standards based;

♦ Applies learning to an authentic situation

♦ Asks students to provide a solution to an open-ended problem;

♦ Includes an audience other than the teacher and classmates;

♦ Focuses primarily on the curricular content;

♦ Connects the content to students' lives;

♦ Elicits an emotional response where possible;

- ◆ Introduces vocabulary or concepts to deepen students' understanding of the content;
- ◆ Presents a choice of product for the students to complete.

REFERENCES

Adams, J. (1990). *Conceptual blockbusting: A guide to better ideas* (3rd ed.). Reading, MA: Addison-Wesley.

Geurin, D. (2017). *Future driven: Will your students thrive in an unpredictable world?* Bolivar, MO: David Geurin.

Howkins, J. (2013). *The creative economy: How people make money from ideas.* London: Penguin Books.

Smith, F. (1998). *The book of learning and forgetting.* New York: Teachers College Press.

Sousa, D. A. (2017). *How the brain learns* (5th ed.). Thousand Oaks, CA: Corwin Press.

3

Engaging Students Through Clearly Articulated Expectations

A first-grade teacher meets with her students in the morning with a three-column *analytic rubric* printed in large letters on flipchart paper, the columns being "I Am Working On It," "I Did It!" and "I Did It And. . . ." She uses this opportunity to review the rubric for their *problem-based task* about how frogs, turtles, and fish can help people.

Funny Frog, Terrific Turtle, and Fast Fish live in a pond. They spend their time playing, eating, breathing, moving, sleeping, and more. Human beings live their lives in much the same way but in a different place than a pond. Could Funny Frog, Terrific Turtle, and Fast Fish help us in our lives? Students are to design an invention to help human beings in some way that is based upon the abilities and life functions of a frog, turtle, and/or fish. The teacher leads a discussion offering the example of how hard a turtle shell is and how that could inspire the design for bike helmets. But first, she challenges, they have to learn all they can about frogs, turtles, and fish so they can come up with some great inventions! She talks about the work that lies ahead using the rubric, which is shown in Figure 3.1 and Appendix D.

Kindergarten students wanted to conduct a food drive to collect food for those in need in their community. They are learning about food categories, counting and adding, and writing opinions through this unit. They are using a rubric (Figure 3.2) that they designed with their teacher to guide their development of their letters to the community asking for donations.

Figure 3.1. Rubric: Can a Frog, Turtle, and Fish Help Us?

	I am Working on It!	I Did It!
Frog Drawing	I named at least 4 frog body parts.	I labelled at least 4 frog body parts. ❑ I did it! I wrote how they help the frog. ❑ I did it!
Turtle Drawing	I named at least 4 turtle body parts.	I labelled at least 4 turtle body parts. ❑ I did it! I wrote how they help the turtle. ❑ I did it!
Fish Drawing	I named at least 4 fish body parts.	I labelled at least 4 fish body parts. ❑ I did it! I wrote how they help the fish. ❑ I did it!
Idea Chart	I made a chart of animal body parts.	I made a chart of at least 10 animal body parts. ❑ I did it! I wrote about how they could help a human. ❑ I did it!
Invention Drawing	I drew my invention to help humans.	I drew my invention to help humans. ❑ I did it! I wrote about how it came from what I learned about the body parts of animals. ❑ I did it!

Figure 3.2. Rubric: Numbers and Words to Feed Others

Using Numbers and Words to Feed Others
Rubric for the Food Collection Letter

	I am Working on It! 	I Did It!	I Did It And . . .
Food List	I wrote a list of foods we can collect.	I wrote a list of at least ten different foods we can collect ❏ I did it! I chose foods that that will not spoil over the next month. ❏ I did it!	I made sure my foods are healthy.
Food List Categories	I put each of the foods I listed in the correct Food Plate category.	I put each of the foods I listed in the correct Food Plate category. ❏ I did it! I used my list to create a sample meal using the Food Plate. ❏ I did it!	I identified foods that fell into more than one category on the food plate.
My Opinion	I wrote a sentence about why people should donate to help us collect the foods on our food list.	I wrote at least two sentences about why people should donate to help us collect the foods on our food list. ❏ I did it!	I explained why the different types of food are important.
Pictures for My Letter	I drew a picture of the food items.	I drew pictures of at least three food items with numbers of what we hope to collect. ❏ I did it!	I drew a picture of the Food Plate with pictures of at least one food item in each category and numbers of what we hope to collect.

Figure 3.2. (Continued)

Using Numbers and Words to Feed Others
Rubric for the Food Collection Tallying

	I am Working on It!	I Did It!	I Did It And . . .
Counting and Recording Donations	Each day, I count up to 100 foods when they are in rows and write down the total number.	Each day, I count up to 100 foods when they are in rows or when they are scattered and write down the total number. ❏ I did it!	Each day, I count up to 100 foods in rows or scattered and tell how many more we need to make our goal.
Comparing Donations to Food List	Each week, I count and record the number of foods collected for two food categories.	Each week, I count and record the number of foods collected for each food category. ❏ I did it!	Each week, I count and record the number of foods collected for each food category and write down how many more we collected for each.
Weekly Progress Report	Each week, I write one statement about how many items we collected for one or more categories.	Each week, I write at least three comparison statements about how many items we collected in various categories. ❏ I did it!	Each week, I write comparison statements for items collected and order them from least to most.

The teacher co-created the project with students in a group meeting, identifying with them what they will have to do. To focus their efforts, she now provides them with one row of the rubric at a time (Figure 3.3). This way, young students learn to work with rubrics and not be overwhelmed by the amount of information on the rubric.

Figure 3.3. Rubric: Two Rubric Rows

Write Your Food List

	I am Working on It! 	I Did It! 	I Did It And  . . .
Food List 	I wrote a list of foods we can collect.	I wrote a list of at least ten different foods we can collect ❏ I did it! I chose foods that that will not spoil over the next month. ❏ I did it!	I made sure my foods are healthy.

Put Your Food Into Categories

	I am Working on It! 	I Did It! 	I Did It And  . . .
Food List Categories 	I put each of the foods I listed in the correct Food Plate category.	I put each of the foods I listed in the correct Food Plate category. ❏ I did it! I used my list to create a sample meal using the Food Plate. ❏ I did it!	I identified foods that fell into more than one category on the food plate.

Loss of habitat is threatening butterflies, so third-grade students are designing butterfly gardens to help butterflies find suitable places to lay their eggs. The students use a four-column *analytic rubric* to guide their learning activities. Given that they are using an engineering design process to solve the problem, the first part of the rubric guides them in the design process steps. (A portion of the rubric is shown in Figure 3.4; the full rubric is in

Figure 3.4. Rubric: A Butterfly Garden

Design Process Journal:				
	Novice	**Apprentice**	**Practitioner**	**Expert**
Formulate	states the problem to be solved and why it is important to solve it	describes the problem to be solved, why it is important to solve it, and known causes	describes: ❑ the problem ❑ known causes ❑ how other living beings are affected ❑ what will happen if we do not solve it	all of *Practitioner* plus: includes facts and statistics to show how the problem has worsened over time
Explore	❑ reads 1 non-fiction book on butterflies and records important information	❑ writes down at least 2 questions to answer through reading ❑ reads at least 2 non-fiction books on butterflies and records important information ❑ reads at least 1 fiction book on butterflies and records important information	❑ writes down at least 5 questions to answer through reading ❑ reads at least 3 non-fiction books on butterflies and records important information ❑ reads at least 2 fiction books on butterflies and records important information ❑ records information on the life cycle of butterflies ❑ makes a list of plants that attract butterflies, noting which grow in the local climate	all of *Practitioner* plus: keeps a table, while reading, to write down ❑ questions that come to mind to answer and then ❑ the answers, once found
Ideate	each group member generates one idea to use in designing the garden	each group member generates a list of at least 3 different ideas to use in designing the garden	❑ each group member generates a list of at least 3 different ideas to use in designing the garden with why the idea will be good for attracting butterflies ❑ each group member generates a list of at least 3 different ways to get people to want to build a butterfly garden	all of *Practitioner* plus: group member sketches ideas for gardens

Figure 3.5. Rubric: Oh, The Places We Can Go!—Version A

	I Am Just Getting Started	I Am Working On It	I Did It!	I Did It And …
Brainstorming Notes	☐ I listed two possible places to visit. ☐ I explained my selection. ☐ I listed at least one book or website I used to gather notes.	☐ I listed three possible places to visit, including in other states. ☐ I explained my selection based on the interests of my family members. ☐ I listed at least two books or websites I used to gather notes.	☐ I listed four possible places, including in other states and other countries. ☐ I listed the pros and cons of each. ☐ I explained the selection based on the interests of my family members. ☐ I listed at least four relevant books and valid websites I used to gather notes.	I identified two similar locations and compared them with my selection. I included an explanation of my selection.
Map of Area	I created an original map with: ☐ a title ☐ the general outline of the area ☐ the location of hotel	I created an original map with: ☐ a title ☐ compass rose ☐ landscape of area with landmarks (train station, landmark, museum, etc.) ☐ location of hotel	I created an original map with: ☐ a title ☐ compass rose ☐ landscape of the area with landmarks at least five labeled points of interest ☐ map key	I included one or more insets with details of an area that contains a point of interest.

Figure 3.6. Rubric: Oh, The Places We Can Go!—Version B

	Novice	Apprentice	Practitioner	Expert
Brainstorming Notes	includes ☐ two possible places ☐ explanation of selection ☐ at least one book or website used to gather notes	includes ☐ three possible places, including in other states ☐ explanation of selection based on the interests of all family members ☐ at least two books or websites used to gather notes	includes ☐ four possible places, including in other states and other countries ☐ pros and cons of each ☐ explanation of selection based on the interests of all family members ☐ at least four books or websites used to gather notes	all of *Practitioner* plus two similar locations with notes that compare and contrast them with the selection, including an explanation of selection
Original Map of Area	includes: ☐ a title ☐ the general outline of the area ☐ the location of hotel	includes: ☐ title ☐ compass rose ☐ landscape of area with landmarks (train station, landmark, museum, etc.) ☐ location of hotel	includes: ☐ title ☐ compass rose ☐ landscape of the area with landmarks ☐ at least five labeled points of interest ☐ map key	all of *Practitioner* plus includes one or more insets with details of an area that contains a point of interest

Appendix B.) When the teacher sits down with her students, she expects them to identify where they are at and what they need to do next. She then initials certain boxes on the rubric, indicating that she agrees with the progress thus far. By the time students hand in their final plans, she'll pretty much know their level of success, as she's worked with them all along to help them to achieve at the higher levels.

A teacher sits down with a fourth-grade student to discuss his progress on a problem he wants to solve. He indicates that he thinks he's done. The teacher asks, "Did you check this against the rubric?" The student responds, "Yes," to which the teacher persists, "And you're absolutely sure you're going to score in the Practitioner column?" The student looks down at the rubric, smiles, and admits he could do a bit more work. The teacher then suggests he see where he might be able to even reach Expert! She is training her students to rely on the *analytic rubric* and double-check their work before relying on the teacher for affirmation or before handing it in.

Second-grade students are developing family vacations to pitch to their own family and, optionally, to share with a Chamber of Commerce or travel agency. Their teacher is offering a *benchmark lesson* explaining how they are going to begin using rubrics like those they'll be seeing in third grade. She has the students look at the current rubric for the project (a portion shown in Figure 3.5) and the new rubric (a portion shown in Figure 3.6).

The teacher points out how the new rubric has different, more "grown-up" headings. She explains each heading, offering examples and explaining how they relate to the students' work. After some discussion on this, she asks the students to share what else is different. She points out how their current rubric indicates what *they* will do to create their vacation plan and how the new rubric describes the product itself. In second grade, students are transitioning from the primary-level rubric to a style of rubric they'll use throughout their school career.

Fifth-grade students are considering how we could colonize Mars. One group of four students decided to design a model biodome to support life on Mars. As a precursor to their final design, they are experimenting with an indoor greenhouse to see if they can grow food-bearing plants in a contained space. The group members designed and conducted two experiments each and are now meeting to discuss their data. As they share, one student talks about plants that grow well together and the space they need. He then asks what the dimensions of their greenhouse have to be. The students then turn to the rubric they designed, with the teacher's help, to find out. They notice that to be in the expert column, their greenhouse needs to have at least one curved side, with them calculating the area (see Figure 3.7). They decide they are definitely going for the expert level.

Figure 3.7. Rubric Row for Greenhouse Design

	Novice	Apprentice	Practitioner	Expert
Greenhouse Design	includes scale drawing of footprint w/ actual-size dimensions	includes: ❑ scale drawing w/ actual-size dimensions noted for footprint and height ❑ accurate calculation of area and volume	includes: ❑ scale drawing w/ actual-size dimensions noted for footprint and height ❑ accurate calculation of area and volume ❑ supporting reasons for dimensions based on selected plants' needs (spacing, height, etc.)	all of *Practitioner* plus one curved size with accurate calculation of area, including description of approach to the calculation

CONSIDER

Years ago, a principal with whom I consulted shared an idea he used in a faculty meeting, and we at IDE Corp. have used it with success ever since in training teachers to design *Learner-Active, Technology-Infused Classrooms*. In conducting workshops, we'll group teachers into fours and hand them a bag of gumdrops and a box of toothpicks. The instructions are to build your dream house using only gumdrops and toothpicks within the next fifteen minutes and then be prepared to offer a two-minute presentation on your creation.

Consistently, teachers get right to work, creating some amazing dream houses. At the end of the time period, each group of teachers shares its creation. Everyone is proud; applause is loud.

Unbeknownst to the teachers, we are carrying an *analytic rubric* that has criteria such as "includes five different geometric shapes." Most groups' creations include squares, rectangles, and triangles; some use an additional shape; few use five. Another criteria has to do with color-coding areas of the house; another with including interior and exterior walls. As we grade these marvelous creations, the scores, based on the rubric, are typically quite low.

I recall one workshop in which I was announcing the scores as I was handing out the scored rubrics. "Team A achieved a 29 percent; Team B achieved a 42 percent; Team C achieved a 36 percent , and so forth." As I read each score, I dropped the scored rubric on the table. Teachers quickly reached for the rubric to see how they were scored. The anger welled up, and they indicated that they were treated unfairly. Soon someone called out, "Well, if we had the rubric ahead of time, we could have gotten an A!" I didn't say a word but just waited. A hush fell across the room and then, with a sigh, someone said, "I get it." I cannot tell you how consistently this happens with groups of teachers. The teachers' own emotional response to the unfairness of judging them without first clearly articulating the expectations leads to the connection that that's what teachers do to students every day. In our consulting work, we often have teachers tell us they will never teach again without first handing out an *analytic rubric*.

In one workshop, the scores of four teams were below fifty percent; the fifth team received a fifty-six percent . The latter started cheering and exchanging high-fives for their success. When all quieted down, I pointed out they were cheering for an F. They stopped, admitting that they hadn't even thought of that; they were just so happy to have achieved the highest score. When you neglect to give students clearly articulated expectations up front, you set them up to accept and justify failure.

One of my colleagues was in a classroom decorated with Native American masks. She commented on how beautiful they were, to which a student responded, "Oh sure, I got a B. But I could've gotten an A if we had a rubric for *that* project. Who knew you'd get extra points if you laminated it?" Without clearly articulated expectations up front, students are left to read your mind; and if they repeatedly fall short of doing that, they stop trying.

"Without clearly articulated expectations up front, students are left to read your mind; and if they repeatedly fall short of doing that, they stop trying."

The Task–Rubric Partnership

While the *problem-based task* statement is intended to be motivational, creating a *felt need* to build content mastery, the *analytic rubric* details the targeted curricular content and provides students with clearly articulated expectations for their work. It should drive student action in the classroom. That means that students should regularly review the rubric and, based on what they need to accomplish next, take action to learn that content (Figure 3.8).

Figure 3.8. The Task–Rubric Partnership

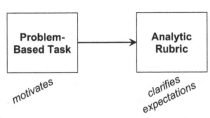

Rubrics were originally designed as a way to assess performances on standardized tests. The goal was to have multiple people assess a piece of student work and arrive at the same grade, producing interrater reliability. In an *Authentic Learning Unit (ALU)*, you are going to use an *analytic rubric* to drive instruction at the start and throughout the completion of the student's work on the *problem-based task*. In this case, the *analytic rubric* offers clearly articulated expectations for the finished piece of work and a "roadmap" for getting there. Students will use the rubric before beginning any work to gain a better understanding of their goals. They will use it throughout the unit to self-assess and set intermediate goals. As the teacher, you will use it to facilitate learning: to confer with the students regarding their current progress and guide them with further instruction and resources to achieve their goals. Essentially, the *analytic rubric* should be visible or easily accessible to students at all times; it should provide enough specific information regarding expectations for the final product to make it useful.

Using Analytic Rubrics to Drive Instruction

The rubric describes the solution that you're expecting students to develop. That final product might be a prototype, model, article, performance, presentation, and so forth. The rubric should reflect mastery of content standards as they would be evident in the final product, the outcome of the unit of study. While the rubric offers increasingly high-quality descriptions of performance as you read across, it should not be used as a list of activities for the student to complete. It is important for the *analytic rubric* to describe what students will hand in at the end of the unit to demonstrate their understanding and application of the content.

As just mentioned, holistic rubrics were designed for large-scale assessments in which multiple raters would be grading work. The rater refers to a rubric, typically of six columns, to determine which column in its entirety best describes the work. With an *analytic rubric*, each row can be assessed independent of the other rows, thus allowing the scorer to select a different column score for each row of the rubric.

Holistic rubrics are often difficult for students to use as a guide for their work because they have to be able to assess all of the components at once, as a whole. With students being able to focus on just one aspect of the work at a time, *analytic rubrics* are particularly effective tools for driving instruction. The student assesses progress and then determines the steps to take to move to the next level.

The structure, therefore, of the *analytic rubric* is a collection of rows that represent components of the final product and columns that represent levels of performance quality. Each cell in the rubric offers criteria for completing one component at a specific level, offering clarity for students. Given that the rubric is used by the student throughout the unit to drive learning and action, when designing an *analytic rubric*, you—and your students when you eventually engage them in cocreating—should be mindful of six important considerations:

1. *Titling Performance Levels:* Consider headings that describe developmental levels of increasing mastery that serve as a path to increasingly greater success, such as Novice, Apprentice, Practitioner, and Expert. When you are a novice at a skill, you push on to become more masterful. Avoid labeling the columns (levels of quality) as grades: A, B, C, D, and F. That is more reflective of a final grade and not conducive to using a rubric to engage students in the learning process. The message should be that it is okay to be a novice when you're first tackling a new concept or skill; in fact, it is to be expected. An *analytic rubric* with developmental headings encourages students to celebrate their progress and keep going. Note: for kindergarten and first-grade students, you might want to include only three performance levels as they learn to use *analytic rubrics* to drive their actions and use headings such as Working on It, I Did It, I Did It And. . . .

2. *Creating a Progression of Success*: To create a progression of increasingly higher-quality performance criteria related to a row component, label the columns with the performance levels (e.g., Novice, Apprentice, Practitioner, Expert) from left to right, with the highest-quality performance level being on the right. We read from left to right; therefore, increasing performance levels as one reads across the page sends a message that learning is a progressive journey. This allows students to first succeed at the Novice level then move to the Apprentice level and so forth.

3. *Titling Row Content:* Label the rows with the various components of the final product. For example, an opinion-writing rubric might have row titles of stating an opinion, reasons for opinion, use of linking words, and conclusion. Each row should represent a focused aspect of the final product such that you can describe it well enough for the student to succeed in performing to your level of expectation.

4. *Ordering Criteria:* Arrange the rows to mirror a reasonable order of components in building to the final product. This will help students envision how to tackle the challenge. In the opinion-writing rubric example, you would label the first row "Stating an Opinion" rather than labeling it "Conclusion." Keep those components that are most connected to the target content near the top, and use the lower rows for related components. For example, if students are creating a multimedia presentation of

their solution to the challenge of encouraging people to vote in elections, your curricular content is understanding government and civic responsibilities, so those rows should be near the top. The look of the presentation, while important, is secondary to the curricular content; thus, that row should be near the bottom so as to not draw too much attention to the presentation at the start.

5. *Keeping Rubric Language Positive:* Given the purpose of the rubric is to guide learning, as opposed to evaluating an already-completed assignment, use language that describes positive steps toward the goal. Avoid using negative criteria, pointing out what's missing. Instead, use positive descriptions as to what *does* exist. If you want students to write descriptive sentences, the first column might simply read, "all complete sentences." The second column might read, "all complete sentences using adjectives." The third might read, "all complete sentences using adjectives and adverbs." The student masters one developmental level and then considers what must be accomplished to master the next.

6. Build on a description of increasingly higher-quality performance as you move from left to right. Keep the criteria focused on describing the performance as opposed to activities to accomplish. Be sure that each column focuses on improving on the performance directly to the left of it.

It may be difficult to take all of this in at this point. As you review rubrics in the Appendices and then write your own, return to this list so that you gain a better understanding.

The Balance Between Quantitative and Qualitative Criteria

It is tempting to design an *analytic rubric* solely from quantitative criteria. However, it will fall far short of your academic goals for your students. Consider the (not recommended) *analytic rubric* in Figure 3.9 for writing a paragraph about oneself.

Using the rubric in Figure 3.9, assess the following two paragraphs:

Paragraph 1: My name is Paul James. I was born in Boston, Massachusetts in 2001. I have brown hair and brown eyes. I like playing with my dog, Mopsy. I like riding my dirt bike. I don't like vegetables. I have a sister named Natasha.

Paragraph 2: My name is Paul James, actually, Paul James III, as I was named after my grandfather and my father. I was born on a snowy

Figure 3.9. Quantitative Criteria

	Novice	Apprentice	Practitioner	Expert
Spelling	some words are spelled correctly	no more than two errors	no more than one error	no spelling errors
Grammar	some correct grammar is evident	no more than two errors	no more than one error	no grammatical errors
Punctuation	some correct punctuation is evident	no more than two errors	no more than one error	no punctuation errors
Content	at least two criteria from expert level	three of five criteria from expert level	four of five criteria from expert level	includes name, birthplace, physical description, likes, and dislikes

night in January in Boston, Massachusetts in 2001. My mom told me that I woke her up at two o'clock in the morning and said, "I'm ready to enter the world!" Ten years later, I stand four feet tall and weigh in at seventy-five pounds and, like my parents, I have brown hair and brown eyes. Needless to say, being ten, I attend school. After school, I enjoy playing with my dog Mopsy. She is a Hungarian sheep dog, so she spends most of her time trying to herd my friends and me into groups. At night, she sleeps at the foot of my bed to protect me. I also like riding my new dirt bike through the trails behind my house. I have few dislikes, but if I had to tell you what I liked least in the world, I would have to say, "Vegetables!"

Using this rubric, both students would be considered expert writers. However, clearly, the second paragraph was written by a student who possesses a greater command of the written language. This level of writing must be described qualitatively. Consider the modification of the rubric, presented in Figure 3.10.

The second *analytic rubric* successfully differentiates between the two writing samples. Compare the criteria in the rubrics in Figures 3.9 and 3.10. The former contains solely quantitative criteria, whereas the latter offers descriptive criteria to capture the quality of writing beyond sheer quantity. While it is easy to become fixated on filling in the grid, be sure to read through your rubric criteria carefully to ensure that they describe the quality of the performance.

Figure 3.10. Qualitative Criteria

	Novice	Apprentice	Practitioner	Expert
Content	includes name, birthplace, and physical description	includes full name, birthplace city and state, and physical description	includes ☐ full name ☐ birthplace city and state ☐ physical description (at least hair and eye colors) ☐ likes and dislikes ☐ at least one other piece of information	all of *Practitioner* column plus more detailed information about at least two of the criteria listed
Sentence Quality	sentences include a simple subject and simple predicate	sentences follow a similar structure but include descriptive words	☐ some variation in sentence structure ☐ use of descriptive words ☐ proper use of clauses and phrases	all of *Practitioner* plus use of one or more other writing strategies
Sentence Flow	each sentence focuses on topic	some sentences relate to one another	use of transition words and phrases to enhance paragraph flow	sentences follow one another with smooth transitions based on content and writing strategies
Mechanics	includes correct spelling of grade-level words, and correct end punctuation	includes correct spelling, present-tense grammar, and end punctuation	includes correct spelling, grammar, and punctuation throughout	all of *Practitioner* plus includes spelling, grammar, and punctuation challenges

CREATE

The first step in designing your *ALU* was to develop a *problem-based task* challenging students to create a solution or "product" (article, prototype, performance, presentation, etc.). Now use the steps that follow to design your analytic rubric, keeping in mind that you want your students to use the rubric to drive their actions. Your goal is to describe a final product or performance so that your students can assess their progress and plan to get to the next column. As you begin designing your *Learner-Active, Technology-Infused Classroom*, you will design an *analytic rubric* for the *problem-based task* you designed in Chapter 2. As your students gain familiarity with rubrics and begin to identify their own problems to solve, involve them in the *analytic rubric* design. Eventually, students will be able to present you with a rubric for you to review and advise them on enhancing to meet curricular goals.

Step 1: Determine the Structure of the *ALU* Solution

Given the *problem-based task* you developed for your *ALU*, think about what that final product would look like, as the job of the rubric is to describe the final product. Will it be a prototype? Letter? Drawing? Oral presentation? Essentially, what will students hand in at the end of the unit? Will you be able to assess student mastery simply by considering that product? Sometimes the product itself won't tell you enough about the student's abilities. This is the reason for the "show your work" approach on a math exam. In that case, you can have a portion of the final product be a log, journal, or notebook, such as, the scientist's log, the artist's notebook, the writer's journal, design process journal, and the like. Students would hand in a notebook of sorts with specific aspects of their work that led to the final product, much as an actual scientist, writer, engineer, artist, and other professionals would keep. Decide if you need such subproducts, such as the product itself and a log, journal, or design notebook for a closer look at the student's process in developing the solution. Sometimes a final product is a collection of multiple subproducts, for example: a product prototype, a designer's notebook, and a letter to pitch the product to a company. Your rubric can be divided into sections to accommodate each of these. Decide on the various aspects of the *ALU* solution for which you will need performance criteria so you can structure the rubric in one or more sections.

Step 2: Identify What Grade-Level Performance Would Look Like

Given that the purpose of the *analytic rubric* is to offer clearly articulated expectations, begin rubric design by asking yourself what you would consider to be a strong, grade-level performance. For each product or sub-product to be developed by the student, write down a list of descriptive phrases, focusing more, at first, on the curricular content demonstrated in the product than on the product appearance. If you allow students to choose their final product form, some may create multimedia presentations while others offer oral presentations and still others written work, but the same subject-area content should be evident in all. What would a strong, content-rich solution look like?

In the *ALU* "Using Numbers and Words to Feed Others" (Appendix C), the students will create a donation list, write a letter to inspire others to give, and collect and categorize donations. What would a strong donation list look like? You might decide that the student should generate at least ten different types of food and put them into categories. For the letter, you might want the student to give two reasons someone should donate to help feed others.

If you're asking students to develop various fractional pizza slices for the *ALU* "Designer Pizza" (Appendix A), you may want them to conduct a survey of twenty people to determine popular types of pizza, develop eight different-sized pie slices, and create twelve sample meal options, combining different pizza slices based on a theme.

As you think through the final product and imagine looking at high-quality examples, identify what you would expect to see. At this point, don't attempt to categorize the criteria. Just create a list of what the final product and subproducts would look like. Be as specific and descriptive as possible.

Step 3: Define the Rubric Categories

Next, group the criteria into categories. In the primary example, "Using Numbers and Words to Feed Others" (Appendix C), you might find that some criteria deal with developing a list of foods, then categorization of foods, then writing an opinion letter about donating food, and so forth. In the example "Designer Pizza" (Appendix A), you might find that some criteria deals with conducting market research, some with developing pizza slice options, some with designing a menu, and so forth.

A strong *analytic rubric* generally has four to seven categories, or rows. If you have too few categories, you may not be asking for a rigorous enough demonstration of learning. If you have too many, the rubric may appear overwhelming. However, when you have multiple subproducts, you can consider each to have a set of rows, so you would most likely exceed seven categories overall. In that case, I'd recommend each subproduct have its own rubric page. Review your categories to ensure that they are heavily oriented toward the desired subject-area content. If your content is not presentation, avoid dedicating more than one row to that. Better yet, let the students make the presentation in any format they like; your rubric, then, can just be focused on your content. In the "Designer Pizza" example (Appendix A), all five of the rows are packed with math content, and there is no specified format to present the menus, focusing students more on the math than on the aesthetic aspects of designing a menu.

In self-contained elementary grades, however, mixing content in one rubric is actually preferred. That is, even though a particular *problem-based task* is about science, include the writing aspects and math aspects, as you teach those subjects as well. It is only with departmentalization that you have to take care to focus primarily on the subject-area content. Optimally, a team of teachers would design a unit that allows the student to focus on content from multiple subject areas while addressing the same task. For example, if the science teacher has students writing a proposal to add a ride they design to an amusement park, the language arts teacher might provide assistance on writing techniques and coach the students from that perspective.

Step 4: Define the Rubric Columns

Your rubric should have four columns (possibly three if you're writing for kindergarten or first-grade students.) The column next to the rightmost column should represent grade-level mastery, and the rightmost column should provide a reach to challenge your academically advanced students. That leaves the first column or two to represent steps toward grade-level expectations. The purpose of the columns is not for students to complete the first column before moving on to the second. It is so that when they look at the grade-level column, if it seems overwhelming, they can take a step back to get started. It also increases the likelihood that, as they are working, they will find themselves somewhere on the rubric so they can celebrate progress toward the end goal.

Step 5: Write a Developmental Progression for Each Row Across the Columns

The next step is to write an individual row or category. You should form your Practitioner (or "I Did It") column from your brainstormed list of expectations. Based on each row category, fill the Practitioner column with a description of what you expect. Be sure to review your state or district curriculum standards to ensure that you reflect them in the description. Figure 3.11 offers the Practitioner column of a rubric on designing a new playground.

Once the Practitioner column is written, consider the developmental levels of quality students would follow to arrive at that level of performance. Where might they start? What naturally follows? Use this line of thinking to develop the Novice and Apprentice columns. Keep in mind that as you

Figure 3.11. Planning a Playground Rubric: Practitioner Column

	Novice	Apprentice	Practitioner	Expert
Calculations			accurately determines: • length of schoolyard • width of schoolyard • perimeter of schoolyard • area of schoolyard	
Playground Diagram			uses graph paper to chart: • perimeter and area of schoolyard • perimeter, area, and placement of sports fields • perimeter, area, and placement of basketball court • dimensions and placement of equipment	
Equipment Data			includes: • survey questions • survey of 50 students • data displayed in bar graph • graph labels and key • predictions made for entire student body based on sample polled	
Budget			accurately determines cost of playground equipment	
Written Proposal			• includes explanation of design • supports design with references to calculations and data • builds an argument with several points and supporting statements for each	

Figure 3.12. Rubric Criteria Progression

	Novice	**Apprentice**	**Practitioner**	**Expert**
Graphic Organizer	includes opinion and one supporting reason	includes opinion and three supporting reasons	includes: ❏ opinion ❏ three supporting reasons, each with facts or details ❏ a conclusion	all of *Practitioner* plus includes at least one opposing claim

read from Novice to Apprentice to Practitioner, you want to see a natural progression of learning, the way you would instruct students. Review the Practitioner column to ensure that all of your expectations are included. If you expect it, it must be articulated in the rubric.

Also note that the progression across the columns should not represent different activities. For example, you would not have one column indicate that the student makes a graphic organizer, the next an outline, and the next a rough draft. These are different stages in the overall product development; as such, they would each have a row dedicated to that subproduct. Within the graphic organizer row, you might indicate, as depicted in Figure 3.12, the beginning level would be that the student fills in their opinion and one supporting reason. The next level includes three reasons. All reasons are not alike, however, so rather than simply adding the next component, you'll note that at the next level, the student includes facts or details to strengthen those reasons. The student must also include a concluding statement. The expert column has them tackling writing found at a higher level, which is that of acknowledging possible counter arguments. Each successive column should describe a higher quality of performance.

Step 6: Write the Expert Column

Writing the Expert column is slightly different from writing the others, as you're looking to inspire students to achieve at levels that are higher than grade-level expectations. Essentially, there are four ways to move from the Practitioner column to the Expert column.

1. The first and least powerful is to make a quantitative leap, that is, have students produce more. If the Practitioner column asks for four facts, the Expert asks for more than four. If the Practitioner column asks for varied sources, including books, journals, and the Internet, the Expert column asks for two of each. Sometimes, asking for more is the appropriate approach; however, always

challenge yourself to make a qualitative leap, modifying the quality rather than quantity of response.

2. The second option is to make a qualitative leap of *extended content*, that is, content that may not typically be introduced at the grade level or at all. If students engaged in an interdisciplinary unit are asked to draw a compass rose on a map with four directions (i.e., N, S, E, and W), the Expert column might require them to use a protractor to accurately construct the compass rose. If first-grade students are writing a slogan for keeping skin safe, the Expert column might be to have that slogan rhyme. If the Practitioner column of a rubric asks students to use prepositions in their writing, the Expert column might ask them to use hyperlinks to identify phrases serving as adjectives and those serving as adverbs. If music students are asked to play a song within a single scale of notes, the Expert column might require them to play a song that covers notes in two octaves.

3. A third option is to make a qualitative leap of *higher cognitive level*, that is, requiring a more sophisticated level of thinking. If students are asked to list cause-and-effect relationships of an event, the Expert column might require them to include primary, secondary, and tertiary effects. For example, if students are to identify cause-and-effect relationships of the increase in water temperature on Caribbean coral reefs, an obvious response from some research might be the death of the microscopic plants that feed the coral reefs. A secondary effect would be the death of the coral reefs. A tertiary effect would be the loss of the fish that thrive among the coral reefs. A quaternary effect would be the devastation of the economies of the Caribbean nations. Thinking through related levels of events, including projecting future effects, requires higher cognitive skills. In "Can a Frog, Turtle, and Fish Help Us?" (Appendix D), students must list the main body parts of a frog, turtle, and fish. At the expert level, they compare and contrast these parts to those of humans.

4. A fourth option is to make a qualitative, *metacognitive leap*, that is, asking students to reflect on their own thinking process. This usually takes the form of asking students to talk or write about how they went about solving a problem, explaining a process to others, or reflecting on their plan to manage a project. If the Practitioner column requires the students to use at least three geometric figures to make a new shape, the Expert column might ask them to describe how they went about making the design.

A common misconception when addressing the needs of gifted learners is that because they are so capable, they should produce more. Quantitative and extended content leaps from the Practitioner column to the Expert column do not challenge gifted learners as do higher cognitive and metacognitive leaps. A well-crafted rubric will present varied ways to move from the Practitioner column to the Expert column throughout the rubric.

Figure 3.13 presents two columns from a rubric on designing a playground. For "Storyboard Dimensions," to be an Expert, students are challenged to think at a higher cognitive level by explaining the relationships between two different measurements. "Playground Diagram" requires extended content of scale conversions. "Written Proposal" makes a metacognitive leap, requiring students to explain how they decided upon their argument points. As you design your rubric, be mindful of the ways in which students will move to become Experts and use these different approaches throughout.

Step 7: Foster High Academic Standards

Review the rubric you have just designed. As previously detailed, you'll want to make the Practitioner column grade-level performance and fill the Expert column with a description of truly exemplary work. Use these two columns to foster high academic standards. Refer to your state standards to ensure you're using the language and including the nuances of the standards. Consider what understanding and application of content would look like and include that criteria in the rubric. If it is too easy for students to achieve at the Expert level, there will be little or nothing to challenge those who are able to move beyond the norm, and average students will be satisfied with their performance rather than pushing themselves to achieve more. Be comfortable knowing that few if any of your students will be able to score completely in the Expert column.

Step 8: Ensure Objectivity

It is important to write the criteria in as objective a manner as possible so that student and teacher alike will assign the same performance level. "Neat" means something different to everyone. "All lines drawn with a ruler or straight edge" means the same thing to everyone. This aspect can be a challenge. However, taking the time to define a performance allows you to raise academic standards. Read through your rubric to ensure that you have clearly defined all criteria. Where space is an issue, use a checklist or a nested rubric. For example, if you use the term "neat" in your rubric, provide a separate checklist that describes what neat looks like. If the unit content is social studies, but you are asking students to write an argumentative essay, keep your rubric focused on social studies content and

Figure 3.13. Planning a Playground: Expert Column

	Novice	Apprentice	Practitioner	Expert
Calculations			accurately determines: • length of schoolyard • width of schoolyard • perimeter of schoolyard • area of schoolyard	all of *Practitioner* plus explains the relationship between area and perimeter
Playground Diagram			uses graph paper to chart: • perimeter and area of schoolyard • perimeter, area, and placement of sports fields • perimeter, area, and placement of basketball court • dimensions and placement of equipment	all of *Practitioner* plus includes key for scale
Equipment Data			includes: • survey questions • survey of 50 students • data displayed in bar graph • graph labels and key • predictions made for entire student body based on sample polled	all of *Practitioner* plus percentages are displayed for each category
Budget			accurately determines cost of playground equipment	all of *Practitioner* plus includes state tax in total cost
Written Proposal			• includes explanation of design • supports design with references to calculations and data • builds an argument with several points and supporting statements for each	all of *Practitioner* plus uses calculations to argue against a different proposal

include a reference to a rubric for writing an argumentative essay that is a separate rubric unto itself. When students encounter the reference to the nested rubric, they retrieve that *analytic rubric* for further guidance. This is particularly helpful when offering students options for the final product. You may write a math unit task that allows students to create a multimedia presentation, three-dimensional model, or written report. Focus on the math content in the rubric and refer students to a separate *analytic rubric* for the type of final product. You can utilize those rubrics throughout the year as students design various products.

Step 9: Include Executive Function Skills

You can promote executive function skills throughout any unit. Consider your *ALU* task and include rubric criteria that will build executive function skills. While there are forty executive function skills that are important for students (Sulla, 2018), here are some that will fit almost any unit:

- **Cause-and-effect relationships:** Have students identify primary and secondary cause-and-effect relationships. Tertiary effects and beyond could be reserved for the expert column. As an example, rain causes runoff (primary), which causes soil erosion (secondary), which causes soil to fill rivers and streams (tertiary), which causes flooding (quaternary). You can have students identify existing cause-and-effect relationships and project future effects.

- **Seeing multiple sides to a situation:** Have students consider different points of view related to the *ALU* task. It might be of those affected by the problem; it might be those to whom students will advocate for their solution.

- **Categorizing information:** Have students categorize information related to the *ALU* task. While you may give younger students the categories; have older students decide on categories to use.

- **Predicting outcomes:** Have students engage in predicting outcomes to experiments and thinking through future events related to the *ALU* task.

- **Considering future consequences in light of current action:** Have students consider unintended consequences of their or others' decisions.

A Closer Look at the Complete Rubric

Let's recap some of the important features of a high-quality rubric. Consider the second-grade rubric for "Oh, The Places We Can Go!" (Appendix F) shown in Figure 3.14. (Note: the choice of this rubric is for illustrative

Figure 3.14. Rubric for the Places We Can Go!

	Novice	Apprentice	Practitioner	Expert
Brainstorming Notes	includes ❑ two possible places ❑ explanation of selection ❑ at least one book or website used to gather notes	includes ❑ three possible places, including in other states ❑ explanation of selection based on the interests of all family members ❑ at least two books or websites used to gather notes	includes ❑ four possible places, including in other states and other countries ❑ pros and cons of each ❑ explanation of selection based on the interests of all family members ❑ at least four books or websites used to gather notes	all of *Practitioner* plus two similar locations with notes that compare and contrast them with the selection, including an explanation of selection
Original Map of Area	includes: ❑ a title ❑ the general outline of the area ❑ the location of hotel	includes: ❑ title ❑ compass rose ❑ landscape of area with landmarks (train station, landmark, museum, etc.) ❑ location of hotel	includes: ❑ title ❑ compass rose ❑ landscape of the area with landmarks ❑ at least five labeled points of interest ❑ map key	all of *Practitioner* plus includes one or more insets with details of an area that contains a point of interest
Itinerary	includes: ❑ location (city, state, country) ❑ distance from home ❑ length of travel time	includes: ❑ location (city, state, country) ❑ distance from home ❑ times and dates for arrival and departure ❑ at least two activities with specified dates	includes: ❑ precise location ❑ distance from my home using the most precise standard measurement ❑ relation, in terms of direction, to my home ❑ dates and times, to the nearest five minutes, for arrival and departure to hotel ❑ list of at least one activity per day with schedule for each day	all of *Practitioner* plus at least two restaurants each for breakfast, lunch, and dinner, with the distance from the hotel, using the most precise standard measurement, and why I chose them

	Novice	Apprentice	Practitioner	Expert
Budget	Itemizes costs for transportation and hotel for entire duration of vacation	Itemizes costs for entire duration of vacation, including: ❑ transportation to and from the destination ❑ hotel ❑ meals (three per day)	Itemizes costs and calculates total cost for the family for the duration of vacation, including: ❑ transportation to and from the destination and for each day ❑ hotel ❑ meals (three per day plus snacks) ❑ activities on the itinerary	All of *Practitioner* plus provides alternative activities for at least two activities that include cost comparisons
Presentation of Information	❑ states an opinion as to where to go on vacation ❑ includes the map, itinerary, and budget ❑ explains some of the activities and the prices	❑ states an opinion as to where to go and why this vacation is worth taking ❑ includes the map, itinerary, and budget in a way that makes sense to the reader or viewer	❑ states an opinion as to where to go and why this vacation is worth taking ❑ includes several reasons for taking the vacation, using linking words to make connections between ideas ❑ includes the map, itinerary, and budget in a way that makes sense to the reader or viewer, including an introduction for each ❑ explains the daily list of activities and prices, utilizing a chart, graph, or visual aid ❑ includes a concluding statement ❑ includes images of points of interest	all of *Practitioner* plus includes personal statements from family members regarding selection (written or videotaped)

purposes; you'll want to think through the points made here as they relate to your grade level and subject area.) Students are proposing a family vacation. This is an interdisciplinary unit addressing map skills, addition, and writing an opinion paper. Read down the Practitioner column; it is full of criteria related to these topics. It includes language from the standards, such as "the most precise standard measurement" and "using linking words to make connections between ideas." The first step in assessing the quality of your rubric is to read down the Practitioner column to ensure that it details the curricular content being studied. If there are any curricular skills you want students to tackle, they belong in the rubric.

Next, look at the developmental movement from Novice to Apprentice to Practitioner. In the first row, the Novice is acknowledged for identifying two possible vacation spots and beginning to gather information. The Apprentice must expand the vacation spot search beyond the local area and explain the selection based on family interests. The Practitioner column introduces a level of reasoning, asking students to make a list of pros and cons of the possible vacation spots.

For the row "Presentation of Information," the first level of achievement includes stating an opinion as to where to go on vacation. At the Apprentice level, the student must include why this vacation is worth taking. At the Practitioner level, the student must support the opinion with reasons.

In each row, the rubric designer is considering how one would go about achieving the goal of designing a worthy final product, breaking it down into progressive steps. Note that the steps would not be the assignments:

♦ Fill out a graphic organizer;

♦ Write a rough draft;

♦ Write a final draft.

While those are steps in a process, they describe student action more than a final product. Instead, you could have a rubric row for graphic organizer to be submitted with the final product that might look like this:

	Novice	Apprentice	Practitioner	Expert
Graphic Organizer	includes at least two topics on the subject	includes at least two topics on the subject with at least two detail points off each	includes at least four key topics on the subject with at least three different detail points off each, including some details that are not widely known	all of *Practitioner* plus includes a third level of detail

Given that you'll be using the rubric to drive instruction and guide your students, keep in mind that they will read each column and decide what they have to do to achieve at that level. Essentially, you are mapping out the path to success for them. Note the developmental progression in each row.

The Grading Dilemma

The key to teaching through an *ALU* is realizing that your role as the teacher is to ensure that *all* students achieve at the Practitioner level. Your job is to provide high-quality, varied learning experiences so that all students succeed; consequently, grading students on the final product is more like grading your own performance. The unit rubric is not intended to produce a grade as much as it is to drive instruction. If you do grade the performance, and if you succeeded in your role in the classroom, it should earn an A or a B; essentially, you are grading yourself as a teacher. If the authentic, open-ended unit task is compelling, students will engage for that reason alone and not for the grade. After all, when students play after school and engage in various sports and online activities, they're not doing so for a grade.

Throughout the unit, the students will engage in a number of activities, both collaboratively and individually. You should grade individual assignments and individual contributions to the final product. Intermediate deadlines for various stages of the final product will help students manage the project more successfully, and related individual assignments should also be graded. You should additionally administer quizzes and even tests across the course of the unit. All of these grades will allow you to see how each student is progressing with individual content mastery.

You will know whether *you* have achieved your goals as a teacher by the success rate of your students in achieving at the Practitioner column. Some teachers make the mistake of handing out the *problem-based task* and *analytic rubric* and then expecting students to achieve success on their own. Given that at the start of the *ALU* you will have offered your students no prior instruction, they would be hard pressed to succeed. The purpose of the *problem-based task* and *analytic rubric* is to offer an instructional roadmap as to what lies ahead on the learning front for your students. As the teacher, your job is to provide students with nearly limitless opportunities to learn, such that, in the end, all of your students succeed.

Once the students have fulfilled the requirements of the Practitioner column of the *analytic rubric* and have met with success, however, what assurance do you have that the students have mastered the content? After all, you provided ongoing instruction and guidance so that students *would* succeed; but what happens in the absence of that level of support?

Assessment Through the Transfer Task

Wiggins and McTighe (2005) used the term "transfer task" to describe an end-of-unit assessment. In the *Learner-Active, Technology-Infused Classroom*, the transfer task would be a focused, performance-based task that can be accomplished by an individual student in a short period of time, typically one or two class periods. The intent is to assess how well the student can transfer the knowledge learned to a new situation. The *problem-based task* introduced to launch the unit is intended to build a *felt need* to study the unit content. The students then spend two to five weeks, depending on the length of the unit, delving into subject-area content, with your guidance. At the end of the unit, they should be able to complete a transfer task in a shorter period of time, now possessing the knowledge they need to solve the problem.

The transfer task should be authentic and cause students to apply their learning, thus demonstrating understanding of the content. It should not require a significant amount of time. As an example, you could use "Designer Pizza" (Appendix A), in which students develop inventive pizza menus offering patrons various-sized slices, as both a *problem-based task* and as a transfer task. When used as a transfer task, the student is asked to develop a set of menu combinations for a local pizzeria. Given that students have already studied fractions using a different *problem-based task*, it will not take them long to develop their solution. When used as a *problem-based task* for learning content, it takes approximately four to five weeks, as the students are learning and practicing key math skills across that time period.

You will want to consider what resources (e.g., charts, maps, formulas), if any, to make available to your students while solving the problem. The transfer task should be assessed by a rubric or a scaled checklist. In the case of pure evaluation, you could use a holistic rubric or an *analytic rubric*. The rubric should focus heavily on curricular content more than the presentation of information. Typically, the end-of-unit transfer task asks students to simply offer a solution rather than create a multimedia presentation or other time-consuming product.

RECAP

The *analytic rubric* presents students with clearly articulated expectations so that they can take responsibility for their own learning; it drives instruction. Use this list to ensure that your *analytic rubric* includes these points:

♦ The Practitioner column accurately and completely represents the content that is the focus of the unit;

- The Novice and Apprentice columns offer a developmental progression toward the Practitioner column;

- The Novice column captures what a beginning performance might look like without using negative language;

- The rubric is mostly written with qualitative as opposed to quantitative criteria;

- Criteria are written to be objective, with little or no room for subjective assessments;

- The progression from Practitioner to Expert utilizes a combination of approaches (extended content, higher cognitive level, metacognitive) where possible;

- The rubric includes related executive function skills.

REFERENCES

Sulla, N. (2018). *Building executive function: The missing link to student achievement*. New York, NY: Routledge.

Wiggins, W., & McTighe, J. (2005). *Understanding by design*. Alexandria, VA: ASCD.

4

Engaging Students Through Differentiated Learning Activities

Fifth-grade students are designing pages for a website titled "What If They Didn't?" that profiles those from World War II who helped to save people of the Jewish faith from the Holocaust. They are reading *Number the Stars* by Lois Lowry. In writing their courage profiles, they have to compare and contrast a person of their choice who made a difference with the actions and beliefs of the characters in the story. They will then share how people today can make a difference in standing against current and future genocide. According to the *analytic rubric*, they have to quote accurately from text. Shadi isn't sure he knows what this means, so he looks at his *activity list* and chooses a video to watch to help him out.

Kindergarten students want to design animal containers to collect recyclables, based on the animals in the book *Brown Bear, Brown Bear, What Do You See?* Their teacher launches the unit by having students discuss what items can be recycled and talking about why it's important to put them in a recycling container. Together, the class makes a list of ways they can help others recycle. They will then choose from activities to learn more about recycling, including watching a video, going to a learning center, and reading a book.

Fourth-grade students are becoming "Ambassadors of Friendship" for students who are new to the school, developing "Thrival Guides" with maps of the school and tips for having the best school experience. Their *analytic rubric* details what they must include on their map of the school; the Expert column indicates the map must be drawn to scale. One student created a *how-to video* of how he created his scale drawing using grid paper. The teacher is offering an advanced *small-group mini-lesson* at 2:00 for all those who have already drawn a map and are looking to learn how to convert measurements to scale. Justin and Amelia decide to sign up so they can work on becoming Experts in the map category.

A kindergarten student who struggled at times with reading and math came in excited to prove he could tie his shoes. The teacher had quietly offered him this challenge, with the opportunity to become the first peer expert for shoe tying. He succeeded and beamed with pride as he was able to help others. He dove into learning that day with new energy, determined to become a *peer expert* again soon! The teacher made a note on her executive function *facilitation grid* to give him an academic challenge next that he could work on at home.

CONSIDER

Beyond the *Problem-Based Task* and *Analytic Rubric*

A well-constructed *problem-based task* builds a *felt need* for students to learn; it motivates them. The corresponding *analytic rubric* provides clearly articulated expectations so that students can set and pursue goals. The next step is to consider how students will learn the concepts, skills, and content needed to complete the task. In a conventional setting, teachers spend much of class time presenting information to students, feeling comfort in knowing they covered the curriculum. In the *Learner-Active, Technology-Infused Classroom*, the students spend much of the time engaging in *learning activities* that they've chosen or found, thus taking charge of their own learning. These might include *how-to sheets, videos, screencasts, learning centers, peer experts, small-group mini-lessons*, and more. Masterful teachers focus less on teaching to the whole class and more on identifying and developing appropriate *learning activities* and empowering students to take charge of their own learning, thus ensuring that instruction is appropriate for individual students' needs. Students remain engaged in learning when they receive instruction in skills and concepts they need in order to solve a bigger problem and when that instruction is matched to their ability level and learning style strengths. The educational Twitter chats in the spring fill up with questions about how teachers are going to keep students engaged until the last day of school; my response is always: in the *Learner-Active, Technology-Infused Classroom*, the last day of school arrives and students exclaim, "It's over already?" Teachers don't engage students; purpose, autonomy, and mastery do (Pink, 2011). As Einstein believed, teachers create the conditions through which students learn.

Learning Activities Versus *Practice Activities*

As you move away from providing instruction from the front of the room in order to design a more differentiated learning environment, you will have to consider other ways through which students will learn concepts and skills. Oftentimes in a classroom, the teacher presents the content while students attend, follow along, and, sometimes, take notes. Students then engage in independent activities aimed at practicing what they learned. The problem is that not all students are at the same cognitive level and are, thus, not necessarily ready to learn that whole-group lesson at the time and in the way the teacher is presenting it. This leaves some students bored and others frustrated. In the *Learner-Active, Technology-Infused Classroom*, students continually engage in instructional activities that are just above their ability level, thus maximizing the probability of success and building momentum toward achieving the standards. Through this learning environment, all students can succeed at high levels in one classroom, including special education students, new language learners, and gifted students. This level of differentiation requires a variety of independent activities that provide students with direct instruction, thus mirroring what the teacher would, in the past, have presented to the whole class. It is, therefore, important to realize that the former practice activities used after the lesson cannot serve as learning activities, as students would have to discover answers and teach themselves, neither of which are goals of the *Learner-Active, Technology-Infused Classroom*. This is why it is important to ensure you provide *learning activities* before *practice activities*.

"Learning activities have three components: a specific content focus, directions, and feedback" (Sulla, 2015, p. 113). They may be videos, printed directions, learning centers, interactive websites, and more. The key is to ensure that students are being offered explicit instruction in the target concept or skill, just not from the front of the room in a whole-class setting.

Vygotsky's Zone of Proximal Development

As stated earlier, but worth repeating, it is ineffective to attempt to teach skills from the front of the room via a whole-class lesson. The diversity of students' cognitive readiness, even in homogeneously grouped classrooms, is too great. Cognitive psychologist Lev Vygotsky (1978) introduced the term "zone of proximal development" (ZPD) in the early 20th century. Vygotsky claimed that everyone has a current body of knowledge. Based on your own body of knowledge, you have a proximal zone: that which you are cognitively ready to learn. Outside of that is your distal zone: that which you are not yet ready to learn. Consider a student who understands the concept and process of multiplication. The skill of division lies in her proximal zone because, based on her current body of knowledge, she is ready to learn that skill. Quadratic equations are in her distal zone because she does not possess the cognitive readiness to understand them.

Figure 4.1 offers a summary graphic for ZPD. When you consider standing in the front of your class of students, ready to present a skill, for some, that skill is in their proximal zone, the middle ring, so they will gain from your lesson. For others, that skill already lies in their current body of knowledge, the center circle, so they will be bored and feel like their time is being wasted, or they will feign attention and daydream about other things. For others who do not possess the prerequisite skills to tackle what you are about to teach, that skill lies in their distal zone, the outermost ring, so they will be lost and frustrated and potentially become behavior problems. So at any point when you are teaching skills to an entire group of students, chances are you are reaching roughly a third of the class. Consequently,

Figure 4.1. Zone of Proximal Development

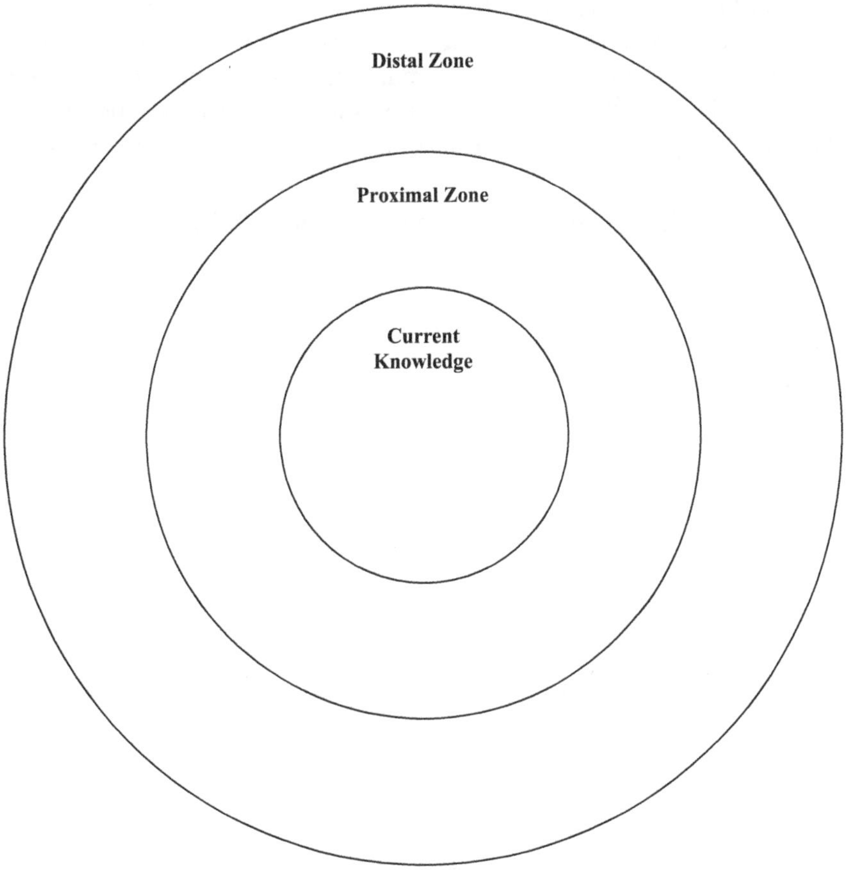

whole-class, *benchmark lessons* are best used to introduce concepts, not skills, that relate to the *Authentic Learning Unit (ALU)*. *Benchmark lessons* should build students' awareness of what they need to learn and why, related to developing a solution to the problem-based task. In the *Learner-Active, Technology-Infused Classroom*, whole-class lessons are not intended to be used for skill instruction.

Mihaly Csikszentmihalyi (1990) found that people learn best when they are in a state of flow—when they are so engaged in an activity that they lose track of everything else around them (Figure 4.2). Building on Vygotsky's work, he points out that for every task in which we engage, we have an ability level that determines how successful we will be. When tasks are just above our ability level, allowing us to be challenged but also achieve success, we are more likely to experience a state of flow. That state of flow, however, is very individual. A set of activities that evokes flow in one student will not necessarily evoke flow in the next, presenting the need for differentiation.

Marc Prensky (2006) draws a parallel between Vygotsky's and Csikszentmihalyi's work and video gaming. Teachers may report that students cannot maintain their attention throughout a lesson. When considering the hours that students engage with a video or computer game, one cannot assume today's students have a minimal attention span. Prensky concludes that video and computer games are successful, in part, because they use a "leveling up" approach to skill building. When the student starts playing

Figure 4.2. Csikszentmihalyi's "Flow"

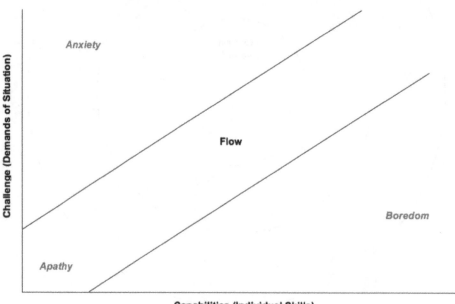

the game, she is at a particular level. She may have to replay the level several times until she masters it, at which point she advances to a slightly more challenging, and thus motivating, level. Video game designers have a vested interest in maintaining the attention of their players. If the game were too difficult, their players would abandon it with frustration. If it were too easy, their players would become bored and opt to play something else. Leveling up ensures that as the players meet with success at each level, they are compelled to attain the next. Teachers would do well to apply this leveling-up concept to their classrooms, which again presents an argument for purposeful differentiation.

Over the years, most of the regular education teachers I've interviewed have reported some level of frustration in not being able to meet the needs of all of their students. When I ask if they only had one student, could they ensure success, they respond affirmatively. When I suggest that if they had two students, they could ensure success, they also agree. As I continue to add to the number, generally the number four or five seems to be the cutoff for feeling successful in ensuring that all students achieve. If, as a teacher, you feel strongly that you could succeed with one student, teaching to that student's proximal zone, then you already have the keys to success for each student! What you need in order to differentiate instruction are "teacher-cloning tools"—ways through which students can learn other than through an in-person encounter with you.

As you prepare to introduce a curricular skill to your class, plot your students on a graphic like the one in Figure 4.1 so you can see who already knows the skill (center), who is ready to learn it (next ring out), and who doesn't have the prerequisite knowledge to learn the skill right now (outermost ring). Make sure you have enough differentiated *learning activities* to teach to the middle, challenge the center group, and support the outer group in being ready to learn the skill.

The *Learning Map*

You're about to develop a set of *learning activities* through which students will achieve the level of demonstration of knowledge outlined on the *analytic rubric*. The best way to start the process is with a *learning map*, which is essentially a roadmap to producing the solution for the *problem-based task*.

Start with a piece of blank paper or digital canvas. Visualize your students tackling the *problem-based task* that's at the core of your *ALU*. Write down what your students might do first to provide a solution to the problem. Be very specific. For example, in "Using Numbers and Words to Feed Others" (Appendix C), to get started, students must first generate a list of foods to collect; but that's not specific enough. Break it down into smaller steps (Figure 4.3).

Once you have your *learning map* for a portion of the *ALU*, at each step, decide what concepts or skills students will need and the ways in which

Figure 4.3. Learning Map: Using Numbers and Words to Feed Others

Identify foods to collect that do not require refrigeration.
Determine food categories.
Classify foods to collect by food categories.

they could learn them. To identify foods to collect that do not require refrigeration, students might use reference charts, watch videos, read books, use a learning center, interview parents, and so forth. Once they have a list or collection of pictures, they need to categorize them; but first they have to identify the major food categories. They might use videos and pictures of the food plate, read books, use a learning center, or attend a *small-group mini-lesson* with the teacher.

Next, using their list of food items and the food groups, they will sort the food into categories. This may require *learning activities* around the skill of categorization, including categorizing items other than foods. Remember that the *learning map* focuses on what students will need to accomplish in steps to achieve the overall *problem-based task*. The *learning map* is not a list of skills but a breakdown of the solution and ways in which students will learn the skills to accomplish each step (Figure 4.3). The intent is to help you, as the teacher, think through the steps students will have to take to achieve the solution to the problem so that you can be a powerful resource and support person in that process. In the *ALU* "Designer Pizza" (Appendix A), first students must construct a survey, then gather survey data, then graph the survey, then analyze the survey. These would be included on the *learning map* (Figure 4.4).

To accomplish these steps on the *learning map*, students will need specific skills, which will be included as *learning activities* on your *scaffold for learning* and ultimately on their *activity lists*. Note that teacher-given *small-group mini-lessons* are not included here; you will most likely offer them for almost every skill. The *learning map* focuses on ways to learn independent from the teacher. Note, too, that while you may see a lot of repetition, there are nuances. For example, I do not want a *peer expert* helping to construct a survey, as it's a complex skill and I fear the *peer expert* may do more of the work than I want. However, for learning about the best way to get people to respond to the survey, a *peer expert* might have some great ideas. The more deliberate and purposeful you are in determining how students will learn, the greater success your students will have.

Figure 4.4. Learning Map: Designer Pizza

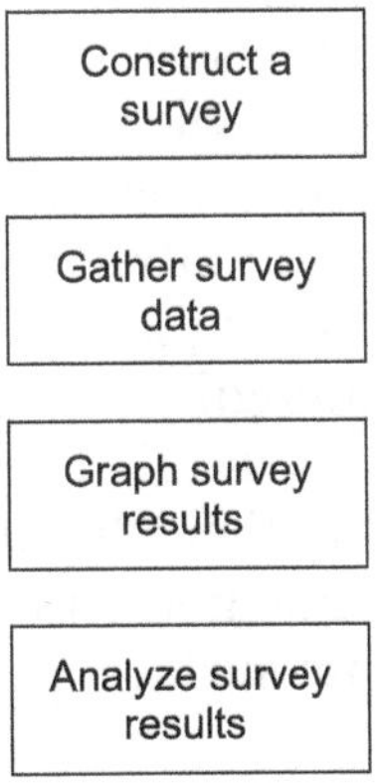

Construct a survey

Gather survey data

Graph survey results

Analyze survey results

A *learning map* can also give you a sense of where you will need *benchmark lessons*. In this example, you would offer an early *benchmark lesson* on marketing strategies: why companies use surveys when they have a new idea. You might then have *learning activities* on how to write a good survey question and survey, tallying responses, and graphing data. You might run a *benchmark lesson* on analyzing data: what you can learn from data. Next students would need to build a menu. So the *learning map* would include identifying pizza choices, assigning fractional slices to pizzas, understanding fractional parts, creating the list of slice options, and constructing menu items of combinations of slices. To assign fractional slices to pizzas, students will need a concept of sizes of fractions, comparing fractions, and if-then decision making (e.g., if a lot of people really like pepperoni pizza, maybe that should be offered as a quarter slice; however, if few people listed mushroom pizza as a choice, maybe it should be offered as a twelfth slice so people might be convinced to try a small piece. To create menu combinations, students will need to learn to add fractions. As you can see, the *learning map* really makes you think through the learning process.

You will not end up building a *learning map* for every aspect of every unit, but to provide for purposeful differentiation, as you begin this journey of instructional redesign, it's a great way to truly visualize the path your students may take. Even though different students will approach the problem from different angles, begin with one path that you can imagine. You can then teach students to develop *learning maps* as well, having them then identify possible resources at each step.

Lesson-Level Differentiation

Fourth-grade students are proposing a new design for a section of the playground to be constructed at the school. They need to learn to calculate the area of various shapes. The teacher has given the class a three by three grid of *learning activities* for calculating area. Each successive column provides more difficult experiences; the rows represent visual, auditory, and hands-on activities. (Figure 4.5 is an example of IDE Corp's "Learning Styles and Readiness Grid," also referred to here as a differentiation grid.) The students recently completed surveys to identify their learning style strengths, and the teacher encouraged the class to pay attention to their strengths but to also challenge themselves to strengthen other modes. One student decides to follow a hands-on activity in the first column, using manipulatives to explore the concept of area. Another already knows how to calculate the area of regular and irregular polygons and chooses an auditory offering of a podcast to learn to calculate surface area of three-dimensional shapes.

Figure 4.5. Calculating Area

	Need Some Help	Ready for This	I Know This Already
Visual	Follow the "Filling the Figure" *how-to sheet* to explore how many area blocks fit inside various shapes. Then draw 10 polygons and calculate how many area blocks fit inside.	Follow the "What's Inside?" *how-to sheet* to learn how to calculate the area of regular and irregular polygons. Then draw ten polygons and calculate their area, showing your work.	View the "Fill It Up" presentation to learn how to calculate the volume of 3D shapes. Then find five objects in the classroom and calculate the volume of each.
Auditory	Listen to and watch the "How Much Space?" video to explore how many area blocks fit inside various shapes. Then draw 10 polygons and calculate how many area blocks fit inside.	Watch and listen to the "Finding the Area" podcast to learn how to calculate the area of regular and irregular polygons. Then draw ten polygons, calculate their area, and record your explanation of how you calculated each.	Attend the "Beyond Polygons" *small-group mini-lesson* to learn how to calculate the volume of 3D shapes. Then find five objects in the classroom and calculate the volume of each.
Kinesthetic/Tactile	Use the "Shape Explorer" *learning center* App to explore how many area blocks fit inside various shapes. Then construct and cutout 10 polygons to add to the *learning center* with area blocks glued onto the back.	Using the "Calculating Area *learning center*, follow the direction sheet to learn how to calculate the area of regular and irregular polygons. Then construct and cutout ten polygons to add to the *learning center* with your calculations on the back.	Use the "Fill It Up" *learning center* to explore how many cubes fit into various 3D shapes and learn how to calculate the volume. Then find five objects in the classroom and calculate the volume of each.

Differentiation is a natural process; we all tend to gravitate toward that which suits our interest level, skill set, and learning style. A person may not know how to video conference using a phone, but when that person's loved ones are away traveling or off at college, she has a *felt need* to learn. Armed with a *felt need*, she pursues the way in which she knows she will learn best. She may look for an app to download and follow the directions, search the Internet, or ask a friend to show her.

In the early 1980s, I was offering beginning computer instruction to teachers who claimed that word processing seemed useless, as it took much more time than handwriting (clearly based on their lack of technology skills). Instead, I introduced how the computer could allow them to shop and email their college-aged children. Before I knew it, everyone was engaged in using the computer in ways that were purposeful for them. After that, they saw word processing as a more powerful tool. It is contrary to human nature to ask a group of diverse individuals to all sit and listen to instruction on a concept or skill they may or may not need and in a way that may or may not address individual learning styles. Yet this is what occurs in classrooms every day.

> **"It is contrary to human nature to ask a group of diverse individuals to all sit and listen to instruction on a concept or skill they may or may not need and in a way that may or may not address individual learning styles. Yet this is what occurs in classrooms every day."**

Whole-class instruction may seem easier for the teacher and may appear to give the teacher a sense of control, but the only control in place is over physical bodies, if even that, not minds. A student can sit and pretend to be listening while thinking about something totally different from the lesson. A teacher might assume a lesson is going well because five students are asking and answering questions and are excited about the skill; but videotape the next lesson you offer and you'll see the reality of your audience. Differentiation is a combination of providing a variety of activities through which students can engage in learning, teaching students to self-assess and make appropriate decisions about their learning, and allowing students to make choices and have some control over their learning. I once had a group of students tell me that they felt that when teachers just present the same lesson to everyone, it is disrespectful of them. That's a powerful sentiment! For differentiating instruction for a particular skill, plan out learning choices using a learning styles and readiness grid (Figure 4.5).

The *Scaffold for Learning*

To achieve a high level of student engagement in learning through differentiation, you'll want to ensure you offer students a variety of possible *learning activities* and *practice activities* across *participatory structures*: different ways to participate in learning. Students may engage in whole-class lessons,

Figure 4.6. Scaffold for Learning

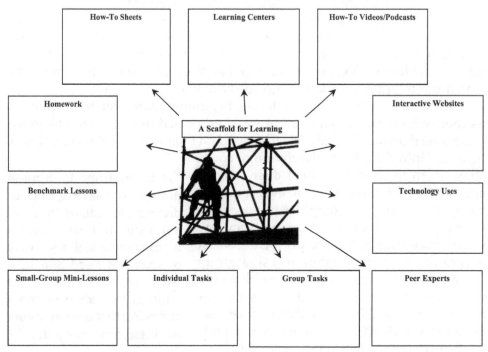

small-group lessons, pair work, individual work, hands-on activities, technology activities, and so forth. Your *analytic rubric* defines what your students need to learn to accomplish the task at hand. You're now going to consider all the ways in which they can participate in the learning process; I refer to this as a *scaffold for learning* (Figure 4.6). It becomes the foundation for providing students with myriad opportunities to learn, thus differentiating learning to ensure success for each student. As you design your *ALU*, use the *scaffold for learning* to brainstorm various ways in which students could build content mastery. You don't typically share the *scaffold for learning* with your students. It serves as a planning tool for you.

CREATE

The learning process is not set in stone; it's different for each learner and varies with the content, which is what makes teaching such a complex craft. As the teacher, you'll want to decide on the best approach to introducing a topic, the goal being to make students aware of new learning they will want to pursue. In some cases, an inspirational kickoff *benchmark lesson* is

Figure 4.7. The Path to Learning

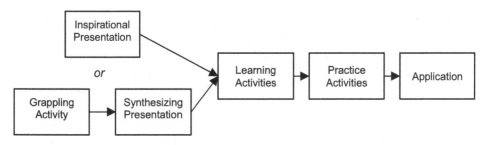

the best. In others, having students grapple with the content in advance of the *benchmark lesson* allows the teacher to then synthesize those experiences for students during the *benchmark lesson*. Loosely, Figure 4.7 offers an instructional path that relates to the *scaffold for learning*.

For example, when introducing students to the concept of tessellations, you might present a *benchmark lesson* to inspire and intrigue students. You would show them tessellated items from nature: a honeycomb, a turtle shell, tessellated windows on a building, tessellated tiles in a walkway, and pieces of art. You would then engage students in a discussion of what is similar about these images, drawing their attention to the faraway look and the close up look. Once you've triggered students' awareness (Gattegno, 1987) of this special type of pattern in nature, architecture, and art, you can have them engage in a variety of *learning activities* around understanding and designing tessellations.

Alternatively, you might start with an individual, pair, or small-group activity that allows students to grapple with the content before you introduce it. You would give students bags of tessellation pieces and ask them to assemble them to fit on a larger piece of paper with no open space showing inside the design. This could range from triangles to more complex geometric configurations. After students explore, you would offer a *benchmark lesson* to synthesize what they discovered and introduce them to the term "tessellation." You would then have them engage in a variety of *learning activities* around designing tessellations.

Regardless of the entry point to skill acquisition, students should be able to engage in a variety of *learning activities* and *practice activities* related to the content, as are represented on the *scaffold for learning*. As you work through each section of *participatory structures* in what follows, stop and add to a *scaffold for learning* for your *ALU* by considering how each mode of engagement can support student learning. Note that the *scaffold for learning* examples shown in this book each address a portion of a unit. Over the course of a three- or four-week unit, you would need several pages to capture all of the possibilities. This is like your new *Learner-Active, Technology-Infused Classroom* planbook: ways through which students will learn the content you are responsible for teaching.

The *Benchmark Lesson*

One way students participate in learning is through a *benchmark lesson*—a whole-class lesson focused on triggering awareness of what students need to learn at different points (benchmarks) throughout the *ALU*. Whole-class instruction is not an effective venue for engaging students in learning specific skills, no matter how talented and engaging the teacher. It can, however, be a powerful venue for inspiring students and making them aware of the skills they need to learn to accomplish the *problem-based task* at hand. Thus, in the *Learner-Active, Technology-Infused Classroom*, teachers are challenged to think differently about that whole-class lesson. Just because you're presenting content to the whole class does not mean you're conducting a *benchmark lesson*. The intent of the *benchmark lesson* is to "trigger awareness" (Gattegno, 1987) of what skills and concepts students need to accomplish their *problem-based task*.

Consider a *problem-based task* in which students are surveying their peers to make recommendations about the school lunch program. The teacher may offer a *benchmark lesson* to the class to introduce them to the concept of opinions, surveys, and the types of questions to use. The teacher wouldn't begin the unit with the concept of displaying data, as the students have no data to present yet; that skill would come later. Introducing concepts to the class at key developmental checkpoints in the unit, or benchmarks, is accomplished through the *benchmark lesson*: a ten- to fifteen-minute whole-class lesson to introduce students to a concept that is essential to the problem-based task.

As teachers, we have a tendency to think that we must directly "teach" content or students will not learn it. Often, that teaching is presented to the whole class from the front of the room, which may be more efficient for teachers, but it is not effective for student learning. Students' brains must construct knowledge. This is accomplished by having students grapple with content, often individually or in a pair or triad. The *benchmark lesson* is not the venue for having students learn and retain content; it is not the place to check for understanding. It is, however, a perfect venue for providing inspiration, whetting appetites, and piquing interest. The best *benchmark lessons* produce "aha" moments for students that drive them to want more information and learning. This is a very different approach to whole-class instruction with which *Learner-Active, Technology-Infused Classroom* teachers must grapple.

Conducting the *Benchmark Lesson*

To maximize the brain's potential to learn, keep your *benchmark lessons* to ten to fifteen minutes. As teachers, we are notorious for being able to stand in the front of the room and talk about a subject to our seemingly captive audience. It is critical to remember that while you may be enjoying your own presentation, your students most likely will not be absorbing all the content you think they are. The key is to make your lesson count!

Start with a clear, focused, and narrow objective. Avoid covering too much in one *benchmark lesson*. It's better to offer several *benchmark lessons* to build on the concept. During a lesson, the first couple of minutes involve getting the brain engaged. The next ten to twelve minutes are prime brain activity time: students are most likely to absorb what you are teaching. Then the brain begins to enter a lull (Sousa, 2017). Stop talking!

Be mindful as well of the primacy-recency effect: a "phenomenon whereby, during a learning episode, we tend to remember best that which comes first (prime-time 1), second best that which comes last (prime-time 2), and least that which comes just past the middle (down time)" (Sousa, 2017, p. 139). If you think about it, that means the first point you make and the last will be remembered; everything in the middle may be lost. That is why it is so important to begin your *benchmark lesson* with a compelling point you want to make, build it, and then repeat it at the end.

When offering a *benchmark lesson*, use the first minute or so to focus your students' attention through some sort of personal reflection. Your students have come to this lesson from other activities and, most likely, their minds are still focused on those, whether walking through the hall, finding a piece of paper, or working on another assignment. When you begin talking, your students' brains may not be focused on you. As students are settling into their seats for the lesson, have them reflect on a life experience or existing knowledge they have regarding the concept you are about to teach. If you are going to introduce seasons, ask students to think about how they dress at different times of the year based on the weather. If you are going to present the characteristics of polygons, ask students to write down five geometric shapes they see in the room. For elements of a musical composition, ask students to think of a favorite song. The purpose of the personal reflection is to get the students focused on the topic at hand as their brains are engaging so that when you begin to speak, they will be ready to hear.

Make your objective known; write or project it on the board. Use your lesson to create connections among the concept, real life, and students' experiences. Where possible, utilize technology; for example, find a compelling video clip or image. Make your point, write it, restate it. Do not assume that saying something once ensures that all students will remember it.

As an example, students who are writing directions to design their own adventure games must understand the power of the preposition: how just one word changes the meaning of a sentence. As students assemble for the lesson, have the following questions projected: "Where is the floor in relation to your feet?" "Where is the ceiling in relation to your head?" After allowing students to consider the two reflection questions, project several

Figure 4.8. Benchmark Lesson on Prepositions

The book is _____	the desk.
The book is _____	the desk.
The book is _____	the desk.
The book is _____	the desk.

incomplete sentences on the board involving two objects with the preposition missing (see Figure 4.8).

Note: in this example, you'll need to have a desk handy that has an inside compartment for the sentence "The book is in the desk." Obviously, you can change the two objects to work for your classroom.

Tell your students to watch what you do with the book as you place it on the desk. Then ask them where the book is. Once students answer, fill in the blank in the first sentence with the word "on." Then tell them to watch again and place the book under the desk, asking students where it is. Fill in the blank in the second sentence with "under." Next, place the book inside the desk and continue filling in blanks. Next, hold it hovering over the desk. Based on the items you choose, see how many different sentences you can complete with different prepositions. Then draw students' attention to those now filled blank lines. Discuss what the words tell the reader and how changing just that one word changes the meaning of the whole sentence and clarifies exactly where the book is in relation to the desk. Introduce the term "preposition" as a powerful word that describes the relationship between two items. Offer an example from the *ALU* task to show how different their adventure game directions would be if they simply used a different preposition and how the success of their game is going to depend on how well they use prepositions to offer clear directions. That's it! *Benchmark lesson* is over. You introduced a concept, you demonstrated it in a visual way as well as through your words, and you related it back to the *ALU*. Students will now have access to a variety of *learning activities* through which they can learn to recognize and use prepositions (the skill part of the process) based on their ability level. For students who are just grasping the concept, they'll engage in *learning activities* focusing on the most common prepositions; those who already understand the concept may engage in *learning activities* requiring them to determine the six types of prepositions (time, place, direction, agent, instruments, and phrases.)

As you offer a *benchmark lesson*, make sure your students are in a position to pay attention. That may include scanning the room to make sure all are seated or standing so that they can see you and whatever props you might have, asking students to close their laptop computers, and asking them to close any notebooks and put down any writing instruments. During a *benchmark lesson*, all that students should be doing is listening, watching, and participating. *Benchmark lessons* are not designed for note-taking except in the case where you deliberately want to build note-taking skills. (Note-taking can occur in *small-group mini-lessons*.)

Given that you have set a time for the *benchmark lesson*, set your expectation that students will be ready at the appointed time. Avoid having to remind students and call them to the lesson, building dependence on you; this would mean other students have to wait for their peers to get ready. Make your expectations clear from the beginning of the school year that they are to watch the time and be ready. In the case of primary students, ring a bell or have some sort of signal for them to start packing up their activities and get ready for the *benchmark lesson*.

During the *benchmark lesson*, make sure your students are following along by using a thumbs-up, thumbs-down signal in response to a question; small whiteboards where students hold up a quick response; or a technology app that allows students to enter a quick response digitally. An exit card would allow students to answer a question on an index card and hand it in before leaving the *benchmark lesson* and returning to their work. It's a good idea, too, to then offer a targeted *small-group mini-lesson* (more on that *participatory structure* next) so that those who did not feel they understood the lesson can receive more instruction from you.

Keep in mind that the purpose of the *benchmark lesson* is to offer well-timed introductions to concepts through short segments of whole-class instruction. Timing should coincide with students' *felt need* to accomplish the next phase of the *ALU*. Imagine students who are designing a roller coaster and are at the initial stages of exploring how a marble runs along rails (physically or virtually on a computer). As they are grappling with how to keep the marble on the rails, how to ensure it can climb the next hill, and how it can avoid falling off a loop, you have the perfect opportunity for a *benchmark lesson* on the physics behind a roller coaster. You can introduce concepts such as kinetic and potential energy, acceleration and deceleration, and the influence of gravity and friction.

You will most likely offer one to three *benchmark lessons* over the course of the day, with different numbers from day to day. Avoid setting a prescribed time for your *benchmark lessons*. Think through the day and plan the number and times for the *benchmark lessons*, being mindful of the flow of work taking place in the *ALU*. At the start of a school year, with students who are not used to *Learner-Active, Technology-Infused Classrooms*, you may want to conduct more *benchmark lessons* with shorter periods of time between them, focusing on both academics and process, so that students feel they are getting the direction they need. As students become familiar with all of the ways in which they can learn and all of the ways in which they can engage with you, they will be more capable of independently using longer periods of time well. If you decide to conduct a *benchmark lesson* at the start of a day or soon after students return from lunch or a special activity, leave at least twenty minutes before the start. This way, students can use the time meaningfully for their work. If you start a *benchmark lesson*, say, five or ten minutes after the start of the day, students can't delve into any other work; you end up causing them to waste precious time waiting for the *benchmark lesson*. Encourage your students, too, to schedule around the *benchmark lesson*, if need be, rather than trying to fit activities into tight time slots. For example, if they are going to spend an hour working on some aspect of an *ALU*, they can start it, attend to the *benchmark lesson*, and return to it. Their schedules do not have to perfectly fit in a way that causes them to finish all activities before the *benchmark lesson*. Note: for students who struggle with focusing or being interrupted, you might want to ensure that they, in fact, *do* schedule their time to complete an activity before the *benchmark lesson*, as they may not be able to pick up with the interrupted activity easily.

Given that you are looking to inspire students and introduce them to a new concept, showing the connections to the *problem-based task* they are working to solve, you or another teacher are the best people to offer it. On rare occasions, you might have a student who understands the concept and wants to create a presentation on it, with your guidance, of course, and offer a *benchmark lesson*. However, *benchmark lessons* are not intended to be offered by students to their peers. This is where the teachers' knowledge of the students and learning process, expertise, and inspirational ability are needed.

Using the *ALU* task you've designed, consider various points along the way at which you should introduce certain key concepts, based on the majority of students reaching a benchmark point in the overall *ALU*. How will you launch the *ALU* to build student interest and intrigue? What might you introduce a few days into the unit? The second week? And so forth. Figure 4.6 provides you with a *scaffold for learning* image to cue your thinking. All of your actual *ALU* activities will not fit in the boxes; you may wish to use a page for each box or some other document layout that works for you. Make a list of all of the *benchmark lessons* you plan to offer. Use the Rubric to Assess a Benchmark Lesson (Appendix H) to guide the development and delivery of your *benchmark lessons*.

Opting Out of a Benchmark Lesson

At times, though rare, you may find that you have a student or two who do not need the *benchmark lesson* you are about to present. Offer those students the option of opting out of the lesson if they wish. They may decide to attend anyway, and that would be their choice. Otherwise, they should move to an area outside the rest of the group and work quietly on another activity they scheduled. This approach honors your students and the use of their time. While *benchmark lessons* should be focused on concept introduction such that any level of student can benefit, the student who, for example, already fully understands the power of prepositions and already uses them in writing should be allowed to opt out of that *benchmark lesson*.

Presenting Skills to Your Students

The *benchmark lesson* is aimed at teaching concepts and triggering students' awareness as to content that will help them in accomplishing the *problem-based task*. Students, however, also need skill instruction! So many of the other structures on the *scaffold for learning* are aimed at skill and content acquisition. Introducing skills requires three essential elements:

1. Activating prior knowledge by focusing students first on the prerequisite skills they've already mastered to succeed in mastering the skill being introduced.

2. Creating a connection to students' lives and the real world to ensure that the skill being presented has meaning and makes sense (Sousa, 2017).

3. Providing a variety of ways through which students can learn and practice the skill, including those geared toward learning styles, cognitive progression (Sulla, 2015), disabilities, advanced learners, and giftedness.

While you can present skills to your students in small groups, and that will be one of the topics that follows, consider the many other ways in which you can provide students with learning opportunities in which they can engage independent of you. Videos, printed directions, picture directions, learning centers, and peers are just some of the ways through which students can learn independent of a teacher. In the *Learner-Active, Technology-Infused Classroom*, the teacher becomes the masterful "bridge builder" who creates varied opportunities through which students can learn, building toward greater student efficacy.

Designing Learning Activities Versus Practice Activities

As mentioned earlier, the key is to identify and design *learning activities* (Sulla, 2015) as differentiated from *practice activities*. A *learning activity* has three distinct characteristics from other classroom activities and assignments:

1. **It is focused on one targeted, discrete skill or concept**; it is not too broad in content. In kindergarten, a *learning activity* might

focus on "words that begin with t" or "words that end with t." One *learning activity* would not address both. "Equivalent fractions" would be too broad a topic; "an introduction to equivalent fractions" would be more focused, perhaps followed by "writing equivalent fractions when the numerator is missing."

2. **It includes directions**. A *learning activity* offers the student directions for completing the skill or grasping the concept. It may offer a demonstration or modeling, as in the case of a video, or step by step directions with images, as in the case of printed directions or a learning center.

3. Where possible, **it includes feedback**. It may include sample scenarios with answers. It may offer a visual. In the case of a video on how to use a glue stick, one kindergarten teacher was careful to point out how to know you succeeded, i.e., no glue pushing out from underneath, no bubbles, the paper is stuck in place, and so forth. In some cases, completing the skill itself is feedback enough, such as in the case of using a compass to draw a circle.

As you move beyond the *benchmark lesson*, you have to ensure you have a broad collection of *learning activities*. In the past, you may have presented content to the whole class and then given them activities to practice what they learned. *Practice activities* presume learning has already taken place; they cannot be used in place of *learning activities*. Without well-crafted *learning activities*, you will be leaving student learning to chance. The following sections offer more detailed descriptions of structures for providing *learning activities*.

How-To Sheets

You can provide your students with direct instruction in skill development using a printed *how-to sheet*. Students who are visual learners and enjoy independent learning may actually prefer a *how-to sheet* to listening to a teacher's lesson. Students can follow the directions at their own pace, re-read as necessary, and refer to diagrams and examples you've included.

A *how-to sheet* should focus on a particular skill, such as reading a map key, setting up a letter format, playing the scale on a saxophone, subtracting two-digit numbers, etc. The buddy-reading checklist in Chapter 1 (Figure 1.2) is an example of a *how-to sheet* providing students with direct instruction in written form. *How-to sheets* are also useful for teaching students how to use various technologies, such as calculators, apps, and interactive whiteboards; and they can be used for instructing students in the structures of the *Learner-Active, Technology-Infused Classroom*, such as how to schedule time.

Figure 4.9. Writing the Letter B

B

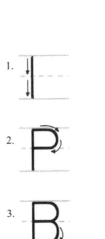

How-to sheets should have clearly numbered steps, with the student taking one action per step. Include screenshots, diagrams, or images to help the student understand the step. For young students or those who have difficulty staying focused, add small boxes to the left of each step for them to check off as they complete the step.

How-to sheets provide "just-in-time-learning." At the point the student has a "felt need" to learn a skill, he or she can retrieve the *how-to sheet* from the *resource area* and follow the written directions. *How-to sheets* can be useful in the upper elementary grades as students build their reading skills; however, for primary students you may need to use video or introduce a *how-to sheet* through a *small-group mini-lesson* using a corresponding printed *how-to sheet* of images and words as cues to the process. For example, a *how-to sheet* for writing the letter B (Figure 4.9) might have a picture of the B at various stages of writing. You might add words as well, as you are introducing students to reading sentences, but primary students may need to rely on visuals and perhaps an accompanying video.

How-To Podcasts, Screencasts, and Videos

Computer technology makes it easy to create your own personalized audio and video files to provide your students with direct instruction in a skill or concept. Podcasts generally consist of audio, while screencasts include images from a computer. Screencasts are easily created using one of a number of apps that capture what is happening on your computer screen or interactive whiteboard while you narrate it. For videos, use a video camera, tablet, or cell phone to capture the video and audio of a lesson or performance offered by you, students, or other adults. Using readily available technology, you create podcasts recording your voice presenting information to your students. Students can listen to or watch these as needed to build a particular skill. Many teachers will use QR codes (though newer technology will soon replace the QR code) either posted on a wall with an accompanying image or as a link on an activity list to bring up podcasts, screencasts, and videos.

Plan out your lesson, focusing on a narrow objective. In creating a screencast, for example, capture the action on the computer or interactive whiteboard using one of a variety of available screen-capture programs. Then add your voice-over to narrate the screencast. The key to recording your voice is to speak slowly. Keep in mind that after the human brain hears words, it has to process them. Sometimes, when you're recording familiar information, it's natural to speak quickly, because your brain has already processed it. When recording your voice for your students, be mindful of their need to process information. Chunk the words so that you pause for your students to process what you just said. In other words, the point is not to speak each word slowly but to speak in phrases followed by pauses. Here is an example of an audio script for a podcast or screencast.

> Adverbs are words that describe a verb (*pause*), adjective (*pause*), or other adverb. (*pause*) John walked slowly. (*pause*) What word does slowly (*pause*) describe? (*pause*) The word slowly describes how John walked. (*pause*) Walked is the verb in the sentence, (*pause*) and slowly is an adverb that describes a verb.

Figure 4.10 offers an accompany set of images that could be used to accompany the text.

Note that the pauses are at points that will allow the listener's brain to process key information that was just stated. Use voice inflection and intonation to capture and maintain the attention of the listener. Carefully pronounce words, and avoid colloquialisms. This will enhance the listener's experience.

Podcasts, screencasts, and videos, like *how-to sheets*, focus on a single skill or narrow set of skills so that each does not require too much time to complete. You might have a corresponding printed sheet to which students refer while listening and/or watching. You might have a sheet for students to complete that demonstrates to you that they understood the skill or concept. In the case of the example, you might have a sheet with a list of sentences and ask the student to read sentence number five and circle the adverb. Then, through the podcast, screencast, or video, offer the correct answer. (Remember that a strong *learning activity* offers directions and feedback.) I would not necessarily offer students a transcript unless reading is the subject and it makes sense for students to follow along with your audio.

Figure 4.10. Adverb Screencast Images

John walked slowly.

John <u>walked</u> slowly.
verb

John <u>walked</u> <u>slowly</u>.
verb   *adverb*

John <u>walked</u> <u>slowly</u>.
verb   *adverb*

However, other visual aids can be beneficial. Your students who are strong auditory learners may lean toward listening to podcasts and screencasts for skill development over following a printed *how-to sheet*. Your students who are fast visual processors may find podcast and screencast explanations too long and opt for the printed *how-to sheet*.

Consider recording *benchmark lessons* or *small-group mini-lessons* for students' later review. This is particularly useful for students who were absent at the time of the lesson. I presented this idea to a science teacher years ago, before the advent of digital video cameras. I walked into his classroom one day to find him working with some students, asking probing questions about an experiment in progress. Other students were looking up information on a computer; still others were meeting in groups to discuss their findings from an experiment. I then heard the teacher's voice on the other side of the room. I walked over to find a group of three students watching a video of the teacher. The screen revealed just his hands folding a paper airplane as he gave verbal directions. He was taking his students outside at the end of the week to learn about the physics behind flight. I later found out that he had set up a video camera in his basement and was filming short clips of demonstrations for his students. He told me that he realized that standing in the front of the room giving an entire class directions for folding a paper airplane was a poor use of his and his students' time. By creating the video, he enabled small groups of students to work on preparing for the flight lesson while he focused on pushing other students' thinking on other experiments. I asked the students how they liked learning this way, and they unanimously agreed it was better than listening to the teacher in the front of the room. One student exclaimed, "When you zone out and miss something, you can rewind him!"

Using podcasts, screencasts, and videos, you can capture skill lessons and demonstrations for students to use when they need them. This style of information dissemination will appeal to your digital generation of students. Plus, you will free yourself from repeating skills lessons in favor of using your time to engage in higher-order questioning and thinking with those students who are ready. Technology provides many opportunities to "clone" the teacher.

Start small: create key videos. Then have students create some, adding to your repertoire; teaching others solidifies one's own learning. Work on expanding your collection to various cognitive levels, including for advanced students who can be given the next challenge.

Note: I strongly recommend checking whether your school has a specific policy and perhaps a permission form for parents to complete if you decide to film their children. All schools handle this differently, but essentially, if you are videotaping someone and plan to use the video with others, you should secure permission in advance, and avoid using any student's last name.

Small-Group Mini-Lessons

You can provide skill instruction to a small group of like-ability or like-interest students through a short lesson on a particular skill. Students sign-up to participate in the lesson in advance (more on the structures to support *small-group mini-lessons* in Chapter 5.) A *small-group mini-lesson* should last approximately seven to ten minutes, after which time you may want to have the students stay together to practice the skill, with you checking in later. *Small-group mini-lessons* are effective for students who benefit from in-person, direct instruction from you, and they appeal to auditory learners. There are four main reasons to conduct academically focused *small-group mini-lessons*:

♦ As a follow-up to a *benchmark lesson*, for those who may continue to have difficulty grasping the concept or have questions that were not answered during the lesson;

♦ To provide an introduction to a skill for those students who may be auditory learners or who benefit from working with the teacher for skill development;

♦ To provide reinforcement for students who may need help in a skill; and

♦ To provide an advanced skill for those students who have mastered the current content.

Also conduct process-oriented *small-group mini-lessons* to help students master the structures of the *Learner-Active, Technology-Infused Classroom*, such as scheduling, which is covered in more detail in Chapter 5.

Structuring *Small-Group Mini-Lessons*

Create an area in the room that is conducive to meeting with a small group. You might set up a table in a corner of the room, for example. Consider whether you want the table near an easel, whiteboard, or interactive whiteboard. It's important to be considerate of the students who are not working with you by keeping your voice to a volume that is loud enough for just those students sitting with you to hear. Be mindful of this when you designate your area. I worked with teachers who created the *small-group mini-lesson* area in the middle of the room. They soon realized that the conversations from that area were disturbing students all around them and relocated the area to a corner of the room to minimize the distraction to the rest of the class.

Drawing on brain research, keep the following in mind as you design *small-group mini-lessons*:

♦ Structure each *small-group mini-lesson* so that it has a very narrow focus on a very specific skill that you can present in a short period of time, which not everyone will need at the same time. Keep your group size to no more than six students, with options for overflow students who also wanted to sign-up. If you find too many students are signing up, you may need to focus the topic better. For example, the topic "spelling challenges" is too broad. Instead, offer *small-group mini-lessons* on "I Before E, and the Exceptions," "Mastering 'ough' and 'augh' Words," and "I Always Get 100 percent on Spelling Tests, Now What?" The latter is to offer students who are strong in spelling some advanced challenges, like deconstructing the longest word in the dictionary: pneumonoultramicroscopicsilicovolcanoconiosis. The focus of your topics will depend on your grade level. By fifth grade, when students have already been introduced to spelling challenging words across the years, you could run a single *small-group mini-lesson* on "tackling challenging spelling words" for those who continue to struggle with the skill.

♦ Make your instruction count! You have a short period of time while your students' brains are highly activated to have them build new skills. The *small-group mini-lesson* must be very tightly structured. Let the students know the objective up front. Ask questions to activate their prior knowledge. Use visual aids and demonstrate what is appropriate. Make every sentence purposeful and deliberate. Have students take notes and repeat back to you certain steps of key points. At the end, summarize and, potentially, allow students to stay in the *small-group mini-lesson* area to practice. While you may know a skill, crafting the best way to convey that skill to others is the goal of *small-group mini-lessons*.

♦ Throughout the lesson, check for understanding. Unlike the *benchmark lesson*, the *small-group mini-lesson* is designed to offer direct instruction in a skill or concept. Ensure that the students are understanding what you are presenting.

♦ Take into account that some students may choose to attend the *small-group mini-lesson* because they are confused, but as you start, the content solidifies for them and they no longer need to participate. In this case, allow students to leave the area when they feel they have the information they need. You can provide "opt out" points at which this happens so as not to disturb the flow of your presentation. One student exclaimed to his teacher, "Wow, you really must respect me that you trust me to know when I can go."

Other Considerations

While they may seem like a simple structure, there are several nuances to *small-group mini-lessons* that will make them a powerful learning opportunity in your *Learner-Active, Technology-Infused Classroom*.

♦ Stick to your time slots. Begin and end *small-group mini-lessons* on time. Otherwise, student scheduling becomes compromised, and your class will not run as smoothly. If you find a topic warrants more time, schedule a follow-up lesson.

♦ **After conducting a *small-group mini-lesson*,** return to facilitating learning in the classroom. Therefore, avoid scheduling back-to-back *small-group mini-lessons*. Given that the rest of your students are most likely working independently, often on *learning activities*, you want to ensure you are offering the necessary facilitation. You want to be careful not to spend too much time with a small number of students off in a corner of the room.

- **Let students know the schedule for** *small-group mini-lessons* **in advance** so that they can plan to attend. In the *Learner-Active, Technology-Infused Classroom*, students take charge of scheduling how they will use their time. Consequently, it is important to give them responsibility for planning to attend a *small-group mini-lesson*. Avoid suddenly announcing one and asking students to attend at that moment, as it interferes with student control of their own schedules.

- **The best time to announce a** *small-group mini-lesson* depends on the grade level of the students. For primary students, post and/or announce *small-group mini-lesson* topics at the start of the morning and right after lunch. For older students in self-contained classrooms, provide the *small-group mini-lesson* schedule at the start of the day or the day before. Based on your facilitation and student requests, you may decide on the need for a *small-group mini-lesson* to be offered in the more immediate future. In that case, you can add it to the list of scheduled *small-group mini-lessons* and alert students in your daily announcement notes. Students would need to then revise their schedules to attend, which is not a problem, as the need to change plans along the way is an important life skill.

- **Sometimes you may need to invite students to a** *small-group mini-lesson.* As your students come to understand the *Learner-Active, Technology-Infused Classroom*, they will learn to self-assess and to determine whether they need to attend a *small-group mini-lesson*. There will be times, even then, when you have to let students know that they must attend a lesson. Depending on the structures you have in place for communicating with your students, you might email them or include a comment in their personal folder.

- It's important to keep in mind that *small-group mini-lessons* are not only for those students who need help; they also can be **an effective way to address your high-achieving and gifted learners**. In fact, a well-timed, advanced *small-group mini-lesson* can be used to motivate average students to raise their level of achievement. If you announce an upcoming advanced *small-group mini-lesson* and indicate a prerequisite assignment or quiz to receive an entrance ticket or gain admission to the lesson, you might find that more of your students will step up to the challenge.

- **Offer a variety of ways to learn a skill beyond the** *small-group mini-lesson* so that students have more options than just attending the lesson to learn the skill. The Web offers a wide range of websites, videos, simulations, how-to pages, and interactive websites that you can use as *learning activities*. You can add a few that you design. As stated earlier, over time, you will enhance your collection with ideas and *learning activities* designed by students and your colleagues.

♦ **Let go of the notion that students must hear something from you in order to learn it.** Otherwise, you will be inclined to offer repeated *small-group mini-lessons* when students could learn through other structures. *Small-group mini-lessons* are one important component of the *Learner-Active, Technology-Infused Classroom*. While there is no one right number of *small-group mini-lessons* to offer each day, over the course of the entire day, you will want to offer approximately three *small-group mini-lessons*, or three across the course of the week if you teach in a departmentalized situation.

♦ **Position *peer experts* to offer some *small-group mini-lessons*.** It's possible for peer experts to conduct some *small-group mini-lessons*; however, it is very hard to unlearn that which was incorrectly taught. So you will want to ensure that they are able to offer the lesson and answer related questions. This is covered in more detail in the *peer expert* section later in this chapter.

Learning Centers

The term *learning center* tends to be associated with the primary grades, but, used correctly, they can serve as an effective opportunity for students to learn at all grade levels. It is important to use them as independent *learning activities* and not as stations in a timed rotation, as the latter would make you a "ferry master" and not a "bridge builder." When teachers move students from center to center in rotations based on an allotted time, they are not allowing students to take charge of their own learning, nor are they differentiating instruction. Rather, students should sign-up for *learning centers*, as they are typically a limited resource only able to accommodate a certain number of students at a time. (*Learning centers* often involve some sort of kinesthetic, hands-on activity that requires keeping all the pieces in one place.) *Learning centers* fall into three categories:

♦ Those that require limited resources, such as a fish tank, a puppet theater, the sole microscope in the room, or a specialized computer;

♦ Those that involve a hands-on experience, such as blocks, working with clay, a pre-set science experiment, math manipulatives, and STEM kits, and;

♦ Those that involve materials that are best kept together, such as sentence strips, map puzzle pieces, and photographs.

You can design *learning centers* for individuals, pairs, or groups. Essentially, students go to the *learning center* or retrieve a container or packet with materials to be taken to a desk, table, or other space.

You might set up an area of the classroom with an experiment, paints, a model, and so forth. Alternatively, you might place a set of manipulatives or other objects in a container for students to take to their location. If the materials are flat, such as cardboard or paper pieces, you could store them in a packet or folder. Students sign-up for a period of time in the *learning center* and add it to their personal schedules.

When teachers rely primarily on whole-class instruction, they need class sets of materials for all activities. In the *Learner-Active, Technology-Infused Classroom*, class sets of materials are not necessary. Instead, students schedule their time to share resources. This allows teachers to make better use of budget funds by providing more varied resources, using them as *learning centers*.

In designing a *learning center*, realize that you will not be there to offer directions. Your printed or videotaped directions must be clear and, as in the case of *how-to sheets*, presented in such a way that each direction asks the student to take one action. Suppose you want students to plant a seed in a cup. A direction such as "plant the seed in the cup" leaves too much up to the imagination of the student. Instead, you might provide a direction sheet that offers clear steps. For example:

1. Using the spoon in the dirt bucket, fill the cup with dirt up to the blue line, being careful not to spill the dirt.

2. Use the spoon to tap down the dirt.

3. Add more dirt up to the blue line and tap down.

4. Keep adding just a little dirt, tapping it down until your dirt reaches the blue line.

5. Take the wooden dowel and push it straight down in the center of the dirt to the red line on the dowel to make a small hole in the dirt.

6. Place your seed in the hole.

7. Using the spoon, cover the seed with dirt, tapping it down to keep the seed in place.

8. Pour water into the cup to reach the top. It will soak in.

Note that each direction requires the student to take one action. This level of detail helps ensure students will meet with success and decreases the need for students to ask for help. In the primary grades, to help students with unknown words, you could read through the directions during a morning meeting as you introduce the *learning center*. You could include a podcast or video to offer an even greater explanation of the directions.

To build writing skills, you might create several *learning centers* in which students retrieve a packet that includes an activity and directions. In art, you might create a *learning center* in which students study a painting and respond to questions. For physical education, you might create a *learning center* in which students video and view themselves practicing a particular skill in a sport. For geography, you might create a *learning center* in which students work with images, descriptions, and a world map to explore landforms. For science, you might create a *learning center* in which students test water samples from local bodies of water. A computer could be designated as a *learning center* with a specific piece of software or website to be used. For primary students, you might stock plastic containers with place-value rods and direction sheets through which students would explore the concept.

Keep a *sign-up sheet* next to each *learning center* or in the *resource area* with enough time for students to retrieve, use, and replace the *learning center* before another student needs it. Students will learn to sign-up in advance and coordinate the use of the resource with others. The *limited-resource sign-up sheet* will be discussed, along with other critical structures, in Chapter 5.

Interactive Websites and Applications

Today's digital world is filled with apps that run on smartphones, tablets, Chromebooks, and computers. They are typically interactive, focused, and visually appealing. You can find apps to practice telling time, work with tangrams, interact with a number line, learn grammar skills, engage in a crossword puzzle, interact with an online version of a magnetic poetry board, translate words to another language, play music on a keyboard, explore the color wheel, see and hear animals, explore maps, learn the laws of physics, learn to read music, and more. The interactive nature allows students to manipulate objects, make predictions, experience cause-and-effect relationships, and create. To locate apps, use your Internet search engine and type the word "app" followed by the subject of interest, for example, "app poetry."

If you have access to handheld computing devices, be sure to search out and load apps related to your curriculum and then make those apps part of your *scaffold for learning*. You may need to create a direction sheet for using an app.

Individual Versus Group Tasks

Learning is social; students learn well from one another. Today's students thrive on social interaction, both in person and through the Internet. Collaborative learning can be a powerful tool in the classroom; however, you must be purposeful in your assignment of group versus individual activities. Students must eventually perform independently, on standardized tests as well as in life. It is your responsibility to ensure that all students have achieved personal content mastery. Consequently, it is important to provide students with individual *learning activities* that allow them to acquire and practice skills.

The best use of collaboration is when the activity is related to *higher-order, open-ended problem solving*. Not unlike the collaborative world of work, students should independently gain a certain amount of content mastery and then come together to collaborate. When work teams come together, each person brings some level of personal expertise. Brainstorming ideas, analyzing problem solutions, and generating questions are some of the types of activities in which learning is enhanced through collaboration.

Computer technology can provide powerful opportunities for collaboration through networked software and Web-based tools. Students can collaboratively build databanks, building on one another's knowledge, and even join with students around the world in this effort. They can collaboratively work on documents, spreadsheets, and other products. Students are no longer limited to working with others in the classroom; email and videoconferencing can expand the student body beyond the walls of the classroom or school.

A key skill to learn in collaborating is reaching decisions through consensus (Sulla, 2018). Instead of students voting and using a majority-rules approach, have them discuss a solution, offering pros and cons, until they can all at least live with, if not fully support, an idea.

Peer Experts

Peer experts provide an effective learning experience for both the student offering the instruction and the one being instructed. First, one of the best ways to ensure retention of learning is to teach someone else. Second, people learn best from those who are hierarchically similar; children learn more readily from other children than from adults. *Peer experts* are designated by the teacher as having mastered a specific skill and having the ability to share the skill with others. Make sure that the student designated as a *peer expert* is adequately equipped to teach others. Simply scoring high on a test is not an indication that the student can explain the concept or skill in an effective way. It is good practice to have the potential *peer expert* walk you through the explanation before showing others. It is also good to train your students, all of whom should be designated as a *peer expert* at some times across the year, that it's important to not simply take over the work. Being a *peer expert* is not about doing the work for others; it's about talking them through it in a way that they understand.

Once you have identified a *peer expert*, have them put their name on the *peer expert board* with their skill of expertise (see Chapter 5 for more on this structure). Students who are having difficulty with the skill can go to the *peer expert* for help. *Peer experts* also tend to check the *help board* in case they have expertise to share to meet another student's need. Avoid having that one student spend an inordinate amount of time teaching others. Students will solidify their own learning after they've explained a concept or skill to others two or three times. Once they present more than that, they run the risk of becoming bored with the topic or not having the time to complete their other work. Have them recommend another student to you as a *peer expert* for that skill so you can rotate students through areas of expertise.

Peer Experts Conducting Small-Group Mini-Lessons

Direct instruction must be offered by someone who understands the skill and knows how to present it to others, and that is usually a teacher. However, given that learning is social and students learn well from one another, students can offer *small-group mini-lessons* if they are well vetted by the teacher.

One third-grade teacher shared with me that she first ensures that her students have mastery of the skill in question. Then she requires them to create lesson plans! She uses a four-quadrant paper, and the students must include an example they are going to use to introduce the skill, one for guided practice, one for independent practice, and one for assessment. Students love to rise to the challenge to conduct a *small-group mini-lesson*, and when you watch the students in the audience, they are rapt with attention. This is serious business!

Homework

Homework should be meaningful and purposeful. There is a cognitive benefit to providing students with homework. During the class period, students learn a new skill, and they spend time practicing it. Once time passes after the initial introduction and practice session, and the students are home after school, a related homework assignment should require the students to recall the classroom experience. This further solidifies the learning. For this reason, I do not recommend that students be allowed to complete homework in class. Doing so eliminates the cognitive benefit of returning to the content after the passage of time.

It is tempting in the *Learner-Active, Technology-Infused Classroom* to allow students to complete unfinished class work for homework. This, however, risks the danger of students engaging in *learning activities* at home that require greater teacher participation. In the *Learner-Active, Technology-Infused Classroom*, you are not delivering information from the front of the classroom. Rather, you are designing a variety of *learning activities* through which students will build content mastery, and you are facilitating learning by working closely with students to monitor their progress and pose probing questions to promote higher-order thinking. Clearly, some, or many, of these activities should be accomplished only in class with your facilitation. If you allow students to complete these *learning activities* at home, they may lose out on the richness of the experience.

Design unique activities to be completed at home, as a follow-up or extension to classroom activities. This may mean providing multiple activities from which students will choose, based on their progress in classroom activities. If students are building map-reading skills, some may be learning to read map keys while others are using the scale to convert the map to actual distances. The homework should be aligned with their cognitive progress. You might want to include *practice activities* throughout the unit that can serve as homework assignments. By labeling activities on the *activity list* as LA (*learning activity*) or PA (*practice activity*), students can then assign themselves the appropriate homework based on their progress and available *practice activities*. Even the youngest students can select an appropriate assignment with your guidance.

Often, *ALUs* have content that is not directly related to the core curricular content (see Figure 4.1). The outer-ring, peripheral content could be a perfect homework assignment. Often, students will be very interested in this aspect of the *ALU*, but it does not address your content and, thus, they need not be learning it with you nearby.

Homework should never be assigned as busy work to fill up students' time. It should satisfy a specific purpose and be meaningful. The purpose for homework might be to:

- ♦ **Activate prior knowledge** before introducing new content. Prior to introducing students to the concept of a noun, you might assign homework asking them to draw or find pictures of persons, places, and things. Just prior to introducing students to the concepts of fractions, you might assign homework asking them to identify items in their homes that are naturally divided into relatively equal pieces, such as candy bars, pizzas, oranges, or window panes. Offer a question or task that enables students to draw upon personal experience to connect to a new concept or skill.

- **Grapple with new content** to create a healthy cognitive dissonance. Prior to introducing persuasive techniques, you might ask students to generate a list of sentences they would use to convince their parents to let them have some privilege. In grappling with new content, the student is asked to actually attempt to solve a problem that you will then address in class. They will be able to relate to the usefulness of the content and share their own ideas.

- **Reinforce content.** It is reasonable to ask students to practice that which they are learning in class. However, ensure that the reinforcement is necessary and not merely "busy work." Also, ensure that the student will have ample directions to rely on if needed. Where possible, have one aspect of the assignment move the performance to a higher cognitive level to offer a challenge after the practice.

- **Generate ideas.** Often in *problem-based tasks*, students need to generate ideas that they can then share with their peers and collaboratively evaluate. Students can be instructed to gather some information from books, articles, the Internet, or interviews and brainstorm ideas to share the next day with their groups.

- **Assemble final presentations.** At times, it will be more advantageous to use class time to focus on the subject-area content required to produce the ALU product rather than on the final presentation. For example, if students in science class are designing a new ride for a theme park, building an understanding of the laws of physics and the related cause-and-effect relationships should be content studied in class, with the teacher's expertise on hand. If part of the *ALU* is for the students to make a pitch to a theme park to include their ride, *and* writing skills are not a part of the teacher's content, then the brainstorming of points to make in the pitch should be developed in class, but drafting ideas for that final pitch could be assigned for homework. If the skills of presentation development are not part of the target curriculum, relegate the development of aspects of the *ALU* presentation to homework time. I say aspects because *ALUs* are designed to be collaborative, so you do not want to place on parents the burden of getting two to four students together after school.

Back to the *Learning Map*

Consider the *learning map* you designed earlier in this chapter. Now that you have been introduced to various *participatory structures* for learning in the *scaffold for learning*, you can begin to map out the various *learning activities* you'll need to provide for the unit. Refer to your *learning map* (see examples in Figures 4.3 and 4.4). At each step, decide what concepts or skills students will need and how they might learn them. Although it may be tempting to "teach" every concept and skill either from the front of the room or in small-group sessions, think about how you can "clone" yourself and provide direct instruction in other ways. A carefully designed *how-to sheet* offers written directions the student can follow. A screencast is great for capturing steps you would take to use a particular app. The student can watch the screen animation and hear your narration while you're explaining how to accomplish the task. They might then follow the printed *how-to sheet* and try it for themselves. Some skills are going to be too difficult for some students to tackle independently. You might film a video using a digital camera and walk students through the steps; however, you also might want to schedule a *small-group mini-lesson* for students who are going to require more personalized assistance.

Add to your *learning map* a column for how students will learn the skills needed to accomplish what you wrote on the left side (see Figures 4.11 and 4.12). The left side should be described in the *analytic rubric*; the right side is the foundation for developing your *scaffold for learning*. If you want to capture specific skills required, list them on the line, moving from what students need to accomplish (left side) and how they will learn (right side) the necessary skills (middle), if not self-explanatory.

Figure 4.11. Learning Map 2: Using Numbers and Words to Feed Others

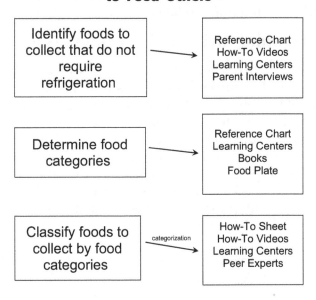

Figure 4.12. Learning Map 2: Designer Pizza

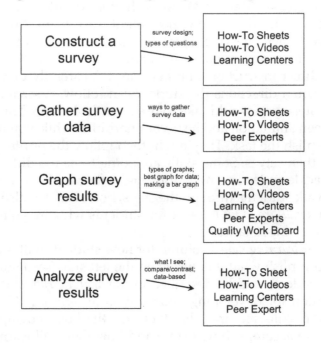

Once you complete the second column, you can begin to identify or design actual *learning activities* to put on your *scaffold for learning*. Use a *learning map* to think through the steps students would take to accomplish the *problem-based task*, to consider how your curricular standards relate to your *ALU*, and to plan *learning activities* for your *scaffold for learning*.

Back to the Learning Styles and Readiness Grid

As you consider the *learning map* you've just created, identify a skill that is a key part of the curriculum for this unit. For example, in science, such a skill might be how to create a food chain (Figure 4.13). It's probably easy to visualize yourself teaching students the skill you selected; but for the moment, let's assume you must create a set of instructional activities for the student to use to build a skill independent of you. Although concepts are often appropriately introduced to the whole class through a *benchmark lesson*, with questions, answers, and discussion; skills are best addressed on a more individual basis when students can personally grapple with the content based on activities that match their cognitive levels and learning styles.

Let's assume that some students are ready to learn the skill, in this case, creating a food chain. According to Vygotsky, that skill would be in their

Figure 4.13. Differentiation Grid for Proximal Zone

Skill: Creating a Food Chain			
	Distal Zone A student who will be challenged to learn this skill/ concept or lacks the prerequisite skills needed	**Proximal Zone** A student who is ready to learn this or is on grade level	**Current Knowledge** A student who is ready to move beyond this or is above grade level
Visual		Follow a printed *how-to sheet* with diagrams to match predator and prey in a four-item food chain.	
Auditory		Watch and listen to a video that describes several food chains existing in the natural world.	
Kinesthetic/ Tactile		Use a set of prey and predator cards with an answer key to create food chains.	

proximal zone. Consider that some of your students may learn best through visual means, others through auditory cues, and still others through a more tactile approach. Figure 4.13 offers three different ways to learn the same skill, based on the designated learning styles. A *how-to sheet* allows you to turn your skill lesson into step-by-step directions for students to access again and again as needed. It's easy to record an enhanced podcast that includes audio and still images. Keep a list of videos that would help your students; then sit down and record all of them. You will have created those "teacher-cloning tools" to which I referred earlier in the chapter. Designing kinesthetic and tactile activities can be more challenging and require additional resources, but be creative, ask colleagues, and search the Internet for ideas.

What about the students who are not yet ready to learn the skill you've identified? In this case, if a student is not familiar with identifying predators and prey, spending some time understanding the concept will make the subsequent skill development easier. Figure 4.14 offers the same grid, with the left column filled in for those students who require some prerequisite work before tackling the skill of creating a food chain. You can offer videos

Figure 4.14. Differentiation Grid for Proximal and Distal Zones

Skill: Creating a Food Chain			
	Distal Zone A student who will be challenged to learn this skill/ concept or lacks the prerequisite skills needed	**Proximal Zone** A student who is ready to learn this or is on grade level	**Current Knowledge** A student who is ready to move beyond this or is above grade level
Visual	Read a book on predators and prey.	Follow a printed *how-to sheet* with diagrams to match predator and prey in a four-item food chain.	
Auditory	Watch and listen to a video that describes various predators and prey.	Watch and listen to a video that describes several food chains existing in the natural world.	
Kinesthetic/ Tactile	Cut out pictures of predators and prey and glue them to a category board for predator and prey.	Use a set of prey and predator cards with an answer key to create food chains.	

of lessons you've offered in the past or create video segments to explain a concept or skill. Small cameras, tablet PCs, and phones can be used to focus on a desktop or paper so you can demonstrate a skill while narrating.

What about the students who have already mastered this skill? It may have been introduced to them in another class or by older siblings, or maybe they discovered it themselves while pursuing other interests. Although it may make the teacher feel better to think that additional practice is always useful, the reality is that asking students to sit through lessons or activities to learn that which they already know will most likely lead to boredom, frustration, and daydreaming. Fundamentally, it's disrespectful toward students. Instead, consider what they could do next. You may or may not wish to allow them to move ahead with curricular content; you could have them apply the learning to another situation, deepen their knowledge of the nuances of the skill, pursue some specific area of personal interest, or even design materials to present the learning to others in a creative way.

Figure 4.15. Differentiation Grid

Skill: Creating a Food Chain			
	Distal Zone A student who will be challenged to learn this skill/ concept or lacks the prerequisite skills needed	**Proximal Zone** A student who is ready to learn this or is on grade level	**Current Knowledge** A student who is ready to move beyond this or is above grade level
Visual	Read a book on predators and prey.	Follow a printed *how-to sheet* with diagrams to match predator and prey in a four-item food chain.	Read a book or web page on food webs.
Auditory	Watch and listen to a video that describes various predators and prey.	Watch and listen to a video that describes several food chains existing in the natural world.	Watch and listen to a video that explains food webs.
Kinesthetic/ Tactile	Cut out pictures of predators and prey and glue them to a category board for predator and prey.	Use a set of prey and predator cards with an answer key to create food chains.	Play an online food web game to exploring placing species in the correct trophic level and spot in a food web.

Figure 4.15 offers the complete grid, now with the right column filled in that provides activities for the students who have already mastered the skill. In this case, the students will move on to explore food webs and the effect of the extinction of a species on the ecosystem. You've just explored a *learning styles and readiness grid* (also called a *differentiation grid*), a key tool for lesson-level differentiated instruction (see Appendix I).

The purpose of designing this *learning styles and readiness grid*, like the *learning map*, is to build your skills in designing truly differentiated activities. You've brainstormed nine activities that address a curricular skill. It would be extremely time consuming to attempt to develop a grid for each skill or concept you teach. As you begin designing your *Learner-Active, Technology-Infused Classroom*, develop grids for key skills to expand your thinking on skill presentation in ways other than whole-class instruction.

Over time, you'll brainstorm a variety of activities naturally to address the needs of your students. If you have ample computer technology available and can locate a variety of computer-based *learning activities* for a particular skill, create the grid as a word-processing document with hyperlinks of the website URLs. Students can then click on a link and access a *learning activity*. In the case of student use, you might want to change the column headings to "Just Learning," "Ready to Dive In," and "I've Got This," or other similarly descriptive headings.

RECAP

Designing a *problem-based task* and *analytic rubric* is just the beginning of an *Authentic Learning Unit* (*ALU*). Implementing the unit requires a carefully constructed plan that provides students with a variety of ways to participate in learning. While short, whole-class *benchmark lessons* can be used to introduce concepts, most of students' classroom time will be spent engaging in activities to learn and build skills and concepts. Review your *scaffold for learning* to ensure that you've included a variety of ways for your students to learn the concepts and skills they will need to succeed at the *problem-based task*. Use this list as you review to ensure that you've included:

♦ *Benchmark lessons* to present unit concepts at key points in the unit;

♦ *Benchmark lessons* that focus on presenting concepts and not skills;

♦ A comprehensive list of printed *how-to sheets* to be designed to teach key skills throughout the unit;

♦ A list of podcasts, screencasts, and videos to be located or designed to offer instruction in skills and concepts;

♦ *Small-group mini-lessons* for focused skill instruction, being careful not to include too much content for any one session;

♦ *Learning centers* for students to explore concepts and skills in a hands-on manner;

♦ Individual *learning activities* and *practice activities* for building core content mastery;

♦ Group activities for planning, brainstorming, sharing, designing, and evaluating ideas;

♦ *Peer expert* opportunities for students to share their learning with and learn from one another;

- Apps to build concepts and skills;
- Homework that is structured to activate prior knowledge, allowing students to grapple with new content, reinforcing content, and encouraging students to generate new ideas.

REFERENCES

Csikszentmihalyi, M. (1990). *Flow: The psychology of optimal experience.* New York, NY: Harper & Row.

Gattegno, C. (1987). *The science of education part I: Theoretical considerations.* New York, NY: Educational Solutions.

Pink, D. H. (2011). *Drive: The surprising truth about what motivates us.* New York: Riverhead Books.

Prensky, M. (2006). *Don't bother me Mom—I'm learning.* St. Paul, MN: Paragon House.

Sousa, David. (2017). *How the brain learns* (5th ed.). Thousand Oaks, CA: Corwin.

Sulla, N. (2015). *It's not what you teach but how: 7 insights to making the CCSS work for you.* New York, NY: Routledge.

Sulla, N. (2018). *Building executive function: The missing link to student achievement.* New York, NY: Routledge.

Vygotsky, L. S. (1978). *Mind and society: The development of higher psychological processes.* Cambridge, MA: Harvard University Press.

5

Empowering Students to Take Responsibility for Their Learning

A group of kindergarten students have been given a sheet with four pictures with words representing *learning activities*. Their job is to cut them out, pick three that they want to accomplish this morning, and paste them onto a schedule sheet to follow. The schedule sheet already has a group meeting placed in the second slot, so the students glue their choices in any order they like in the remaining slots.

A first-grade student is working on writing a new ending to a book he is reading. He is filling out a graphic organizer with the book's characters, setting, and key events. He is not sure about the key events, so he looks at the *peer expert board* to see if anyone is listed as an expert. Since there are no *peer experts*, he walks up to the *help board* and writes his name on it so the teacher will come and help him when she's available.

A pair of second-grade students have surveyed the class for their favorite ice cream flavors and are getting ready to put together a bar graph. Neither student is sure of how to create the bar graph on a computer, so one goes to the *resource table* to retrieve a *how-to sheet* with step-by-step directions.

A group of third-grade students is scheduling their day. One student suggests they get together to conduct the science experiment at 2:00. Another shares that she has a speech lesson at 2:10 and will be back by 2:40. The group members agree to schedule the experiment for 2:40. Individually, they schedule how they are going to use time across the day, including attending *benchmark lessons* and *small-group mini-lessons* and engaging in paired, group, and individual activities.

On the first day of a new *Authentic Learning Unit (ALU)*, fourth-grade students read their *problem-based task* and *analytic rubric* and make the list of what they will need to learn to complete the task. The teacher distributes a unit calendar with intermediate due dates, as well as quiz and test dates. Students use the calendar and *activity list* to schedule each week on Monday morning.

A group of four fifth graders has just finished working for the past half hour on choreographing creative movement to a piece of music they selected by coordinating movement to the beat and dynamics. Before they end this activity, they turn to a *table journal* that has them reflect on how well they worked together, stayed on task, contributed, and reached consensus in decision making. They self-assess and set collaboration goals for their next session.

CONSIDER

Most schools have "lifelong learning" in their mission statements, yet few engage students in learning environments that actually create lifelong learners. A lifelong learner must break down goals into attainable steps, be resourceful, self-assess, manage time, manage a project, generate ideas, reflect, and more. Yet in most classrooms, despite a great emphasis on hands-on, collaborative learning over the past decades, teachers still overtly control much of the activity of students, telling them what to do and when to do it; when to speak and when to be quiet; and what resources to use. Creating lifelong learners means allowing students to take charge of their own learning process and teaching them how to accomplish that.

> **"Most schools have "lifelong learning" in their mission statements, yet few engage students in learning environments that actually create lifelong learners."**

William Glasser (1998) first wrote a book titled *Control Theory* and, in a later edition, renamed it *Choice Theory*, but his message was the same: you cannot control students' learning; students must choose to learn. Glasser presents his theory that, after survival needs are met, students choose to learn based on a sense of belonging, freedom, power, and fun (engagement.)

Students will not necessarily come to school with the skills required to take responsibility for learning. Teachers need to reach beyond content instruction to include instruction in these skills. That doesn't mean ignoring content instruction! It means taking advantage of opportunities to also teach the skills needed to build *student responsibility for learning*.

If you were to use a stopwatch and clock the amount of time you spend giving directions and waiting for your students to follow them and be ready for the next direction, you'd most likely be amazed. How much time do you spend on administrative tasks, transitioning students from one activity to another, addressing behavioral issues? If you could regain that time, you'd have more time for students to spend learning content. The time invested at the beginning of the year to teach students the structures and strategies to take responsibility for their own learning will prove to be well worth it as the year progresses.

The following metaphor presents a key paradigm shift for the *Learner-Active, Technology-Infused Classroom:* moving the teacher from being disseminator of information to the architect of a powerful learning environment that gives students responsibility for learning.

Teacher as Ferry or Teacher as Bridge?[1]

Did you ever stop to consider the differences between taking a ferry or traveling over a bridge to cross a river? Taking a ferry leaves the traveler in the hands of the boat operator and releases the traveler from most responsibility. The ferry operator tells you where to park your car, decides when the boat will leave and how fast it will move, and takes all of the travelers across at the same time and speed. Your only responsibility is to show up on time. Taking a bridge puts the traveler in control and in the seat of responsibility. Different drivers use different lanes and drive at different speeds. All who cross the start of the bridge at one time do not necessarily end up on the other side at the same time. The journey is largely in the hands of the driver. But think about the magic of a bridge: a mass of steel suspended over a large expanse, being held in place almost miraculously, through the laws of physics. And yet probably few travelers hold that bridge in awe as they use it to move from one land mass to another, taking control of their travel, taking the bridge for granted.

As a teacher, are you a ferry or a bridge? Do you carry your students through the day, telling them when to do what tasks and how to do them? Do you present lessons to your entire class, deciding on a pace that seems appropriate? Do you have a "do now" to direct their actions as they walk into the classroom? Or do you create the structures for your students to take responsibility for their own learning? Do you offer expectations and pathways to success? Do you create structures that allow all of your students to achieve based on their differences? Becoming a bridge builder is a key paradigm shift of the *Learner-Active, Technology-Infused Classroom.* Think about your role in your classroom and, as you work through this book, decide on how you can become more of a bridge builder than a ferry master.

IDE Corp. consultants work with teachers who wish to shift their paradigms to being bridge builders rather than ferry masters. These

---

1 Reprinted from the IDEportal (www.ideportal.com) with permission.

teachers design *problem-based tasks* with *analytic rubrics* that allow students to self-assess and set goals. They create *activity lists* that guide students through the day or week, listing the teacher's required *benchmark lessons*, optional *small-group mini-lessons*, group activities, and individual activities. Students begin the day or week by designing a personalized schedule for their work. They monitor their progress and reflect on their work habits in journals. *How-to sheets*, *screencasts*, and *videos* are available for students to use as they need to master a particular skill. They each keep their work in a two-pocket or digital *student work folder* that holds completed and in-progress activities. Teachers become facilitators, moving around the classroom, meeting with individual students and groups to guide learning. They carry grids or handheld computing devices to keep notes on student progress and skill mastery. They review *student work folders* and make comments. Based on the data they glean, they set *small-group mini-lessons* to teach skills and set whole-class *benchmark lessons* to build awareness of concepts and skills yet to be learned.

Masterful *Learner-Active, Technology-Infused Classroom* teachers create a complex system of interdependent structures to put students in charge of their own learning. To see it in action in a classroom is to realize that the students take this system for granted, feeling totally empowered to pursue their education and proud to take control, never realizing the incredible feat their teachers have accomplished in building it.

"To see it in action in a classroom is to realize that the students take this system for granted, feeling totally empowered to pursue their education and proud to take control, never realizing the incredible feat their teachers have accomplished in building it."

CREATE

You've designed a compelling *problem-based task statement*, standards-rich *analytic rubric*, and robust *scaffold for learning*. It's time to think about how that will play out in the classroom. As you read, keep a paper or digital journal of ideas you will want to implement. Take time to develop student materials to use in your classroom to build *student responsibility for learning*. This chapter will introduce you to the critical structures that should be in place in every *Learner-Active, Technology-Infused Classroom*.

The Home Group

One structure for providing students with a sense of belonging is to assign them to a *home group*. In kindergarten, begin with pairs, as you can't get lost in a pair! As students progress in their understanding of learning in a *Learner-Active, Technology-Infused Classroom,* increase the group size to three. Assign a *home group* for each period of time in which you are running your two to three *ALUs* across the day to address the various subject areas, which should be anywhere from two to four weeks in kindergarten. By first grade, I recommend groups of three; however, if your students are new to the *Learner-Active, Technology-Infused Classroom* or if you have a high number of English language learners or students with disabilities, start with *home groups* of two and build from there. In second- through fifthgrade levels, I recommend groups of three or four students who will work together throughout the *ALU,* typically three to five weeks. Never exceed a group size of four, as the ability to collaborate and work together becomes increasingly compromised with a larger group size.

Although the students will have collaborative responsibility for the final product, much of concept and skill building will take place on an individual basis. Students will work in their *home groups* for brainstorming, planning, reviewing, and making some decisions for the final solution. However, much of the learning will take place individually and with other like-ability students. Consequently, it is unnecessary and often unproductive to establish groups of like-ability students as the *home group.* You do not want to create the academically challenged group and the gifted group. That being said, I would not recommend, at the beginning of the year, placing the most academically challenged student in the class in a group with the most gifted student. This situation could become frustrating for both at the start of learning to work in a *Learner-Active, Technology-Infused Classroom.* When designing the groups, seek to create a working mix of students in terms of achievement, gender, learning styles, personalities, and work habits. Spend a considerable amount of time on this: designing the lists, reviewing and modifying them, and perhaps returning to them the next day to ensure that the groups are well constructed.

The *home group* addresses the structures of taking responsibility for learning. Together, students discuss and plan out their time; they help one another find resources and make decisions about how to work; and they collaboratively assess progress. They also assist one another in mastering content, but the group's primary function is to provide each student with a sense of belonging to a group that collectively works together to tackle a *problem-based task.* The *home group* is the first tier for assistance, shifting the power, if you will, away from being primarily with the teacher. Working in a group for an extended period of time allows students to build important life and work skills in collaboration.

Switching groups for the next set of *ALUs* offers students the experience of engaging more closely with many members of the class. Working as part of a *home group* provides both comfort and challenges. Switching groups can minimize the amount of time a student must face any particular challenge when working with a group. For example, one group member might tend to take over the activities of the group. Although it's important for students to learn how to handle such peers, it's also pleasant to sometimes not have to deal with that particular challenge.

Some teachers like to allow students to create their own groups. This is possible after students learn how to work in a *home group* and understand how to best select group members. I would not recommend allowing students to establish their own groups until you are well versed in running your *Learner-Active, Technology-Infused Classroom* and can create the structures to guide students through selecting a productive group.

Launching the *Authentic Learning Unit*

A well-crafted, authentic, open-ended, *problem-based task* should motivate students to learn—and learning is fun. Let me make a distinction here: being *taught* is not always fun, but realizing you've accomplished something you could never do before is. Launch your new *problem-based task* with an opening reflection that consists of a two- to three-minute period of thinking, drawing, or writing to focus students. For example, if you were going to launch a unit on designing kites, as students settle into their seats, ask them to list what they know about kites. Remember, the intent is to help students shift focus from whatever they were doing prior to this group *benchmark lesson* onto the subject at hand: kites. The opening reflection to an *ALU* is not intended to address any sort of learning objective, so keep it to a couple of minutes. This activity can be posted on the wall or classroom website as students enter the room at the beginning of a new *ALU*, so they can get started while everyone settles into the classroom. In the case of the virtual classroom, you'd ask students to complete this reflection before watching the opening video.

Then as you address the group through your opening *benchmark lesson*, you want to build their enthusiasm around the topic. This should be your "hook" that sends your students off looking for answers. Where possible, use world events, video, audio, and images to build a case for why you are presenting the question. Seek to captivate them around the topic. Strive for the "oooooh" reaction. The *ALU* launch and *problem-based task* introduction should only take about ten minutes.

Next, introduce students to the *analytic rubric* that will guide their work over the course of the *ALU*. For kindergarten and first-grade students, walk them through the *analytic rubric*, discussing what their final solution will look like based on the rubric criteria. Introduce new vocabulary words, point out how to use the *analytic rubric*, and offer students an overall introduction to these structures. In the beginning of the year, introduce students to one or two rows each day or to just the section of the rubric that is most meaningful at the time. For example, in "Using Numbers and Words to

Feed Others" (Appendix C), students first make food lists, then write a letter to community members, then collect and tally donations. While you would discuss the full project with your students, start by just introducing the rows addressing creating the food list.

From second grade on, after presenting the *problem-based task*, have students send a materials person to the *resource area* to retrieve copies of the *task statement* and *analytic rubric*. Ask students to read the *task statement* and then read down the *Practitioner* column of the *analytic rubric*, circling or underlining everything they are going to need to learn to accomplish the task. Note that I did not say, "what they don't know." Focus on learning as a positive, productive experience rather than as a gap filler. You can also have them circle any vocabulary words they need to learn and see if others in the group know the meanings. After students read and discuss the *problem-based task* and *analytic rubric* with their group, return to a full group discussion to share what the class needs to learn, writing or projecting the list on the board. Then let your students know you've designed a lot of *learning activities* that will help them accomplish their goals. This process allows students to see what lies ahead and consider what they need to learn, thus taking responsibility for their own learning. Depending on the age and ability level of the students, you might want to first have them review and discuss the *problem-based task* and then, afterward, have them retrieve the *analytic rubric* for a similar reading and discussion.

You may choose to assign students articles or stories to read in advance of class to pique their interest in a topic. Then the opening reflection might be relating their lives to the articles or generating questions from the articles or stories. When you introduce the *problem-based task* and *analytic rubric*, students should already be motivated to tackle it.

At this point, which could be the following day, you're ready to hand out an *activity list* (more on that in a future section) and let them get started. Using these structures (the opening *benchmark lesson*, *problem-based task statement*, *analytic rubric*, and *activity list*) and strategies (having students reflect, presenting a case for the problem, having students read the *analytic rubric* on their own and consider what they need to learn), you will build greater *student responsibility for learning* and, thus, executive function skills related to empowerment.

Student Schedules

In the *Learner-Active, Technology-Infused Classroom*, students take responsibility for scheduling how they will use their time. You've developed a set of *learning activities* and *practice activities* for your *problem-based task*, outlined in your *scaffold for learning* (see Chapter 4). The next step is to create a structure that allows your students to schedule how they will use their time. For primary-level students, begin with them scheduling a half day of activities. Third-grade students and above can schedule a full day. In departmentalized settings, in which class meets for a designated number of minutes each day, have students schedule across the week. For virtual courses, students should schedule a manageable amount of time allocated to work on the course content. The amount of forward-looking activities students can manage will depend upon their grade level, the amount of time they have experienced your *Learner-Active, Technology-Infused Classroom*, and the amount of years they've studied in such classrooms in the school.

The goal across the grade levels is to have students self-assess using the *analytic rubric*, identify what they need to learn, then turn to the *activity list* to find the section with corresponding content, and decide from the available activities what they will do when. Note that it is the *analytic rubric*, not the *activity list*, that should drive student action.

> **"Note that it is the *analytic rubric*, not the *activity list*, that should drive student action."**

If students simply look at an *activity list* and start working through it, they are merely being compliant. Alternatively, if they have the overall *problem-based task* challenge in mind and they refer to the *analytic rubric* to determine what aspect they need to tackle next, they are building efficacy—the ability to produce an intended result.

Years ago, I was redesigning a school one grade level at a time, beginning with fourth-grade classrooms. In the third year, I was talking with some of the students who had begun learning in *Learner-Active, Technology-Infused Classrooms* three years prior, asking them how the year was going. One student said, "It's getting better. At first the teacher wouldn't let us schedule our own time, but we've been doing this for two years now. But she's catching on." The teacher was moving slowly because the idea of students managing their own time was new to her, but it wasn't new to her students.

To schedule time, students need an *activity list* and a blank schedule. (Kindergarten teachers, hang on: there's a section coming up just for you, but it's good to read through this to see how your students will schedule in the future.) The *activity list* is developed from the *scaffold for learning*. Primary students should be given a few activities to schedule across a half day, giving them freedom to decide the order in which to accomplish them. For example, first-grade students, at the start of the year, might decide when to accomplish their buddy reading, journal writing, science experiment, and math practice. When they have mastered this scheduling skill, you can introduce choices within each target skill, such as deciding between playing a math game, listening to a podcast, or attending a teacher-led lesson, all focusing on a single math skill.

By second grade, you can introduce the concept of scheduling start and stop times for activities. Although second graders are typically just learning to tell time, the promise of scheduling one's own time builds a *felt need* to learn to tell time. A group of teachers once told a colleague of mine that second graders were not developmentally ready to tell time. My colleague suggested they provide students with the option of scheduling their own time if they can learn to read the clock. By October, all students were scheduling their day with varying degrees of teacher assistance. By December, the teachers presented students with a test and found that the students could tell time to the minute, at which point the teachers were dismayed to realize the state tests only required them to tell time at five-minute intervals. *Felt need* deriving from autonomy is a powerful motivator.

"The importance of having students indicate start and end times for their planned activities cannot be overemphasized; it is the foundation of time management, and it builds executive function."

If students merely determine the order in which they plan to complete activities and start working, an activity that should require twenty minutes of attention could end up taking forty minutes, and the student will be left believing that the teacher has assigned too much work. The *activity list* of learning options that you design should indicate approximate completion time for each activity. As students begin to develop and/or contribute to *activity lists*, they will need to consider how long an activity should take. If the *activity list* indicates that gathering and graphing the data should take thirty minutes, students who find themselves still collecting data at twenty minutes will know to seek additional instructional supports. By scheduling start and end times, students can reflect on their ability to work productively and schedule realistically: two important twenty-first-century skills.

Scheduling in Kindergarten

Kindergarten is a time of strengthening executive function. Each teacher has to assess individual students and the class as a whole to make decisions about how to approach scheduling time. Ultimately, you want students to consider the *problem-based task* at hand, refer to the *analytic rubric*, and use the *activity list* to decide on the *learning activities* and *practice activities* in which they will engage, putting them into an order of their preference.

At first, you might consider giving students a set of laminated choice cards that they can affix to a blank schedule or board in the order they like. Given that students cannot tell time, only have them schedule for half of the day at a time. Loosely label the times by twenty-minute slots as red, blue, yellow, and so forth or A, B, C, and so forth. You will post what time slot it is, and in the beginning of the year, announce it. That way, if a student selected the math game during the blue time, when you call blue time, she needs to pack up what she's doing and move on. While this is not critical for most activities, if students have signed up for limited resources or a *small-group mini-lesson*, they will have to be mindful of the time slot. While the idea of moving students through twenty-minute slots is antithetical to the philosophy of the *Learner-Active, Technology-Infused Classroom* (because the teacher is managing the action and the student is being compliant), hey, it's kindergarten! You will find that you must start the year more ferry-like as you build in your students the skills and executive function to take charge of their own learning. That being said, never use your perception of students' ability as the reason for not providing them with opportunities to stretch those skills of student responsibility. Many *Learner-Active, Technology-Infused Classroom* teachers have said that they can't believe what five-year-olds can really do.

Once you have students making choices by giving them tactile cards to stick to time slots, move to a paper display of activities that they cut out and glue to a blank schedule (see Figure 5.1). This also exercises the skills

Figure 5.1. Sample Activity List for Kindergarten

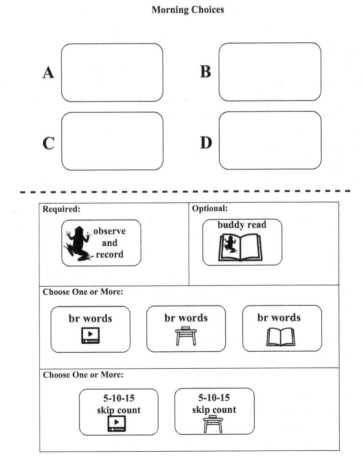

of cutting with scissors and gluing paper. As the students progress in their ability to choose from a number of items and select an order, introduce the idea of choosing the way they learn. For example, if the skill at hand is exploring the letter D, point out that there are several ways they can learn about this letter. Offer various computer games, computer apps, learning centers, and videos. (Remember, at this point, they are learning about the letter; a worksheet in which students match words to the letter based on beginning sound would be considered a *practice activity* assigned later in the day or week.) Now you might ask students to pick two of the five possible ways to learn about the letter D to place on their schedule.

Some teachers use timers to cue students that a new time has started. The problem with timers is that the teacher is setting a time for all students, and students soon simply work to the timer bell, which, again, sets up a compliance model. However, if using timers at the start of the year helps build students' awareness, and you have a transition plan, then that's fine. For example, you might start with timers. Then you would point out to students that you think they can tell their own time using cues on the clock. If you have a clock with hands, each number is five minutes, which involves skip counting. You can let students know that they can use a little more or less time if needed. For example, if they are in one time slot and finish early, they can start their next activity. Eventually, you wean them off dependence on a bell or relying on you to manage their time. Ultimately, in a *Learner-Active, Technology-Infused Classroom*, students work to their own schedules, allowing them to allot different amounts of time to different activities, being mindful of the time to stay on schedule. All of your actions regarding time management should move students toward this eventual state of empowerment.

Early in the year, focus some of your *benchmark lessons* on how to schedule. At first, offer students simply three activities that they must complete in any order. During the lesson, talk about the three activities and ask how many would like to start with a particular activity, directing them to put that in the first spot on their blank schedules. You will use the *benchmark lesson* to introduce students to the scheduling process. Then you can offer *small-group mini-lessons* for those who continue to need your help in building their skills in scheduling their time.

When students simply order a set of required activities, they are mostly compliant, with some freedom to decide when to accomplish which activity. When students have to select which activities they want to complete from a larger list, taking into account how they prefer to learn, they have to additionally make choices regarding activities they like. This builds greater executive function. (Compliance requires only basic executive function skills.) When they have to take into account signing up for *limited resources* and arranging time to work with others, they build even greater executive function skills. When students have a voice in determining which activities to add to the *activity list*, they build further executive function toward empowerment and efficacy.

How your students will complete a schedule in the beginning of the year will differ greatly from how they will complete a schedule at the end of the year; kindergarten is a time of great growth in executive function skills, enhanced by the structures of the *Learner-Active, Technology-Infused Classroom*. I recently had a kindergarten student say to me, "Thank you for inventing scheduling." Even the youngest students want to be empowered!

The *Activity List*

The *activity list*, whether digital or on paper, should provide students with a reasonable number of activities to schedule over the course of the scheduling period (e.g., a half day, day, or week). Each entry on the *activity list* should offer a brief description of the activity, indicate any prerequisites to tackling this activity, provide an estimated timeframe for completion, and indicate if the activity should be completed individually (I), in pairs (P), or as a *home group* (G).

The *activity list* should be organized around the content presented in the *analytic rubric*. As students need to learn about a particular skill or concept, they can look to the *activity list* for opportunities to learn. Design your sections around the obvious content you feel will be needed by your students during the time period of the *activity list*. For example, for students tackling the *ALU* "Butterfly Garden" (Appendix B), understanding the life cycle of the butterfly is one of the criteria on the rubric. The *activity list* would have a section for the life cycle of the butterfly with a variety of *learning activities* from which to choose.

Within each content section, you'll have up to three types of activities:

- *Choice activities*—Students must learn a required skill or concept. However, they have a choice as to how they will learn it. Choice activities should make up the bulk of your *activity list* to ensure an adequate amount of differentiation. For any given skill or concept, offer students a variety of ways to build mastery, including those that address different cognitive levels, learning styles and intelligences, and disabilities. For example, offer a podcast, text selection, *how-to sheet*, interactive website, and/or hands-on learning center. (You've already brainstormed the various participatory structures on your *scaffold for learning* in Chapter 4, though as you design your *activity list*, you will most likely add to the choices.) Group the choice activities for a specific skill or concept and indicate how many of the total you want students to complete. For example, you might indicate one or more from a choice of four, or two or more from a choice of five. Students decide how many and which activities to schedule to build personal mastery. *Small-group mini-lessons* are choice activities. However, I recommend posting them separately from the activity list, giving you maximum flexibility to schedule them as needed.

♦ *Required activities*—These are used when students must learn a required skill or concept through a specific activity or demonstrate their understanding for you through an assignment. For example, if you have a video you want all students to view or a workbook page you want all to complete, you would put them as required activities. Given that they do not allow students choice, keep required activities to a minimum. *Benchmark lessons* are also required activities. As with the *small-group mini-lessons*, I recommend posting those separately from the activity list, giving you the flexibility to make a last-minute change.

♦ *Optional activities*—Most *problem-based tasks* lend themselves to many extensions and digressions. Optional activities allow students to pursue related interests. This is particularly useful for students who are on or ahead of schedule to complete the main *problem-based task* and have the time to delve more deeply into areas of interest. For example, students who are building a butterfly garden may become intrigued with the migration of the monarch butterfly and wish to research that further. Students who are launching a food drive for the poor may wish to build their counting skills beyond the required 100 listed in the rubric.

While there is no one right way to design your *activity list*, Figure 5.1 offers a sample page from an *activity list* for the *ALU* "Butterfly Garden" (Appendix B). Students must learn about the life cycle of a butterfly, so they have several choices of *learning activities* from which to choose. They then have a separate set of choices for a *practice activity*. Notice that they must locate two additional resources (books, websites, videos, etc.) to help them as they draw the butterfly cycle. (Here, you're building executive function skills required for efficacy.) That required activity indicates that they must first complete the *learning activities* and the *practice activity*. The jagged black line indicates that there are more sections missing from your view of Figure 5.1. One of their activities will be a kit with caterpillars for each group that they will set up to raise butterflies. This is a precursor to them designing their own garden. This is so that they can actually see the

Figure 5.2. Sample Activity List for Butterfly Garden ALU

	Butterfly Life Cycle		
Choose three of five (LA)	Read the book, *I am a Butterfly*.	I or P	20 min
	Read the book, *The Life Cycle of a Butterfly*.	I or P	10 min
	Watch the video, "The Life Cycle of a Butterfly," once, then again to take notes.	I	20 min
	Explore and read the website, www.thebutterflysite.com.	I	15 min
	Explore the "Butterfly Learning Center."	P	20 min
Choose one of three (PA)	Play the online game, "Butterfly Life Cycle."	I	10 min
	Take the online "Butterfly Life Cycle Quiz."	I	5 min
	Play the board game, "Butterfly Life Cycle."	P or G	15 min
Required (complete two LA and one PA)	Find two additional resources on the butterfly life cycle as references. Create a drawing of the butterfly life cycle. Cite your resources on the back of your drawing.	I or P	30 min
Optional	Read the book, *The Life Cycle of Butterflies* for a more in-depth look.	I	20 min
	Butterfly Habitats		
Required	Read the book, *Raising Butterflies to Set Them Free* and write down your ideas for your butterfly garden.	I or P	20 min
Optional	Read the book, *Gardening for Birds, Butterflies, and Bees* to learn about more than just butterflies for your garden.	I or P	20 min
	Butterfly Habitat Kit		
Choose one of two to receive construction permit	Meet as a group to complete the "Butterfly Habitat Construction Permit Application" and have all group members sign it.	G	15 min
	Have all group members individually complete the "I Know My Butterflies" online survey.	I	10 min
Required (must have construction permit)	Unpack your butterfly habitat kit and follow the directions to set it up and start observing your caterpillars.	G	20 min

life cycle of a butterfly. Since this requires a certain amount of knowledge and readiness, note that the teacher indicates students must first have a "construction permit," which they obtain by engaging in somewhat of a checkout quiz about the life cycle. Where students have to "cite sources," if they don't know how, they will retrieve a *how-to sheet* from the *resource area*, and, if they still have trouble, seek out a *peer expert*.

This activity list would also include sections on other aspects of the *ALU*, such as using information about plants to map out a scale drawing of a garden. For example, if each box on a grid paper represented one foot, students would read actual or pictures of seed packets to determine how far apart they must be planted, taking into account how tall they grow in order to ensure the plants have adequate sunlight and do not block one another. Students would not necessarily complete the butterfly cycle learning before the math learning related to the garden. The *activity list* would include all activities for all subjects for the day or week and, thus, address two or three *ALUs*.

Using an *activity list*, although you still have control over the activities to be completed, students have the freedom to make choices as to how they will use their time and the resources they will use to meet your academic expectations. Depending on your comfort level, allow students to suggest other activities to add to the list. An ambitious student may, for example, locate instructional websites that are unknown to you. A teacher was having students design scale drawings of a dream house in math class. One student found a 3-D modeling app that allowed him to feed in all of the dimensions and see a rotatable 3-D version of his house. He was excited to share this with the teacher, who then set him up to run *small-group mini-lessons* on this *optional activity* as an extension to the plan design.

Special education students with expressive processing issues may know what they want to do but lack the language to explain it. The *activity list* provides them with that language. For *problem-based tasks* that involve writing, the *activity list* becomes a "word wall" of sorts for terms students might need in their writing.

Using the "Butterfly Garden" (Appendix B) again as an example, after learning about butterflies, their life cycle and habitats, and planning a garden, students will have to spend time developing a plan for a unique garden that they feel will best attract butterflies. The intent is for community members to follow their directions and plant such a garden. This is more of an application of knowledge than a *learning activity* or *practice activity*. Either your *activity list* should include required activity time for students to work on their solutions, or you can let students know that they should also include time in their schedule to work on their solutions.

Teaching Students to Schedule Their Time

Gradual Release

If you are teaching students that have previously attended classes in which teachers told them what to do and when to do it, scheduling their time will be an unfamiliar act. Sometimes, even the best activities, if unfamiliar, can cause students to be resistant. In this case, ease students into scheduling. At first, provide them with a completed schedule, and let them know that you want them to be aware of the order in which you are going to offer and assign instructional activities. This schedule may, for example, indicate that you will start with them completing a journal entry, then offer a fifteen-minute lesson, have students complete a pairs activity for twenty minutes, and regroup for wrap-up for five minutes.

After a few days at this level, introduce some flexibility. Tell your students that the order in which they complete two activities doesn't matter, and allow them to fill in those blanks. Offer them choices as to three ways to accomplish the same learning and allow them to select the best fit for them.

Once your students are succeeding at this level, open up the schedule even further and provide them with a primarily blank schedule, allowing them to complete the rest, referencing the *activity list*. It is important to then approve students' schedules, applying your insights into the project and students' work habits. You may recognize that a student has not allotted enough time to complete an activity or has selected an activity that is too easy or too hard. In these cases, advise the students accordingly. Students will house their activity list in their folders, so you can review them and comment and/or approve.

Having Students Reflect on Their Progress

Upon completing and implementing a schedule, students should reflect on their success. Ask students who did not complete their scheduled activities to identify why. It may be that they did not schedule enough time; it may be that they were distracted. I observed a class in which students were brainstorming ideas for building an argument. They were to cut the paper with their reasons in a shape related to their topic and artistically embellish the edges. I watched as one group of students placed rulers on pencils to create whirligigs; one group spent a short period of time brainstorming and an inordinate amount of time working on the edges; one group stayed very focused and created an impressive list; and so forth. At the end of the activity, the teacher had students respond, using a *table journal*, to a series of questions and assign themselves points for how well they accomplished their task. I was pleased to see how honestly and accurately the students assessed their work habits, with those who strayed from focus indicating so and assessing themselves on the low end of the scale. The teacher ended by saying that the following day, she expected those groups that did not receive the highest score to modify their work habits toward greater success. Sure enough, students raised their performance level based on their reflections. It is important to teach students to manage their own time and to self-assess rather than attempting to control their activities and movement.

Pull-Out Programs

One of the greatest frustrations I hear from teachers is the challenge of scheduling around all of the pull-out programs. They believe that there is precious little time for them to have with the entire class. This is all the more reason to limit the amount of whole-class instruction in favor of providing *learning activities* for students to complete based on individual schedules. If a *home group* includes a student who, for example, attends a replacement math class, then that group should schedule math at that time. That one student's schedule no longer affects the entire class and teacher.

Student Work Folders

Each student should have a physical or digital *student work folder* that remains in class. I suggest that in the case of a physical folder, you use a two-pocket folder labeled "Work in Progress" on the left side and "Work Completed" on the right side. In the case of a digital folder, have students create those two subfolders into which they will place their work. When students arrive at class, they'll retrieve or open their *student work folders*, access their schedules, review any notes left by the teacher, and begin working. They'll move completed work that has been checked by the teacher out of the folder to take home. At the end of the class period, they'll ensure that their completed work is on the right, ready to be checked by the teacher. Managing papers or documents and separating work in progress from completed work will build executive function skills and serve students well in their lives.

Make sure your students keep the work folders organized and thin! The biggest challenge is the overstuffed folder with so many papers it takes additional time to find the work to be reviewed. Use a *benchmark lesson* to introduce this folder management concept, asking students to pull out the papers on the "completed" side, identify which are fully completed based on your comments, and remove those from the folder, placing the ones that may need more work, based on your comments, on the "in progress" side. Then create a *how-to sheet* for those who need more support.

The Student Work Folder–Assessment Connection

Given that running a *Learner-Active, Technology-Infused Classroom* requires a series of paradigm shifts, let's look at the dominant paradigm for checking and grading student work. Teachers tend to have students hand papers in, grouped according to activity. If the goal is to make it easier for the teacher to grade papers, it makes sense to have stacks of papers for each assignment. The teacher then takes a stack of papers, turns to the answer key, and grades them.

Although this approach may optimize the teacher's time, it does little to contribute to student achievement. Raising student achievement requires the teacher to know the abilities of the student as a whole and plan for that student accordingly. When you open up a *student work folder*, you are seeing the student holistically. Consider a third-grade student: when you look at the folder, you see that she is strong in math skills but has difficulty with written expression. She seems to thrive on science and has strong observational skills, based on her drawings of science experiments. She has difficulty with map-reading skills. The folder approach allows you to see and assess the student as a whole, providing you with insights into the student's overall ability and interests. In the case of the third grader, you might assign a writing assignment in which she describes what she observed in the science experiment.

During the course of the day, you may have met with a student to discuss overall progress and are therefore familiar with the contents of the folder. Generally, however, you'll want to check *student work folders* daily (for self-contained classes) or weekly (for departmentalized classes). Even though you are facilitating and engaging with students as they work, your folder review will allow you to consider each student's schedule, completed work, and work in progress. You'll make notes to the student and suggest other activities. You'll use the data you glean from the class set of *student work folders* to schedule *benchmark lessons* and *small-group mini-lessons*.

It is important to instruct students to keep their *analytic rubrics* in their folders when they hand them in at the end of class. Additionally, they should indicate on the rubric what they have accomplished toward the *Practitioner* and *Expert* levels by checking off criteria. This way, you can see how students are progressing and make comments targeted to continued success.

Upon Entering the Classroom

Let's consider the moment when students enter the room. You want them to get started immediately, without any prompting from you. A common approach is to implement a "do now," but consider that a "do now" still has the teacher assigning the students an activity to complete, and the level of responsibility for the student does not extend beyond compliantly following the teacher's directions. In taking a problem-based approach to instruction, you can have students schedule how to use their own time. At the most basic level, that involves asking students at the end of the day to identify what they should start working on the next day and then having them reference that note at the start of the next day. This personal "do now" offers students empowerment and builds executive function. At higher levels of executive function, students map out how they are going to spend their time across a day or week. Students should enter the classroom and work on an activity that they scheduled the prior day. Even though you may need students to schedule their week, day, or morning, have them begin with an activity they decided on in advance. Why? Scheduling requires a great deal of cognitive load (Sweller, 1988), that is, the amount of energy one's brain is using to manage information in working memory. Thinking through one's goals, choices of activities, choices of resources, timeframes, and the like requires a lot of information being manipulated in working memory, and, therefore, a lot of cognitive load. When students first walk in the room each day, their brains are already occupied by many thoughts. Retrieving their folders, reviewing teachers' notes, and getting started on an activity that is already written down will allow them to get started easily. After that first activity, then they can schedule their morning, day, or week, being better able to take on that level of cognitive load.

What administrative functions do you need to accomplish when students enter the room? Attendance? Lunch count? Collection of forms? Consider how you might accomplish these in ways that provide the students with the responsibility. Kindergarten students can enter a classroom, find the clothes pin or magnet with their name or picture on it, and move it to the other side of a cabinet to indicate they are present. (This small act builds executive function.) If students retrieve a physical folder or log onto a class website upon entering class, you'll easily be able to determine who is absent without calling names off of a roster and consuming precious instructional time. If students are assigned to *home groups*, you can have, for example, one student monitor attendance and lunch count and record that information to create a class compilation. Checklists posted on websites or physical classroom walls allow students to report in on issues such as lunch choices and field trip forms.

Analytic Rubrics

Analytic rubrics (see Chapter 3) allow students to self-assess and set goals. Key to using an *analytic rubric* to build *student responsibility for learning* is designing the rubric to drive instruction rather than merely to evaluate the end product. *Analytic rubrics* designed to drive instruction offer students a clear path to success, introducing additional criteria in each column.

As you facilitate, expect your students to have their rubrics nearby with notes as to their progress. This might involve checking off a rubric box or highlighting criteria. As you sit with students, ask them to use the rubric to report on their progress and articulate their next steps.

A well-written *analytic rubric* will free a student to pursue learning independent of the teacher's prompting. For example, an *analytic rubric* involving graphing data may ask students to create a stacked bar graph. The Novice

Figure 5.3. Sample Rubric Row

	Novice	Apprentice	Practitioner	Expert
Bar Graph	includes properly drawn x and y axes with labels	includes three categories of data properly graphed, with axes and labels	includes a properly constructed stacked bar graph with two data sets for each of three categories of data with axes, labels, and legend	all of *Practitioner* plus overlays a line graph of related data

column might require the student to set up properly labeled x and y axes for the graph; the Apprentice might require the student to graph three pieces of data; the Practitioner column might require the student to create a stacked bar graph using two data sets (see Figure 5.3). The student can easily begin to seek out resources for creating the graphs and check off those criteria that are satisfied. The student can then set a goal for mastering the next level of graph design and locate the necessary instructional resources. The *analytic rubric* empowers students to take responsibility for learning.

The *Resource Area*

As students are working on their *problem-based tasks*, they will need a variety of resources, including *how-to sheets*; instructional podcasts, screencasts, and videos; articles; the *analytic rubric*; activity direction sheets; and manipulatives. Typically, teachers hand out materials to students. If you hand out a direction sheet to your students and a student doesn't have one, whose responsibility is it? Yours. If you place the papers on a table and instruct students to retrieve them when they need them, and a student doesn't have the appropriate paper, whose responsibility is it? The student's. The *resource area* gives students responsibility for their own learning. One teacher pointed out that homework completion increased once she placed the assignments in the *resource area*.

Establish an area to place materials that students will need. If your students all have personal computing devices, you might create a digital filing cabinet for files and links to websites. If not, create a physical space. This could be, for example, a table, a filing cabinet, a crate of folders, pockets on a bulletin board that can hold papers, or cubby holes for tactile materials.

So as not to overwhelm students, it's a good idea to display the materials needed for the current set of activities in a prominent place in the *resource area* and avoid putting out materials to be used in the future. Materials used in the recent past that may need to remain for reference should be moved to a less prominent location in the *resource area*, such as the back of the table, or filed in a three-ring binder or file cabinet. Essentially, create an area where students can easily find what they need, are not distracted by materials they do not yet need, and can access formerly used materials if needed.

If you are teaching in a 1:1 technology environment, a digital *resource area* can offer links to video and websites as well as print materials. Begin to build digital resources, for example, by creating screencasts, and then encourage your students to design some of their own.

The *Peer Expert Board*

As described in Chapter 4, *peer experts* serve as powerful learning partners in the *Learner-Active, Technology-Infused Classroom*. As with other key learning engagement strategies, it's important to pair this with a structure to empower students to take advantage of *peer experts*.

Designate an area on the classroom wall or website as the *peer expert board*. As you cover key concepts and skills, post the names of students who can assist in learning them. Once other students become *peer experts*, add their names while removing those of the existing *peer experts*. This allows students to build mastery by teaching others without having them spend an inordinate amount of time on a skill or concept.

One group of kindergarten teachers shared with me that they're trying something new. They are posting the main learning objectives, such as identifying the letter M, writing it, and identifying words that start with that sound, and putting an image of the letter M on a Focus Board. Near the M would be the pictures and names of *peer experts* for those objectives. The teachers felt this would make it easier for kindergarten students to find resources and peer experts related to a specific skill. By the end of the year, students should be able to look at one list of *peer experts* to find a skill and corresponding name.

The *Help Board*

As students begin working on the various activities toward the accomplishment of the *problem-based task*, you will facilitate instruction by moving around the room and sitting with a student or group for a few minutes. It would be extremely disruptive for students to be calling out for help. You want your facilitation to be proactive and not reactive.

Teach your students that their first line of help for academics is looking at the *activity list* and *resource area* to see if a related *how-to sheet* is available. Next, they should check the *peer expert* board. Then they should turn to their *home group*. If they don't understand a direction, are not sure where to find a resource, or need help understanding a concept or skill, they should seek out a *home group* member. In either case, if students find they are in need of *your* help, they should write their names on the *help board*. This can be a space on a whiteboard, a paper on a bulletin board, or a digital comment on a Web-based help page.

Some teachers have students include the focus of their need for help in addition to their names. I recently visited a kindergarten classroom in which the teacher had students move a magnetic nameplate to the *help board* and then use one of two colored markers to write the focus. If students were just looking for feedback, they wrote in blue; if they needed more immediate help, they wrote in red.

The *help board* meets the needs of both the students and the teacher. While facilitating, teachers need to know who is in need of more immediate guidance. When the teacher is meeting with students, other students are not supposed to interrupt. They can, however, add their names to the *help board* to indicate their need. Often students write their names on the *help board* and then erase them, having found alternate ways to answer their questions.

As a teacher, your job is to keep an eye on the *help board* and provide assistance in a timely manner. When you finish facilitating with a group, check the *help board*. In the *Learner-Active, Technology-Infused Classroom*, you're not teaching lessons and then letting students work independently, in which case they would most likely require little of your attention. Rather, they are engaged in challenging *learning activities*, and you are teaching as you facilitate those experiences. Address those who need help in a reasonable period of time; however, teach your students to begin working on another activity if they find themselves in need of your help. No one should ever be simply waiting for the teacher; students should move on to another, less challenging activity while waiting.

Monitor the amount of time you spend addressing the *help board*. Not all students will post their names on the board or feel they need your help. That does not mean, however, that they won't benefit from your facilitation. Students don't always know what they don't know. If you spend all of your time working down the *help board* list, you'll be more reactive than proactive. If you find this is the case, determine if your students have not yet become resourceful and are simply putting their names on the *help board* as a first step. Another problem might be that you do not have clear enough directions in your *learning activities*. If you find your time being driven by the *help board*, work to figure out why and correct that.

The *Quality Work Board*

Teachers often use subjective words such as "neat," "descriptive," "complete," and "compelling" when describing expectations. What does "neat" look like? It helps for students to see examples of high-quality work to gain a better understanding of expectations and to clarify any subjectivity. If you teach in your own classroom, you might use a bulletin board area for this. If you move from classroom to classroom throughout the day, consider a three-ring binder. If every student in your classroom has a mobile computing device, consider a digital folder or website.

Hang student work from previous years; hang your own examples. If you want students, for example, to draw their observations of plant growth, you might draw a diagram of a sliced-open piece of fruit, labeling the parts and including anything you think makes a neat, complete observational drawing. That way, you are showing an example of drawing from observation without doing the actual assignment for them. Post quality work without names, and refrain from posting work completed by students in the class. The point is not to create competition but to demonstrate what quality work looks like.

Obviously, quality work goes beyond those items that can be posted on a bulletin board. What do strong oratory skills sound like? What does a powerful song sound like? What does a well-crafted piece of pottery look like? Be creative! With today's technology, you can capture video and audio and post it to a digital folder. You can videotape yourself holding a piece of pottery and pointing out what makes it quality work.

A teacher who was introducing her students to myths decided to challenge students with selecting a product or sports team named after a mythological figure and writing their own myth as to how this product or sports team got its name. In order to gain a better understanding of the *problem-based task* so she could construct the *analytic rubric*, she decided to write her own myth about how the Honda Odyssey got its name. She wrote a creative and humorous account of how Odysseus was called from his home in Ithaca to address a problem in New York City. He borrowed someone's Honda SUV to drive there. On the way, he encountered various challenges and picked up some traveling companions, such as Zeus, who had difficulty sitting up straight in the vehicle because of his size. Once Odysseus saved the day for New York City, he returned the car but wrote a letter to Honda offering some suggestions for improvements, such as more headroom (for Zeus). And that's how the Honda Odyssey got its name. She decided to have students read her myth as part of the *ALU* activities and found that, because of them reading a sample, high-quality myth, her students produced some of the best writing she'd seen from them. Quality work can produce even greater quality work!

The *Learning Dashboard*

The *learning dashboard* is a spreadsheet that each student uses to track individual progress. It has a tab for each content area and ones for executive function skills and, if applicable, Individualized Education Program (IEP) goals. Grade-appropriate content goals are listed down the first column. Students then place an x in the cell to the right depending on if they are just starting to learn the skill, practicing it, or have mastered it. Using conditional formatting in some spreadsheet programs, you can have the cell automatically fill in with colors (for example, orange, yellow, and green) for a more visual effect. Figure 5.4 shows an image from the ELA tab.

Figure 5.4. Learning Dashboard

Key Ideas and Details:	Just Learning	Practicing	I Got This!
I can ask questions about stories I'm reading			
I can refer to the text to answer questions			
I can retell stories from books			
I can tell you what a fable is			
I can retell fables			
I can tell you what a folktale is			
I can retell folktales			
I can tell you what a myth is			
I can retell myths			
I can identify the main message of a story			
I can explain how a story's message is built through details			
I can name the main characters in a story			
I can tell you some of a character's traits			
I can tell you how a character feels			
I can tell you what motivates a character			
I can tell you how a character's actions contribute to a sequence of events			

You can download a learning dashboard template to use by heading to www.ideportal.com and the free content offering. Then search for "dashboard" to access information and a downloadable version with tabs.

Table Journals

One way to focus students on the effectiveness of their *home group* is with a *table journal*. At the end of a session during which students are working together, have them spend a couple of minutes reflecting on their effectiveness, using a set of questions or indicators. The reflection can be different from day to day, but the goal is the same: have students assess how effective and productive they are and what they can do to become more effective and productive. The indicators will differ depending on the age of the students and will become more sophisticated over the course of the school year to build greater collaborative and executive function skills.

A *table journal* can be created as a digital or paper document. Figures 5.5 and 5.6 offer some examples of *table journal* pages.

Limited-Resource Sign-Up Sheets

You will most likely have some limited resources (introduced in Chapter 4) in the *Learner-Active, Technology-Infused Classroom*, for example: math manipulatives, microscopes, computers, reading center, listening center, aquarium, and/or *learning centers*. The key is that not all students can access the resource at the same time. *Limited-resource sign-up sheets* coupled with *student scheduling* allow students to make use of limited resources easily. Many schools attempt to outfit classrooms with full sets of resources. An advantage of the *Learner-Active, Technology-Infused Classroom* is that you can save money on such resources because you don't have to purchase an entire class set. You can provide students with more diverse offerings if you are willing to have students engaged in various activities at the same time—that

Figure 5.5. Table Journal: Example 1

Table Journal					
Each group member should rank the following statements on a scale of 1 to 5, with 1 being the lowest score and 5 being the highest. Rank independently. Then one person should record the results of the group by marking how many members rated each statement with a 1, 2, 3, 4, or 5. Be honest in your assessment!					
	1	**2**	**3**	**4**	**5**
The group arrived and got started immediately without any prompting from the teacher.					
The group involved everyone in all aspects of the work, but still divided responsibilities.					
Every member of the group participated throughout the work session.					
All members were encouraged to voice their opinions.					
The group worked through conflicts by discussing options and reaching consensus.					
Group members used their time well.					
Discuss how you might work even better as a group the next time and record ideas here:					

Figure 5.6. Table Journal: Examples 2 and 3

Table Journal
As a group, discuss how you have worked differently as a group today as compared to prior days. What have you learned about working in a group.

Table Journal
This is it: Your last chance to reflect on your work as a group! What was most effective about your group during this problem-based unit?
How might your group have been even more effective?
If you were to give other students advice on working well as a group, what would it be?

is, giving up overt control in return for a structured environment in which students take charge of their learning.

As with all situations in the *Learner-Active, Technology-Infused Classroom*, you want to figure out how to build *student responsibility for learning* rather than overtly controlling the limited resources. Use a sign-up process. If you have a limited number of computers in the room, post a sign-up sheet with time slots, allowing a student to sign-up, for example, at most, two slots per day. If you want students to observe fish in the aquarium but not all at the same time, you can have them sign-up for one slot per day. As students schedule the day or week, they determine when resources are available, sign-up at the location of the resource or at the *resource area*, and indicate the time they will be using it on their schedule. This process builds tremendous executive function. See Figure 5.7 for two examples of a *limited-resource sign-up sheet* (also can be used for a *learning center*).

Primary students will most likely not be able to tell time and sign-up using this type of list. Give them a card with their name on it and have them place it in a slot next to the center. You might want to create three time slots labeled red, blue, and green, or A, B, and C (particularly if you have any colorblind students). You then place the color or letter in a prominent place in the room so students know it's "blue" or "A" time and, if they signed up for a *learning center* in blue time, they should get started. At the start of the year, with kindergarten students, you will need to be much more deliberate

Figure 5.7. Limited-Resource Sign-Up Sheet

Measuring Kit (30 minute time slots)

Time	Name
9:00–9:30	
9:40–10:10	
10:20–10:50	
11:00–11:30	

3D Virtual Reality Glasses Sign-Up (30 minute time slots)

Time	Group Members
Mon 1:10–1:40	
Tue 1:10–1:40	
Wed 1:20–1:50	
Thur 1:20–1:50	

and tell students that it is "blue" or "A" time; then walk to each center and point out who signed up, asking them to look at their schedule sheet for the "blue" or "A" time activity. Create the structures that your students will need to take charge of their own learning, with the intent being for you to prompt them less and less as the year goes on.

Limited-resource sign-up is clearly a skill to demonstrate and walk students through during a *benchmark lesson* early in the year on using limited resources. I watched a first-grade teacher in a morning class meeting describe the various *learning centers* students could use right after lunch. Each station had two cardboard pockets next to it. Students had cards with their names on them. When the meeting was over, they calmly walked around the room and selected one center to use that afternoon. In this case, they had to make a decision and sign up in advance to use a *learning center*. If a peer already selected that center, they had to select another and wait for another day to use the desired center. The key is to find a way to have your students sign up for the use of limited resources.

This structure applies to your time as well. Limit the amount of one-on-one conferences you have with students, as they keep you from the rest of the class. However, if you are planning to meet with individual students or groups of students, create a sign-up sheet and have students select a time slot. Leave open time between conferences so that you can circulate the room to engage with students, and see whose names are on the *help board*.

Small-Group Mini-Lesson Sign-Up

As a differentiation structure, introduced in Chapter 4, the *small-group mini-lesson* allows you to provide a short, narrowly focused lesson to a small group of students who are ready to learn a particular skill at the same time. As a structure to build *student responsibility for learning*, the *small-group mini-lesson* requires students to self-assess whether they should attend the lesson and then, if attending, sign-up for it. Here are some more tips for empowering students through structures related to *small-group mini-lessons*:

- Provide the tools for students to self-assess to determine if they should attend the lesson. These might include quizzes, checklists, pretests, and a set of questions.

- Announce *small-group mini-lessons* well enough in advance for students to consider them when scheduling their time. That might be the day before or the beginning of the week. From time to time you will find the need to add a lesson unexpectedly based on your formative assessments, and students will have to adjust their schedules. This should be the exception to the norm, but, as previously stated, an important life skill is the ability to adjust to changing plans midstream.

- To announce the lessons, post them on a specific area on the board, bulletin board, classroom website, or other online venue. Include the start time and length of the lesson so that students can schedule accordingly. (For kindergarten, as with *limited-resource sign-up sheets*, use colored or lettered time slots.)

Given the *small-group mini-lesson* involves students signing up, use a structure that works for you. It might be a sign-up sheet in the *resource area*, a list on the wall, or a digital version. (See Figure 5.8 for an example of a sign-up sheet you could put in the *resource area*.) I've seen kindergarten teachers make laminated circles of students' faces with Velcro on the back. Students then move their circles to the *small-group mini-lesson* sign-up. This is a great transitional structure until students are able to write their names.

Recognizing that you can't always ensure that the students who need it most will sign up, you can include a note in their folders indicating you want them to attend. At the younger grade levels, you can "invite" students. I've seen teachers create very colorful and friendly invitations to *small-group mini-lessons*.

The *small-group mini-lesson* is intended to address the targeted needs of and provide direct instruction to a small number of students; create a

Figure 5.8. Small-Group Mini-Lesson Sign-Up

Small-Group, Mini-Lesson Sign-Up Sheet

Title: _____

Time: _____

Participants
1.
2.
3.
4.
5.

Overflow (I will schedule another session)

sign-up system with only five or six slots for the lesson. Create an overflow section so that others who may have wanted to sign-up can let you know they also wanted to attend. That way you can schedule another *small-group mini-lesson* to handle the overflow. Obviously, you'll want to make adjustments as needed. If you have one student on the overflow list, you might allow them to attend or offer one-on-one facilitation to find out why they wanted to attend and address their challenges. If you encounter overflow situations regularly, make sure your students are aware of all of the options available for learning the skills, and, as stated earlier, make sure your topic is narrowly focused. Sometimes students attend *small-group mini-lessons* because they fear they will not learn if they are not working in person with the teacher, which, as students acclimate, should not be the case in the *Learner-Active, Technology-Infused Classroom*.

It's a System!

The power of the structures of the *Learner-Active, Technology-Infused Classroom* lies in their interdependence. Fourth graders were developing a *how-to* resource for primary students who were starting their *Learner-Active, Technology-Infused Classroom* journey. One group started listing the structures in order of importance, discussing the value of each. As they struggled, their teacher suggested that they consider, instead, how each structure impacts each of the others. They began drawing lines to connect the structures and created a wonderful systems Web highlighting the interdependence of the structures (see Figure 5.9). The students then wanted to send it to me; talk about an authentic audience for a study of the *Learner-Active, Technology-Infused Classroom*!

As you design your *Learner-Active, Technology-Infused Classroom*, consider how your structures are designed to support one another. Resources listed on the *activity list* should be in the *resource area*. Skills on the rubric should be reflected in *learning activities*, those listed as *peer experts*, and *small-group mini-lessons*. The expected solution presentation for *problem-based task* should be defined in the *analytic rubric*, and so forth. The stronger your system, the more effective your classroom.

RECAP

Engaging students in the learning process includes employing a variety of structures and strategies to create greater *student responsibility for learning*. As you design your *ALU* and learning environment, be sure to include the following:

♦ *Home group* designations for students to have a sense of belonging and a first tier of support in their work;

Figure 5.9. Student-Designed Systems Map of the Classroom

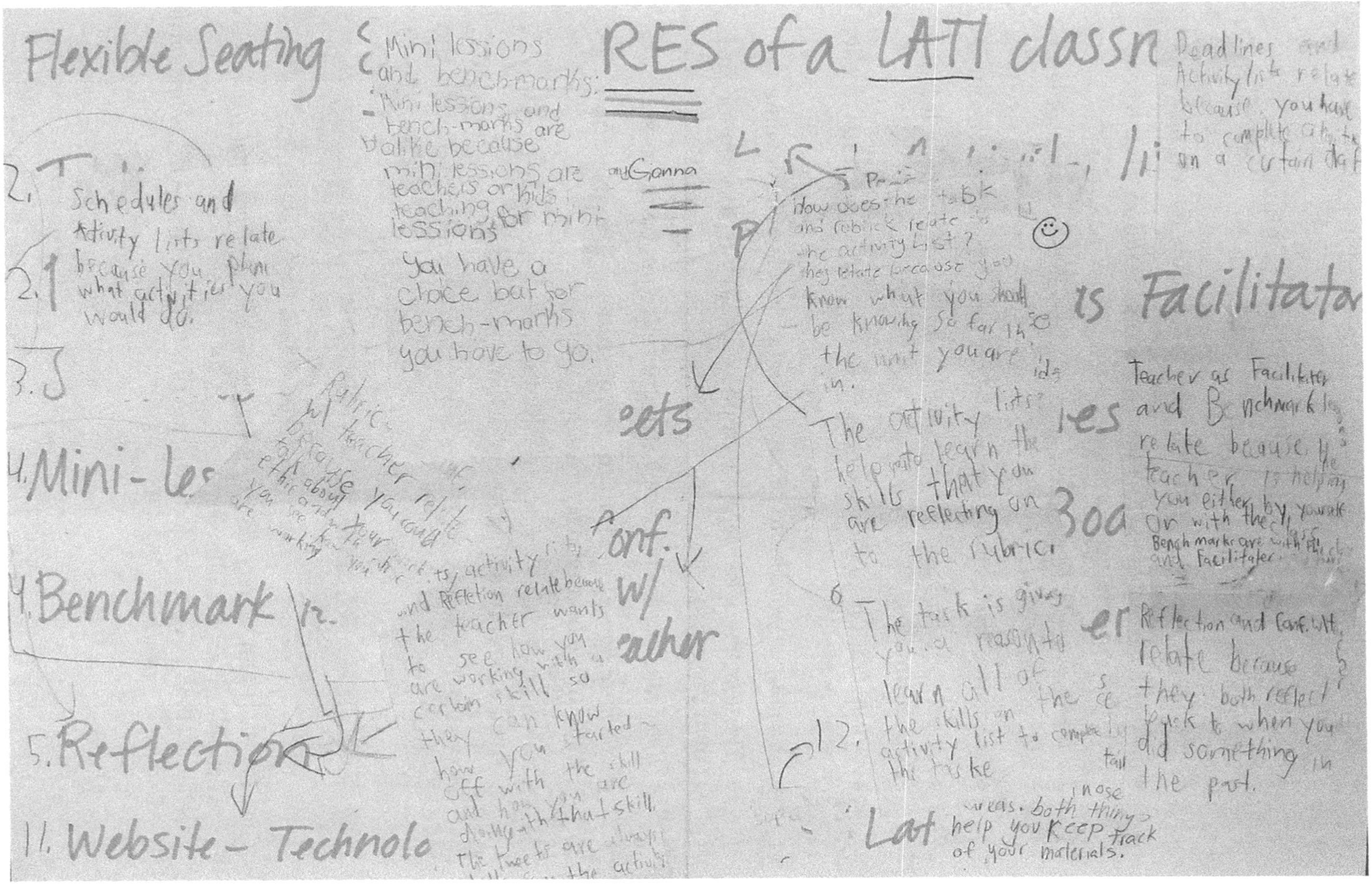

- A compelling launch to the *ALU* that inspires and motivates students;

- Student scheduling of how they will use their time;

- *Activity lists* to guide student scheduling;

- A plan for teaching students how to schedule their time;

- *Student work folders* to encourage organization and teacher–student communication;

- *Analytic rubrics* to position students to self-assess and set learning goals;

- A *resource area* to empower students to gather necessary resources;

- A *peer expert board* to encourage student-to-student learning opportunities;

- A *help board* to allow students to manage their need for teacher assistance;

- A *quality work board* to promote higher levels of achievement;

- The *learning dashboard* to empower students to monitor their own progress;

- *Table journals* to encourage student reflection on process;

- *Resource sign-up sheets* to empower students to manage how they will utilize limited resources;

- *Small-group mini-lesson* sign-up sheets to empower students to avail themselves of teachers' lessons as needed;

- A systems approach to ensuring interdependence among the structures.

REFERENCES

Glasser, W. (1998). *Choice theory: A new psychology of personal freedom.* New York, NY: HarperCollins.

Sweller, J. (1988). Cognitive load during problem solving: Effects on learning. *Cognitive Science 12*, 257–285.

6

Promoting Efficacy Through Facilitation of Learning

IMAGINE

You walk into a classroom to find students actively engaged in diverse activities, clearly attending to the tasks at hand. The teacher is sitting and talking with a student. After a few minutes, the teacher moves to sit with a group of students. Again, after a few minutes, the teacher moves to sit with another student. At some point, you ask the teacher to tell you about a particular student. With ease, the teacher tells you what the student is working on, how he is progressing in his learning goals, where his challenges are, and what she plans to do to address them. How is the teacher able to do this with so much activity in the classroom? The answer lies in masterful facilitation of the learning environment, the subject of this chapter. I frequently use the following GPS metaphor to shed light on the teacher's role as facilitator of learning.

Teacher as GPS[1]

Global positioning system (GPS) is popular navigation partner, particularly in cars, for assisting the driver in meeting a destination. Did you ever stop to consider that a masterful teacher is a lot like a GPS?

First, the GPS identifies the destination. A teacher identifies the destination as the curriculum standards that the students need to meet. Next, the GPS determines the best route for the driver to use to meet the destination.

---

1 Reprinted from the IDEportal (www.ideportal.com) with permission.

A teacher creates lesson plans and activities that are expected to help the student achieve the curricular goals.

During the trip, the GPS continually uses satellite communications to determine where the driver is. Based on that information and the destination, GPS ensures that the driver is "on track" to meet the destination. If the driver makes an incorrect turn, the GPS immediately recognizes that and develops a new plan for ensuring the driver arrives at the destination.

Masterful teachers use continuous formative assessment to determine students' progress and then modify lessons and activities to ensure student success. Quizzes, rubrics, verbal check-ins, gathering facilitation data, online assessments, and the like enable the teacher to track the progress of each student. If a student is having difficulty with a previously taught lesson, the teacher will meet one-on-one or in small groups, utilize a technology program, develop a *how-to sheet*, or use some other means to ensure that the student masters the skill or concept.

Of course, another wonderful aspect of GPS is that it never makes you feel like a failure. At each wrong turn, it merely recalculates the route. My GPS has never told me, "That's it! I'm not going to help you any more if you're not going to listen to my directions!" or "You just really don't have what it takes to get to your destination." On the contrary, my GPS always instills in me great confidence that I will arrive at my destination, as do masterful teachers.

CONSIDER

The goal of the *Learner-Active, Technology-Infused Classroom* is to move students beyond mere engagement in learning to empowerment and efficacy, with efficacy being the ability to identify a problem to solve or goal to achieve and put plans into action to reach a successful outcome. While the *problem-based task* and *analytic rubric* are designed to engage students in the learning process; and the various structures of the *Learner-Active, Technology-Infused Classroom* are designed to empower students; promoting efficacy stems from purposeful and deliberate facilitation by teachers in the classroom.

The Power and Purpose of Facilitation

Facilitating learning presumes that the teacher has already set up clear structures for the learning environment, as discussed in the previous chapters, and students are now engaged in the learning process. In a more conventional model of teaching, the teacher presents information to the entire class, typically from the front of the room, and then students engage in practicing what was presented. The teacher need only walk around the room to ask if students need help, as they are already armed with content from the lesson. In the

Learner-Active, Technology-Infused Classroom, this is not the case. Students are learning in a differentiated environment in which content is presented in a variety of ways, rarely through the teacher in the front of the room. Therefore, the role of the teacher as facilitator during this time becomes critical. It is not enough to ask if students need help, as they may not know that they even need help. Facilitation must be deliberate and purposeful, aimed at the needs of individual students. Teacher facilitation is as important to the *Learner-Active, Technology-Infused Classroom* as are the *ALUs* for engaging students and the structures for putting them in charge of their own learning. There are three aspects to facilitation in the *Learner-Active, Technology-Infused Classroom*:

- ♦ Management: This is the most basic level of facilitation that occurs in most classrooms around the world. Teachers ensure that students are where they belong, address behavioral issues, and overtly coordinate the learning environment. As you shift your thinking regarding the role of the teacher in the classroom, you'll find that *Learner-Active, Technology-Infused Classroom* teachers need to spend little time on this. Instead they focus more of their time toward building student efficacy through the next two categories.

- ♦ Process: Given that the reality of students taking charge means that students must be able to manage themselves and their own learning process, building myriad executive function skills, you'll need to focus some of your facilitation on process. Ask logistical questions to guide students' efforts. Point them to their *analytic rubric* and ask them to share what they've accomplished so far and what goals they've set for the immediate future. Help them learn how to identify the proper resources to select. Work with them to think through how to design their schedule. Continually assess and track students' executive function skills and work to build them through the structures that involve the process of students taking charge: *problem-based task, analytic rubric, activity list, scheduling time, help board, home group*, and so forth. The time you spend facilitating students' learning process will pay off as they become better empowered to take charge of their own learning, using you as a resource in that quest.

- ♦ Content: Given that in the *Learner-Active, Technology-Infused Classroom*, you are not presenting skill instruction from the front of the room, you must provide students with a variety of differentiated *learning activities* through which to learn content. It is then imperative that you use your role as facilitator to ensure that all of your students are receiving the instruction they need and are achieving content mastery. The *Learner-Active, Technology-Infused*

Classroom framework allows for the highest levels of differentiation, and the structures empower students to take charge of their own learning so they can work independent of a total reliance on the teacher. This allows the teacher to provide further, targeted differentiated instruction through facilitation. You'll proactively use formative assessment to track student progress and provide instruction, suggestions, and resources to ensure success. Your facilitation doesn't end with grade-level content mastery; you continue to ask probing questions to stimulate higher-order thinking, inspiring students to higher and higher levels of content mastery. You also need to analyze the formative assessment data you collect during facilitation to drive your own instructional decisions, including what *benchmark lessons* and *small-group mini-lessons* to offer and what *learning activities* and *practice activities* to add to the *activity list*. The time you used to spend in the front of the room offering whole class instruction now gives way to a more deliberate and purposeful engagement with individuals and small groups of students.

Clearly, when you are offering *benchmark lessons* or *small-group mini-lessons*, you are "on stage" in front of the entire class or a small group of students. Beyond that time, you should be engaged as a facilitator. It's important to resist the temptation to think that students are well engaged and you can plan lessons, grade papers, or talk at length with a visitor to the classroom. Your deliberate (you decide when and how) and purposeful (you focus on what is important) facilitation time is a critical part of the teaching process.

Sit Among Your Students

As students are engaged in the learning process, you need to be moving around the room, pulling up a chair to sit with one or a group of students. "Never hover!" Again, if you only had to ask if students needed help, you could lean over their desks. If you are going to engage with them in the learning process in a meaningful way, you should be seated alongside them. When you walk into a well-run *Learner-Active, Technology-Infused Classroom*, it's hard to locate the teacher, as he or she is usually sitting somewhere among the students.

James Coleman (1988) introduced the term *social capital* to mean that which is produced as a result of powerful relationships between adults and young people in a community. In a nutshell, consider a community in which the parents know the youngsters in the neighborhood by name, congratulate them for a sports win, offer a ride home from school, ask about an ill parent, and so forth. In such communities, students build confidence and are secure in the knowledge that there are adults who are interested in them. In such communities, students tend to fare well in school. Juxtapose that with a community in which the adults do not know the neighborhood youngsters and are not concerned about them. Students are left to fend for themselves with little formal or informal adult supervision. In such communities, students tend to fare poorly in school. Coleman's work in defining social capital has led large urban schools to restructure into small learning communities (SLCs). In the *Learner-Active, Technology-Infused Classroom*, it reminds teachers that those critical, caring relationships between adults and students are best fostered during one-on-one and small-group facilitation, not from the front of the room.

The *Learner-Active, Technology-Infused Classroom* is a system of interdependent components. For example, facilitation works best when students are planning their entire day, scheduling activities from all subject areas, tailored to their needs. As you facilitate, some students will be engaged in activities for which they won't need much, if any, of your attention, for example, reading for pleasure, whereas others will be involved in *learning activities* that are more cognitively demanding and could use your involvement. If you limit the choices or only offer students a small amount of time in a day to schedule their own time, you are more likely to run into a situation in which everyone needs you or no one needs you. The power of your facilitation, therefore, begins with the strength of your *activity list*.

> **"The power of your facilitation, therefore, begins with the strength of your *activity list*."**

Be Mindful of Balancing Your Energy in the Classroom

As you move around the classroom, you bring with you your energy. You take on the role of inspirer, cheerleader, coach, helper, guide, and so many others. As you move around the room to facilitate, be mindful of where you've been physically. If you are on one side of the room, move next to the other side. While it may seem to make sense to move, in order, around the room, that would cause your energy to be imbalanced, spending a lot of time on one side of the room and then moving to the other. Instead, move back and forth across the room as you facilitate, unless the *help board* draws you to specific students. Students' positions on the *help board* take precedence. The key is to have few names on the *help board* as students learn to be more resourceful. Then your facilitation becomes more proactive.

Be mindful of your time as you move about the room, spending only a few minutes at each stop. Although at times you will be tempted to engage in a lengthy conversation with one or more students, consider that you would then be absent from the rest of the class. You might suggest that you and the student meet again to continue the discussion at a specified time. You might decide to schedule a related *small-group mini-lesson*.

Your facilitation experience will provide you with insights for further instructional design. If you find yourself feeling like you can't get to everyone, consider more group check-ins in which three students meet with you to share their progress quickly and have you offer next steps. If you find you are not facilitating enough, you might be offering too many *small-group mini-lessons* or *benchmark lessons*, or you might be engaging in too many one-on-one conferences, which take you away from the class as a whole. If you are addressing the same challenges over and over again, you may need to offer more *learning activities* or a *small-group mini-lesson*. Use your facilitation data to inform your practice.

Every Student Will Benefit From Your Facilitation

Facilitation of learning is not about a reactive response to those who need help; it's about a proactive response to determining the best next step for each student. At first, some students may try to push you away, claiming they don't need help. The reality is that they don't know what they don't know; it's your job to help them figure out what they do and don't know and then guide them in the right direction. Elementary school is a time of learning how to learn, not just mastering academic content.

"Facilitation of learning is not about a reactive response to those who need help; it's about a proactive response to determining the best next step for each student."

Three Powerful Tools

Facilitation is an art and a science unto itself; it is a critical component of the *Learner-Active, Technology-Infused Classroom* that cannot be taken lightly. While the more tactile work of designing the *problem-based task, analytic rubric, learning activities*, and various structures may feel like the hard work of the *Learner-Active, Technology-Infused Classroom*, the real power of the teacher is evident through facilitation. It is that which can make or break your classroom. Students should not be teaching themselves; and they should not be discovering content on their own. The difference between an *ALU* in which students teach themselves and one in which teachers and students partner to ensure high levels of achievement is facilitation. This chapter will offer you three powerful tools: a *facilitation roadmap* to challenge your thinking as to how you can address individual students' learning needs; a *content facilitation grid* that you will use to capture formative assessment data and to make instructional decisions; and a guide for designing *facilitation questions* to probe students' thinking related to content. Mastering these three tools will help you focus on the new role of the teacher in the *Learner-Active, Technology-Infused Classroom*.

The Facilitation Roadmap

In order to make your facilitation more deliberate and purposeful, use the *facilitation roadmap* to guide your actions. This tool focuses on honing in on an individual student's state of mind and providing just the right support at the right time. An immediate win in running a *Learner-Active, Technology-Infused Classroom* is being able to look around and see all of your students seemingly engaged. I say seemingly because you don't really know how well they are understanding the content or how well they are managing their time until you sit with them and start asking questions. When you look out at that classroom full of engaged learners, can you identify how each student is feeling about their work at that point? Masterful *Learner-Active, Technology-Infused Classroom* teachers know their students and the work flow so well, due, in part, to the facilitation tools shared in this chapter, that they can tell you who is on tar-

get, who is bored, who is struggling, who is about to give up, and so forth. Each of those students deserves a different response. The *facilitation roadmap* breaks that down. You would not necessarily carry it with you while facilitating, but it can give you some insights into ensuring your engagement with students is deliberate and purposeful. Facilitation is not about moving around the room seeing if everyone has mastered a skill or following some plan that you as the teacher have made; it's about ascertaining what, how, and when a student is learning, and then off ering guidance, information, and new challenges. You are a mentor; a coach.

> "Facilitation is not about moving around the room seeing if everyone has mastered a skill or is following some plan that you as the teacher have made; it's about ascertaining what, how, and when a student is learning, and then offering guidance, information, and new challenges. You are a mentor; a coach."

The *facilitation roadmap* begins with a challenge. Most likely you've given your students a challenge in terms of the overarching *problem-based task* of the *Authentic Learning Unit (ALU)*. The *analytic rubric* should also provide your students with learning challenges along the way. Sometimes in your facilitation, you will offer up a new challenge for the next level of learning. People are engaged and in flow when a challenge is just above their ability level (Csikszentmihalyi, 2008). When students are given learning challenges that are slightly above their ability level, they thrive, demonstrating a powerful level of engagement with content. When the challenges are below their ability level, they get bored; when the challenges are too far beyond their ability level, they get frustrated and give up. The masterful *Learner-Active, Technology-Infused Classroom* facilitator seeks to identify the state of mind of the student and offer support, resources, and challenges to keep them in flow. Seek to ensure that students are engaged in learning challenges that are just above their individual ability levels. As they achieve one level of mastery, they

Figure 6.1. The Facilitation Roadmap

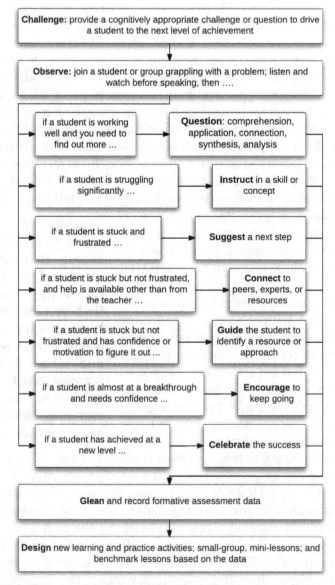

Challenge: provide a cognitively appropriate challenge or question to drive a student to the next level of achievement

Observe: join a student or group grappling with a problem; listen and watch before speaking, then ....

if a student is working well and you need to find out more ... → Question: comprehension, application, connection, synthesis, analysis

if a student is struggling significantly ... → Instruct in a skill or concept

if a student is stuck and frustrated ... → Suggest a next step

if a student is stuck but not frustrated, and help is available other than from the teacher ... → Connect to peers, experts, or resources

if a student is stuck but not frustrated and has confidence or motivation to figure it out ... → Guide the student to identify a resource or approach

if a student is almost at a breakthrough and needs confidence ... → Encourage to keep going

if a student has achieved at a new level ... → Celebrate the success

Glean and record formative assessment data

Design new learning and practice activities; small-group, mini-lessons; and benchmark lessons based on the data

Note: It's easiest to facilitate when students are grappling with a problem to solve or with a new skill or concept.

should be given challenges at a slightly higher level. This "leveling up" (Prensky, 2006) increases the likelihood that students will be in flow and engaged in grappling with content.

As a *facilitator* of learning, focusing on the process and content aspects of facilitation, sit down next to a student or group of students and, at first, **observe** them. Your presence by their sides should not be unusual to them nor cause them to stop and attend to you. Over time, they will keep working until you ask them a question. Watch them work or, if students are engaged in collaborative work, listen to them. Within twenty seconds you will most likely get a sense of what is going on, but those twenty seconds will make what you do next that much more purposeful. Now, as you assess the situation, you decide how to engage with the student(s).

You'll see a list of possible options in Figure 6.1. If the student seems to be working well, **delve further** to determine how well they are understanding the content. Through a series of *facilitation questions* (discussed later in this chapter), you can see if students are at a level of basic comprehension, able to apply learning to new situations, or able to synthesize and invent new solutions or ideas from existing content. Based on your assessment, you'll ask questions at higher and higher levels to probe their thinking.

If a student is struggling significantly with the content, it's important to step in and simply **provide direct instruction**. You do not want to start asking probing questions, making suggestions, or offering resources when a student is about to give up due to excessive frustration; just teach! Show the student how you would go about tackling the challenge. Arm the student with enough knowledge to continue on, meeting with success. That being said, more often than not, you do not want to swoop in with the answer; instead, you want to guide students toward succeeding at the challenge. Those situations are discussed next.

If a student is stuck or frustrated, but not to the point of giving up, **suggest a step**. "What if you tried . . .?" "Remember when we . . .? Let's try that!" The point is to offer an immediate step to take, not have the student attempting to find that step. Your facilitation stops just short of providing direct instruction in the skill or concept. Once the student has that aha moment and you have ensured that the learning momentum will continue, you can move on. If, however, it becomes obvious that, even with a next step, the student is becoming more frustrated, then you switch to providing direct instruction.

If a student is stuck but not really frustrated, rather than you being the critical resource that you would be in the prior two situations, **connect** the student to other resources to provide the content they need, including peer experts, outside experts that are available to them, or various learning resources that are available in the room or online. This is your opportunity to teach your students the powerful skill of resourcefulness. A first grade teacher was sitting with a student who had difficulty finding the right descriptive word for her story; the teacher suggested she might find one on the word wall. The student looked over and did; excitedly, she returned to her writing. In this case, the facilitating teacher provided the student with a resource to which she can turn in the future. A fifth-grade student was struggling with mapping out the physics concepts of the roller coaster he designed, specifically when it came to describing the potential energy needed to create the centripetal force needed to keep the marble on the track around a loop. His teacher shared that another student had just completed her diagram and suggested he ask her to share her diagram and explain it to him. Students learn well from one another, and those who have just completed a challenge are usually proud to share their breakthroughs with others.

If a student is stuck but has the confidence and motivation to figure it out, **guide** the student to finding the needed resource or approach to take. "Where might you find some help?" "Remember what you did the last time you were stuck?" "What are you thinking of trying next?" Note that this is subtly different from pointing the student to a resource or next step. This level of facilitation is more about asking the student to think through how they are going to locate a helpful resource. Often, students who have the confidence to push through are deflated when you give them the answer, as they wanted the thrill of figuring it out on their own. Your role is to simply ask them to share their thinking out loud with you. Often in talking about it, they arrive at the answer on their own.

If a student is doing well and nearing a breakthrough, **encourage** the student to keep going. "You almost have it!" "Keep going and let me know when you figure it out!" Those words of encouragement provide further motivation and let the student know that you are interested.

If a student has just successfully mastered a skill or concept, **celebrate the success**! Share some confirming words. Suggest the student posts something on a "My Best Work" wall if you use one. Depending on the skill, see if the student is ready to be a *peer expert*. Once the student has basked in the success for a few moments, move on to present the next challenge. "Now what if you . . .?" "What's the next level on your rubric that you want to achieve?"

It is important to offer students the most purposeful facilitation to propel their academic achievement. Your words and actions will ensure that your students keep moving in a positive direction, making the best use of their time. It makes no sense for students to struggle futilely when you could help them; it makes no sense to let successful students work on their own, thinking they don't need you. Every student needs you to provide just the right facilitation in the moment.

While you're facilitating learning, you have the perfect opportunity to gather significant formative assessment data for your instructional decision making. The key is to capture the data as it presents itself, not to attempt to move around the room assessing one particular skill or concept with all of your students. The tool for capturing formative assessment data is the *content facilitation grid*.

Content Facilitation Grid

Your *ALU* is designed around specific content that your students need to master. Given that students control when and how they learn, you need a way to capture formative assessment data throughout the day. In one short period of time, you might gather data on one student's math skills, another's science concept mastery, and yet another's reading skills. It may seem easier for you to gather assessment data when, in the more conventional approach, lessons are delivered to the entire class at the same time and all are working on the same content. As you shift responsibility for learning to your students, you give them significant choice and voice over their learning approach, but that comes with the challenge of ensuring you know everything that is going on in the classroom. The *content facilitation grid* allows you to capture data across students and subject areas across the day.

The *content facilitation grid* is a spreadsheet-type grid that includes students' names down the side and content skills and concepts across the top. As you observe and hear evidence of a student's progress toward mastering a skill or concept, you place a letter in the box, noting your assessment. Use the *content facilitation grid* as well to capture formative assessment data from quizzes, tests, and individual, in-class assignments. I do not recommend using it with any out-of-class assignments, as it will be difficult to know the extent to which you are assessing the student's mastery given you won't know what kind of help was offered from others. The *content facilitation grid* will be described in more detail in the Create section that follows.

Facilitation Questions

As you sit with students, observe them in action, and then partner with them in the learning process, you will move between offering them instruction, guidance, and resources and asking questions. Questions aimed at promoting content mastery, as opposed to those focusing on the learning process, should foster a culture of "leveling up" described earlier in the chapter.

When facilitating, most teachers tend to ask comprehension questions to ensure that students have a grasp on the basic content. Educational psychologist Benjamin Bloom worked with colleagues in the 1950s to develop a classification for intellectual activities inherent in the learning process. Bloom acknowledged that first someone must be able to *recall* information, then *comprehend* it, then *apply* it to various situations, then *analyze* it, which leads to the ability to *synthesize* and thus to create new information, and finally *evaluate* the creation of new information. Bloom's Taxonomy remains a viable guide for teachers when considering *learning activities*. Also use it when considering the types of questions to ask students to probe their thinking. Note: a newer version flips the order of the last two categories, making synthesis a more higher-order skill than evaluation. I think you could argue both ways; the point is, however, give your students ample experience with both!

In the *Learner-Active, Technology-Infused Classroom*, teachers essentially ask five types of questions, somewhat mirroring Bloom's Taxonomy, though not entirely:

♦ Comprehension—to determine basic mastery of the content;

♦ Application—to determine the extent to which the student can apply the learning to another situation;

♦ Connection—to determine the extent to which the student can connect and/or apply the learning to their own life;

♦ Synthesis—to determine the extent to which the student can use the knowledge to generate new information, solutions, or ideas;

♦ Metacognition—to determine the student's ability to reflect on the learning process.

"The road to efficacy is supported by the teacher's facilitation of learning, helping students identify problems to solve, set goals, decide on a path, locate resources, self-assess, consider further options, and so forth."

Your development of *facilitation questions* is intended to expand your thinking on the content and arm you with various levels of questions to ask. Unlike the *facilitation grid*, the *facilitation questions* are not necessarily intended to be carried around with you and are not intended to be used to ask every student these questions as you move around the room. They are meant to spark your own thinking. As you engage in conversations with students, your comments and questions should flow from that discussion. Thus, you may end up asking other questions similar to those you originally designed as a result of your conversations with students. The development of *facilitation questions* will be described in more detail in the Create section that follows. A well-run *Learner-Active, Technology-Infused Classroom* provides students with a differentiated, personalized learning environment. Students are engaged in solving real-world problems and empowered with the structures to support them in taking responsibility for their own learning. The road to efficacy is supported by the teacher's facilitation of learning, helping students identify problems to solve, set goals, decide on a path, locate resources, self-assess, consider further options, and so forth. As you design various tools to support your role as the facilitator of learning in the classroom, keep in mind that your ultimate goal is to propel students to academic success as efficacious learners.

CREATE

So far, you've developed a *problem-based task, analytic rubric, scaffold for learning*, and *activity list*. Once all this learning activity gets underway, you'll want to rely on your facilitation tools to gather formative assessment data to drive your instructional decisions. Avoid relying solely on your intuition, observations, or memory—gather the data!

Facilitating Process

The *Learner-Active, Technology-Infused Classroom* offers students many structures for managing the process of learning, including the *analytic rubric, activity list, schedule, help board, peer expert board, quality work board*, and more. Building greater *student responsibility for learning* involves expecting students to self-assess, make decisions about which activities to choose and when to complete them, select instructional resources, and make many other decisions. Part of the facilitation process is ensuring that students are carrying out these tasks successfully. When facilitating and sitting with students, ask them to show you where they are on their *analytic rubrics* for the *problem-based task*. Ask them what their next step is going to be and why. Ask how they decided upon the activities they've chosen. Ask how they will know when they've accomplished the next column in the rubric. Ask them if they are attending a particular *small-group mini-lesson* and why or why not. Ask them how they decided upon the resources they selected.

These types of questions will help you feel confident in their decision making and will model for them the types of internal conversations they should be having surrounding their learning decisions. The more you teach your students how to take responsibility for decisions in the learning process, the more time you will have to spend on content mastery as opposed to process. You don't want to be the teacher reading off names to check whether students completed their homework. You don't want to be the teacher who asks students to put their homework on their desks and then walks around with a gradebook recording the presence of homework. You don't want to be the teacher who is reprimanding individual students for not being on task or for not following directions. All of these actions take precious time away from what you do best: impart knowledge to your students and help them become lifelong learners. Have students self-report on homework. If they are inaccurately reporting, you'll know it from their performance and can talk with them about the importance of and your expectation for accurate reporting. The more you create structures that allow students to take responsibility for logistics, the more time you'll have to spend on content, which will have a direct, positive impact on achievement.

Advancing Content Mastery Through Facilitation Questions

Consider the following examples. A kindergarten student brings in a collection of fall leaves and classifies them according to color. The teacher asks, "Can you also classify them according to the type of edges?" This challenge pushes the student to focus on a more subtle feature of leaves than color.

A group of fifth-grade students are analyzing data collected on the bald eagle in their state to determine what might threaten the species toward extinction. They share their mappings of how the bald eagle ultimately obtains its energy from the sun, showing the food chain leading up to the bald eagle. The teacher shares two articles with them: one on toxic algae blooms and one predicting the near extinction of saltwater fish by 2048. She then asks what impact these events might have on the food chains and, ultimately, the bald eagle. This challenge sends the incredulous students off to explore these threats.

Two second-grade students just finished reading Judith Viorst's book, *Alexander and the Terrible, Horrible, No Good, Very Bad Day*. They share their thoughts on the story with the teacher. He then asks them what if the book were named *Alexander and the Wonderful, Fabulous, Awesome, Very Good Day*? Could they write a page or two? Their eyes light up and they decide to write their own storybook.

A fifth-grade student exploring space and the discovery of water on Mars suggests NASA should fly a manned spaceship to Mars to further explore how to colonize it. The teacher points out that a serious obstacle that exists for human travel to Mars is the amount of radiation between the Earth and Mars and its potential disastrous effects on the astronauts. Assuming this is new information to the student, it will put her mind in motion thinking about where the radiation is coming from and how to overcome that obstacle.

These types of questions probe students' thinking, sending their minds swirling with questions and ideas to pursue. Usually, one good question will send students off to pursue the next challenge and keep the learning momentum going. Before you can ask questions that probe higher-order thinking, however, you have to ensure that your students have a foundational understanding of the content they are studying. Using the *problem-based task* and *analytic rubric* you've designed for your *ALU*, select a content focus and develop a set of questions that you might use with students. Strive to write five to eight questions for each category:

1. *Comprehension Questions*—It is important to ask questions that ensure students understand the content and skills needed to solve the problem. Examples:

a. What sound does the letter B make?

b. What does the time signature tell you in this piece of music?

c. What is the formula to calculate the area of a square?

d. What do living things need to survive?

e. How can you move across the court with the basketball in a game?

f. What type of graph would show your data as parts of a whole?

g. What is the definition of an adjective?

2. *Application Questions*—Ask questions that ensure the ability of students to apply the learning to new situations.

a. Identify other urban areas in our state.

b. What is the area of *this* classroom?

c. In what ways would human beings on Earth have to evolve to live on Mars?

d. What are at least ten adjectives you could use to describe this school?

e. What other words start with the letter D?

f. What type of graph will you make to display your data?

3. *Connection Questions*—Ask questions that ensure the ability of students to apply learning to their lives.

a. What skills learned here could you use in other places outside of school?

b. How did Martin Luther King Jr.'s work affect your life?

c. Which artist's work here do you like the most and why?

d. Under what circumstances would you be ready to live on Mars?

e. What are at least ten adjectives you could use to describe yourself?

f. What letter and sound is at the beginning of the names of members of your family?

4. *Synthesis Questions*—Ask questions that encourage students to create new information from existing data.

a. How might you ensure your plants have enough water while we are on vacation?

b. Given our classroom is not a perfect rectangle, how might you find the area?

c. How could we count and represent amounts if you could only use the numerals zero through four?

d. What would happen if the character in this story made a different choice?

e. What will you write to persuade your audience to take your advice?

f. Which paints will you mix to make a light orange?

5. *Metacognition Questions*—Ask questions that prompt students to think about their own thinking processes.

a. What was the hardest part of this task for you?

b. How did you arrive at the solution?

c. When did you realize your idea was not going to work?

d. How might you go about solving this differently?

e. How did you figure out how to change the color combinations in this graph?

f. What did you like the most about this activity?

g. What do you find most challenging about playing soccer?

When you finish writing up your questions, reread them and/or share them with a colleague and see if you can improve upon them. Again, once you've designed them, you typically don't need to carry them with you while facilitating. These are not meant to be a script nor answered by every student; they are meant to be used in the context of conversations. The process of crafting the questions focuses more on deepening your understanding of content and its application to the real world. While at first you may want to carry the list of questions as a reference, as you engage in content-rich conversations with students, you'll recall the relevant questions in the moment.

Using Formative Assessments to Drive Instruction

A GPS is constantly sending out satellite signals to determine the progress of the driver and modify the route if necessary. Masterful teachers use formative assessment constantly to determine how students are progressing. This is a key concept in the *Learner-Active, Technology-Infused Classroom:* teachers do not take comfort in the fact that they presented the content well; they only take comfort in the evidence that students learned the content well.

I heard a great analogy that states: formative assessment is to summative assessment as a physical is to an autopsy. Summative assessments are administered at the end of a unit of study or year in school to evaluate the level of success of the student. The understanding is that the teaching–learning process for this content is completed. The best information a summative assessment can offer the teacher relative to improving student achievement is in helping the teacher rethink the unit for the next group of students. Similarly, an autopsy will do nothing for the person being autopsied; however, the data can be used to advance the future of medicine. Alternatively, a physical is meant to assess the patient's condition and lead to prescribed actions aimed at improving patient health. Likewise, formative assessments are intended to provide data that will be used to prescribe learning activities that will lead to greater student success.

Formative assessments can be classified as follows: temperature gauges, breakpoints, student-directed assessments, and comprehensive assessments (Figure 6.2).

Figure 6.2. Four Types of Formative Assessment

Temperature Gauges—Immediate, in-the-moment assessments that allow the teacher to get a sense of current student status. This often takes place while the teacher is presenting a lesson.
Based on student response, the teacher can adjust the lesson content and pacing, and identify any urgent student needs.
Examples: Adjective Check-In, Three-Finger Check-In
Breakpoints—Brief assessments given at a stopping point in instruction (such as the end of the class period or lesson), allowing the teacher to step back and revise the instructional plan.
Based on student response, the teacher can plan instructional activities and whole-class lessons.
Examples: Exit Cards, One Sentence Summary, Do Now, Higher-Order Questioning, Quizzes
Student Directed Assessments—Self-evaluative student reflection, giving the teacher insight into perceived needs.
Based on student response, the teacher can direct the student to appropriate resources—small-group or one-on-one instruction, websites, learning activities, and how-to sheets.
Examples: Checklists, Self-Assessment on a Rubric, Peer Evaluation, Student Journals
Comprehensive Assessments—Systematic data collection on individual skill & concept attainment.
Based on student response, the teacher can offer targeted small group instruction, re-teach core concepts, and provide additional resources.
Examples: Rubrics, Tests, Facilitation Grids, Individual Conferences/Oral Interviews, Student Folders, Notebook/Portfolio Check

Consider these four categories and design assessments that you will use with your students.

1. *Temperature Gauges*—When you are presenting to the whole class, it's easy to take your cues from the handful of students who are smiling, nodding, and answering and asking questions. It's important not to be lulled into thinking this means your lesson is effective for the entire class. A quick check-in will provide you with important data. If you're talking about nutrition, for example, you can use a couple of temperature gauges. You can ask for a three-finger check-in: "Tell me how you're doing. Raise one finger if you're not yet sure of the food groups, two fingers if you can name most of them, three fingers if you can name all the food groups and give an example of each." Some teachers believe that students will not be honest if others are looking on, so they begin with, "Eyes closed." I'm assuming I need not go into the danger of "finger" check-ins with older students. This formative assessment tool must be carefully explained in advance; that is, which finger to raise if you're just raising one finger and so forth. You could also use a thumb-up, thumb-down signal. If you're introducing a unit of study and have just handed out the *problem-based task, analytic rubric*, and *activity list*; you may want to see how students are feeling. Use the adjective check-in to have each student offer one word of how they are feeling. You'll hear words like interested, excited, confused, and overwhelmed. This allows you to get a read on the class. If you have a lot of students who are confused and overwhelmed, offer a *small-group mini-lesson* directly after the *benchmark lesson* for those who want to ask more clarifying questions and get more assistance before diving in. Keep in mind that students have to get used to these Temperature Gauge formative assessments. At first you might not get data as accurate as you want. Over time, students will realize this is critical feedback they are providing that is going to benefit them, and they will respond accordingly. The purpose of a Temperature Gauge is to provide you with the data to shift the focus of your lesson immediately. If you've just introduced the concept of foreshadowing, offer a three-finger check-in on whether a student could give an example of foreshadowing. If you find that few can provide one, you'll want to rethink your approach and offer perhaps some more examples.

2. *Breakpoints*—At the end of a day, class period, or whole- or small-group lesson, take the opportunity to gather assessment data. An exit

card offers students a single, short question or request for information. The students write on an index card and hand it in on their way out the door or upon leaving the lesson. If students are working on a variety of activities around biomes and habitats, ask them to list something they learned today, or ask them to list a biome that interests them and why. Avoid closed-ended questions such as "list the major biomes," as, given that exit cards are completed as students are packing up or transitioning, students might simply ask a peer for the answer. Quizzes are also Breakpoint assessments. At the end of the day or class period, you might offer a ten-question quiz to assess learning. The key to Breakpoint assessments is that they offer you valuable data to use to plan subsequent lessons, offering you more time to adjust than a Temperature Gauge assessment does.

3. *Student-Directed Assessments*—These are powerful because they not only provide you with information, but they force students to become aware of their own progress. Prior to handing in an assignment, have students complete a checklist to ensure they've included all of the learning objectives you expected. A reflective portfolio allows students to set goals, gather examples of progress, reflect on them, and share their insights with you. Sit with individual students and ask them to use the unit rubric to tell you where they are in their progress and how they are going to move to the next column. Student-Directed Assessments tend to take a little more time than the previous two categories, but they provide valuable data about the students' perceptions of their learning as well as data on their actual progress.

4. *Comprehensive Assessments*—Not to be confused with summative assessments, Comprehensive Assessments gather data across a variety of concepts and skills. Rubrics are one example, as they contain indicators for all aspects of the unit performance. *Facilitation grids* gather data from across a set of concepts and skills. These allow you to get the big picture of how the unit itself is progressing so that you can provide clarifying information and new instructional activities as needed. In order to meet overall curriculum standards for the year, an *ALU* can only be allocated a specific amount of time. Even if students are thoroughly engaged in a particular unit, you cannot afford to let it simply continue, as you have other units to launch. If students are not progressing adequately, Comprehensive Assessments will make that obvious, allowing you to provide additional information on a classroom blog or website; offer some targeted *benchmark lessons* or *small-group mini-lessons*; or modify some activities or add new ones.

Formative Assessment Grids

The beauty and challenge of the *Learner-Active, Technology-Infused Classroom* is the level of activity going on in the classroom at any one time. A common fear of teachers is tracking classroom activity: how are you going to track everything that is going on? Two very effective tools are the *task management grid* (for facilitating classroom management) and the *content facilitation grid* (for facilitating content acquisition). These grids enable you to easily track and analyze assessment data. Both can be designed on a spreadsheet or with a table in a word-processing document. Both can be invaluable when speaking with parents, colleagues, and students about academic progress.

Task Management Grid

The *task management grid* allows you to easily see which activities a single student or the class has completed. Across the top are the various activities presented to students; down the left side are the students' names. To design your *task management grid*, consider the various subtasks students will accomplish to complete the problem. What assignments will students hand in? These should be on the *task management grid*. You may choose to include all of the *learning activities* you've assigned to build to each of the subtasks. Just remember that all students will not complete all *learning activities* because of the many choices you'll provide, but they will have to complete all subtasks or assignments. Design the *task management grid* to help you best track student progress toward the final *ALU* project. For example, you may have students researching a topic and writing an opinion letter to be shared with someone who could make a difference. Figure 6.3 is a sample *task management grid* for writing an opinion letter. Once students have researched the topic, they will hand in note cards for you to grade. Then they will hand in a graphic organizer for you to grade. Given the use of linking words is one of the standards for opinion writing, you may have an assignment in which they create their own reference of linking words they might use to connect their thoughts. In this case, the *task management grid* includes all of the handed-in or graded assignments. For students who need more direction, you might include more of the activities listed on the grid, not all of which will necessarily be graded. Use whatever system works best for you in tracking each student's activities.

Reviewing students' folders will give you an idea of how well they are progressing in the curricular content, but it's not always easy to see which activities have been completed. The *task management grid* allows you to glance across a row to see how productive a student is. If you include all *learning activities* and *practice activities*, it will also allow you to identify very popular activities (those completed by many students) and unpopular activities (those

Figure 6.3. Task Management Grid

	Note Cards	Graphic Organizer of Information	Strategy Chart	Draft Letter	Peer Editing/Two Students	Final Copy
Alicia C.						
Jamal C.						
Joshua D.						
Trent F.						
Madison F.						

✓ = Completed   S = Submitted   R = Return for Revisions

that are not typically chosen). Some teachers hang a large poster-board *task management grid* on the wall so that students can check off their progress; others use a digital file students update; and others record the data themselves based on students' *folders*. Although not assessing success in content mastery, it will provide you with data that you can use to guide students. Those who may have completed a lot of activities may not be spending enough time grappling with the content to receive the benefit of the activities. In this case, you'll want to slow them down and perhaps ask them to complete a reflection card or a learning journal on what they learned. Students who are not completing enough may need assistance in scheduling their time or on content mastery itself. You might want to encourage some of these students to sign-up for a *small-group mini-lesson* with you to build scheduling skills.

Content Facilitation Grid

Perhaps the most important tool for using formative assessment to drive instruction is the *content facilitation grid*. When students are working and you are not offering a *benchmark lesson* or *small-group mini-lesson*, you should be facilitating learning. The *content facilitation grid* is similar in structure to the *task management grid* except that, instead of activities across the top, you enter concepts and skills (Figure 6.4). The highlighted columns are for prerequisite skills that you know were addressed in a prior grade or unit. As you pull up a chair next to a student or group of students, you'll be gathering valuable assessment data. Use the grid to make notations. For example, it you see evidence that a student has mastered a skill, write an "M" in that part of the grid. If a student has not only mastered the skill or concept but can explain it to another, use "PE" for peer expert. If a student seems to have an adequate knowledge base but you feel they could use some practice, use "HW" to indicate that you should assign a specific homework assignment on that skill. "ML" indicates the student needs help and should attend a *small-group mini-lesson*.

Given that an *ALU* spans several weeks and involves a number of concepts and skills, it's best to design separate *content facilitation grids* for each week. You might want to carry them on a clipboard with the current one on top or use a handheld computing device with digital grids. Most of the data you'll be collecting will be from the current week's grid; however, sometimes you'll need to refer to past or future grids.

In addition to making notations while moving around the room, you can also use the *facilitation grid* to track assessment data when reviewing student work. As you review *student folders*, you can add notations under specific skills and concepts. I caution you against using homework to make notations regarding mastery, as you cannot always determine how much help the student may have received at home. You could use a small check or slash to indicate the student completed homework on the concept or skill and still add an assessment notation later.

As the *content facilitation grid* fills up, you can use it to assess students' progress and your own effectiveness. By looking horizontally, across a row, you can assess how an individual student is progressing on content mastery. This allows you to encourage a student to complete specific activities or attend specific *small-group mini-lessons*, assign homework, meet with the student to explain content, arrange for a *peer expert* session, and so forth.

By looking vertically, down a concept or skill column, you can assess your own success in designing the learning environment. If many students are having difficulty with a particular skill, you will want to rethink how you're delivering the instruction. You may need additional activities, a different explanation, an additional *small-group mini-lesson*, and so forth.

To get started, think through the concepts and skills students must master in this unit. Be sure that you are specific enough that you can assess a student effectively. For example, "knows parts of speech" could be an appropriate skill set for a fifth-grade student, but for a fourth-grade student, you would probably want to use one column for each part of speech and enter the description as "defines, can recognize, and can use nouns."

As demonstrated in Figure 6.4, you could highlight initial columns you consider to be prerequisite skills. That way, you know that most students should be able to easily demonstrate mastery of those skills, with the unit concepts and skills beginning in subsequent columns. See the *problem-based tasks* in the Appendices for sample *content facilitation grids*. You could also group columns according to overarching topics such that the skills for each topic are easily found under a larger column heading.

Figure 6.4. Content Facilitation Grid

Student	M mastered PE peer expert R needs reinforcement HW needs homework ML needs small-group mini-lesson	Locates words / phrases to define and research	Explains what government is	Explains how America was governed before the Revolution	Explains the purpose of the Constitution	Names and describes sections of the Constitution	Explains how Constitution came to be	Names five rights protected by the Constitution	Applies the Constitution to current situations	Locates evidence from multiple resources	Expresses meaning in own words	Makes explicit connections to text in descriptions	Creates definitions appropriate for audience	Creates scenarios to explain portions of the Constitution	Explains what life might be like without a Constitution

Figure 6.5. Executive Function Skills Mapped to Increasing Levels of Complex Thinking

Conscious Control (CC)   Engagement (En)   Collaboration (C)   Empowerment (Em)
Efficacy (Ef)   Leadership (all)

Working Memory Storing and manipulating visual and verbal information (CC) Identifying same and different (En) Remembering details (CC) Following multiple steps (En) Holding on to information while considering other information (CC) Identifying cause-and-effect relationships (En) Categorizing information (En)	*Problem Solving* Defining a problem (Ef) Analyzing (Ef) Creating mental images (Ef) Generating possible solutions (Ef) Anticipating (Ef) Predicting outcomes (Ef) Evaluating (Ef)
Cognitive Flexibility Shifting focus from one event to another (CC) Changing perspective (En) Seeing multiple sides to a situation (C) Being open to others' points of view (C) Being creative (Ef) Catching and correcting errors (Em) Thinking about multiple concepts simultaneously (En)	*Inhibitory Control* Attending to a person or activity (CC) Focusing (CC) Concentrating (CC) Thinking before acting (CC) Initiating a task (En) Persisting in a task (En) Maintaining social appropriateness (C)
Planning Setting goals (Em) Managing time (Em) Working towards a goal (Ef) Organizing actions and thoughts (Ef) Considering future consequences in light of current action (Ef)	*Self Awareness* Self-assessing (Em) Overcoming temptation (C) Monitoring performance (Em) Reflecting on goals (Em) Managing conflicting thoughts (CC)
Reasoning Making hypotheses, deductions, and inferences (Ef) Applying former approaches to new situations (Ef)	

Adapted from Appendix A of *Building Executive Function: The Missing Link to Student Achievement* by Nancy Sulla (2018), published by Routledge.

It is important that you *use* formative assessment data daily. As a result of this data, you should make adjustments to the instructional activities you are offering. You'll want to allocate time to review each *student folder* and the *facilitation grids* in order to write a note to an individual student, providing direction for future activities.

Facilitating Executive Function

Your *problem-based ALU*, the structures you put in place to put students in charge of their own learning, and your facilitation work together to build greater student efficacy. In my book *Building Executive Function: The Missing Link to Student Achievement* (2018), I map specific executive function skills to key life skills, one of which is efficacy. Figure 6.5 offers a *facilitation grid* for those skills. While you are facilitating to build students' process skills in your classroom and their academic skills, you can also carry a grid to note their advancement in key executive function skills, like the ones included in Figure 6.5. While it's important that students know their letters, planets, geometric shapes, and all of the other content taught in elementary school, the ultimate goal of education should be to build efficacious learners.

RECAP

In the *Learner-Active, Technology-Infused Classroom*, teachers thoughtfully plan for the use of deliberate and purposeful structures and strategies to facilitate instruction. Together with the *ALU* and structures you've put in place, teacher facilitation can and should promote student efficacy. Review the following list to ensure that you have a plan for each in your *ALU*:

♦ Ask logistical questions about the student's goals, schedule, resource choices, activity completion, rubric progress, and so forth;

♦ Ask probing questions to push higher-order thinking, beginning with comprehension questions and then moving to application, connection, synthesis, and metacognition. Brainstorm questions in advance so they'll come to mind easily during the facilitation process;

♦ Plan for a variety of daily, formative assessments, including temperature gauges, breakpoints, student-directed, and comprehensive;

♦ Use a *task management grid* to track students' progress in completing activities;

- Use *content facilitation grids* to track students' progress in mastering concepts and skills;

- Use the data gleaned from the *content facilitation grids* to schedule *small-group mini-lessons* and modify the unit's *activity list*;

- Use a *facilitation grid* to track executive function skills toward student efficacy.

REFERENCES

Coleman, J. S. (1988). Social capital in the creation of human capital. *American Journal of Sociology, Supplement 94*, S95–S120.

Csikszentmihalyi, M. (2008). *Flow: The psychology of optimal experience.* New York, NY: Harper Perennial.

Prensky, M. (2006). *Don't bother me Mom: I'm learning!* St. Paul, MN: Paragon House.

Sulla, N. (2018). *Building executive function: The missing link to student achievement.* New York, NY: Routledge.

7

Physical Classroom Design

The "Big Room" was a collaborative effort among three teachers who taught fifth grade. Based on their school's structure, the teachers taught their homeroom students language arts literacy, and then each of the three teachers taught all of the students either math, science, or social studies. Students moved from one class to the other throughout the day, sharing three teachers, as an introduction to greater departmentalization that was to come in subsequent years. My colleagues and I had been working in the school for three years, designing *Learner-Active, Technology-Infused Classrooms*, after which time these three teachers approached me indicating that they finally "got it" and wanted to run an amazing classroom by taking down the walls between the classrooms. I spoke with the superintendent, who had a knack for supporting teachers with great ideas, and he had the impeding wall taken down.

That summer, the teachers and I brainstormed, designed, and prepared for the fall, incorporating a lot of paradigm shifting. I questioned whether every student needed a seat facing the front of the room. If sometimes students are in their seats, sometimes at a computer, sometimes conducting an experiment at a lab table, sometimes reading a book, why not design the room to be functional? The teachers agreed. In the end, the room had a discourse center with five couches (donated by parents), science lab tables, study carrels from the library for "quiet work," computers, collaborative work tables, a *small-group mini-lesson* area, and individual desks.

Elementary school students are used to having a desk in which to store their belongings, but that would not be the case in this classroom. Instead, students received two personal-space structures. A set of cubbies was used for them to store their books. To personalize their cubbies, students designed thin strips of paper to decorate the left and top sides of each cubby. Additionally, the teachers marked off boxes on the cinder block walls so that each student had a "My Best Work" area to post whatever work they wanted.

That was around twenty years ago. Today, everyone is talking about flexible seating, so it's not so hard to think that you could redesign your classroom to be more student driven!

CONSIDER

In the *Learner-Active, Technology-Infused Classroom*, many of the decisions you make will be focused on the question "Why?" The physical layout of the classroom is no exception. The dominant paradigm for classroom layout is to provide each student with a seat and desk or tabletop space and then provide additional areas such as lab tables, reading corners, specialized computer stations, meeting area, and so forth. The result is often a crowding of furniture in the room.

Instead, consider designing your class functionally so that when students enter the room, they go to the area that matches the function of the activity in which they will be engaged, based on the schedule they designed.

"Consider designing your class functionally so that when students enter the room, they go to the area that matches the function of the activity in which they will be engaged."

In the *Learner-Active, Technology-Infused Classroom*, where students are scheduling their own time and learning activities are differentiated, using space functionally gives you the greatest number of options in the classroom. Of course, it begs the question: how do you offer a *benchmark lesson* to the entire class? As you design the space, think about what that particular learning situation might look like. If you have tables in the room, it may mean that more students sit at a table than usual in order to listen to your lesson. It may mean that students sit around the periphery of the room at lab tables or computer tables. It may mean students are sitting on a couch and listening. You need to make it work for you. I'm not suggesting that you should only have one available spot in the classroom for each student; but I am suggesting that you do not have a seat at a desk for each student in addition to many other work areas in the room.

I've seen teachers focus so heavily on the concept of every student facing front to listen to a lesson that they declined other furniture, such as round tables and couches, so as to preserve the desks facing the front of the room. My response to that is that you should design your classroom for what occurs in it ninety percent of the time, not ten percent. The amount of time you address the entire class should be minimal, so take the opportunity to design a rich and engaging physical environment for the more student-centered activities.

It may turn out that you have little control over your physical space. I have been in science labs where the tables were bolted to the floor. It may be that you share a classroom with other teachers and cannot make a lot of physical changes. If you are limited in the amount of control you have over physical space, read through this chapter to get a sense of the thinking behind the suggestions. You never know what change you may be able to effect over time. Remember that the three teachers in the Big Room managed to get their school district to take down a cinder-block wall!

The challenge today is that furniture companies are heeding the call to develop more flexible seating for classrooms, and they are designing very attractive furniture. However, the dominant paradigm of teacher as lecturer still prevails in many of the choices. Small student tables on wheels roll together to form larger collaborative spaces. While new furniture is attractive and the idea of flexibility, ensuring a seat for everyone in the whole-class lesson is appealing, it may actually not offer you the best solution in the end. As you read through this chapter, focus on the purpose of different types of furniture so you can make decisions that make the most sense for creating a culture of student engagement, empowerment, and efficacy.

> "The amount of time you address the entire class should be minimal, so take the opportunity to design a rich and engaging physical environment for the more student-centered activities."

CREATE

Create a functional and inviting space in which your students can work, offering them options that fit the activity. Students should be able to move around the room and work in a space that is most fitting for the activity: sitting comfortably to read, gathered together for a discussion, sharing a table for collaborative work, moving to an individual desk for individual work when quiet is needed. Try to wipe from your mind all of those images of classrooms in your past and envision students taking charge of their learning, using the space in a room so it makes the most sense in the moment.

A great way to start is to take a piece of paper and draw out your current classroom or, if you don't yet have a classroom, how you expect to set up your classroom. Include all of the various areas, furniture, and structures. Then, on a separate piece of paper, for each area of the room, write about *why* you chose to set it up that way. After you complete this reflective exercise, you'll be in a better position to rethink the physical layout of your classroom. Think through each of the following sections and consider how you could arrange your room. Be open to possibilities, but don't commit to anything until you've finished reading through all of them.

Some physical space could be used to serve the purpose of two or more areas. As you read through each, focus on the purpose and then find the physical space to address the need.

Collaborative Work Space

Engaging in learning in the *Learner-Active, Technology-Infused Classroom* is often a collaborative effort. Outside of school, students naturally learn from one another. Brainstorming and higher-order thinking are typically enhanced through collaboration. Students need a place with an unbroken tabletop surface to write, draw, and work with their peers. This tends to be the largest amount of physical space allocated in the *Learner-Active, Technology-Infused Classroom*. You will probably want to provide enough collaborative space to accommodate approximately fifty to sixty percent of your students at one time.

Moving student desks together does not provide the best collaborative environment as students still have their own desktop and clearly delineated personal space. Collaboration means working closely together, so the space between students needs to be minimized. Pushing desks together often results in students sitting forty-eight inches or more apart, which is too far for voices to carry without adding considerable noise to the classroom. Collaboration means sharing ideas and resources and grappling with ideas to reach consensus. When students sit in arrangements in which they still have their individual desks, they are not pushed to think as one unit as they are when they share an unbroken tabletop surface. Round tables that are forty-two inches in diameter are my choice, preferably with a writable surface to enhance the collaborative experience. Students share the tabletop surface, no one has a specific, marked area, and the roundness and smallness foster a small-group environment. Although schools have a tendency to purchase forty-eight-inch round tables, that extra six inches adds tremendously to the overall noise in the classroom. Tables less than forty-two inches in diameter can be useful for conversations but not necessarily for having laptops, notebooks, and other materials in front of students. Consider a combination of forty-two-inch round tables and thirty-six-inch round tables. Rectangular and square tables tend to take up more space, and they do not engender a feeling of collaboration as well as a small, round table. Some teachers prefer the trapezoid tables that when paired create a hexagonal table. With these, however, the final table size tends to be very large, and there's still a break down the middle, which I find does not foster collaboration as well as an unbroken, flat surface.

Clover tables are a more recent option. They are circular in overall appearance with an indentation where students sit. Students end up sitting forty-two inches apart from one another for better discussion and collaboration, but the table juts out on the sides of the students to provide more space for materials. At this wider diameter, the table is forty-eight inches wide.

A French teacher wanting to ensure that her classroom was conducive to considerable conversation in the target language designed her classroom with small café tables so that students sat in pairs for discussions. On the first day of school, she welcomed students to her café and served croissants.

Individual Work Space

Students need to work alone to build individual content mastery, particularly when it comes to skill building. They can certainly engage in individual work at a round table, but sometimes they will want to be separated from their peers to work on their own. Students can also work individually on beanbag chairs or other soft seating, using a lap desk, but sometimes it's just best to have a place to work at a desk away from everyone else. I advocate having two or three individual desks in the classroom for this purpose. This also allows students who have difficulty focusing or self-regulating to move to an area apart from the distraction of their peers.

Teachers ask me about students who are diagnosed with attention-deficit disorder (ADD) or attention-deficit hyperactivity disorder (ADHD) and may not be able to concentrate with the amount of stimulation that is typical of collaborative and student-centered classrooms. My answer is always that students need to learn to accommodate for their personal challenges, and what better place to learn this skill than in the classroom. The teachers in the Big Room borrowed a few study carrels from the media center. When students knew they needed to remove themselves to concentrate on their work, they moved to a study carrel.

The idea of "hoteling" has become popular in the corporate world. It speaks to the idea that not everyone is always in the building all of the time, so cubicles, desks, and offices should not remain vacant when they can be used by others. For example, if a company has 100 employees, but many of them are in sales or otherwise on the road such that no more than sixty are in the office at once, why should forty percent of the physical space always remain vacant? Some of your students' parents may be working in such a situation; and your students may face this when they enter the work world. In the case of "hoteling," workers sign-up to reserve a particular office, cubicle, or desk. This also can apply to certain areas in the classroom. I once saw a student move to a study carrel, pull out a picture of her family and a stuffed toy, set up her "office," and get to work. These items added a personal touch to the work environment. Note that a study carrel or other furniture may become in demand and require a *limited-resource sign-up* sheet.

Discourse Centers

Oral communication skills are important yet not always supported in the conventional approach to classrooms. Verbal acuity is one of the outcomes of learning in a *Learner-Active, Technology-Infused Classroom* through both collaborative work and meaningful discussions.

Suppose students need to sit and have a discussion about a *problem-based task* or a book they are reading. A couch area can provide a wonderful discourse center, making students feel like they're at home engaging in a conversation in the living room. When the area is not used for discussions, students may use it to work collaboratively or independently. I was in one classroom in which I sat down next to a young man on the couch who was surrounded on the couch and floor by graphic organizers. I asked him about his work, and he explained the writing project in progress. Then he looked up at me and said, "Aren't you the one who said to get couches in the classroom?" I responded, "I am," at which point he patted the couch surface next to him and said, "Nice touch." A couple of couches can give a nice, comfy feeling to a classroom. You can also create a discourse center using a carpeted area and/or beanbag chairs. Think about the best arrangement for you to provide your students with an area to have a discussion with you or among themselves.

Computer Areas

Nowadays, more schools are turning to laptops and a one-to-one ratio of computing devices to students, so you may not need to allocate as much space to a computer area. In the Big Room, each teacher originally had four computers in the classroom; so together, they had twelve. They designated eight of them as available for students to sign-up for up to a forty-minute block. The remaining four were in a "Quick Lookup" area. Students could go to a computer to conduct a quick search for information, spending no more than five minutes at a computer. This way, there were always computers available to answer that spontaneous question or need for information.

Even if you are using laptop computers, you may want to have a desktop computer or two that offer special-purpose peripherals like a scanner, MIDI keyboard, or video camera. This could serve as a work area for multimedia production. You might have a STEM flight simulator computer; that would be in a specialized computer or STEM area.

Resource and Folder Area

In an effort to encourage students to take greater responsibility for their own learning, you'll need a *resource area* from which students can retrieve the printed materials, such as *how-to sheets*, and small resources they may need for their work. Additionally, you will need a place where students will deposit their two-pocket *student work folders* at the end of the day or class period and pick them up when they return to class.

Often, teachers utilize a rectangular table, located in some area of the room, sometimes using tent cards to label materials or sections. Some teachers staple folders on a bulletin board so that students can retrieve papers from there. Others use storage boxes with file folders. Although it is more difficult to easily locate the desired material, storage boxes take up less room and can be stored away or moved if you share a classroom with other teachers. Storage boxes or crates also make a good receptacle for collecting student folders. In a 1:1 computing environment, the *resource area* becomes a Web-based or networked folder for most materials.

Small-Group Mini-Lesson Area

You will need a space that will accommodate approximately up to six students attending a *small-group mini-lesson* with you. Keep the space condensed enough that students can hear you without you having to speak so loudly that the rest of the class can hear you. You'll want the ability to display information for the group. Some teachers create this area near a whiteboard. Others use an easel pad on a tripod stand.

You want to be a part of the group, building *social capital*, so you would not want to sit behind your desk with students in front of you. Some teachers use kidney-shaped tables, others use round or rectangular tables, and still others use a set of individual chairs with an attached table surface. Given that students will be building skills, ensure that they will have a writing surface on which to work. Thus, having students sit on the floor around you is probably not the best arrangement for this area.

Meeting Area

You may decide to create a meeting area in which your students can gather to meet with you for concept development or overall direction in approaching a unit of study. In primary classrooms, this is often a carpeted area in the center or a corner of the room. It allows the class to sit in a concentrated area to meet with the teacher. Primary teachers often have morning meetings in which they post a large letter to the students for the day. By reading this together, students learn about any announcements for the day while building reading skills and becoming familiar with letter format. In the upper grades, the meeting area might double as the discourse center. In the case of a couch area, it may involve having students pull over additional chairs, as you need to fit the entire class.

Limited-Resource Area

I heard someone describing to me just recently how in her school, students used manipulatives to explore certain math concepts, but then, when the lesson was done, the manipulatives moved on to another class. If some students hadn't quite yet grasped the concept, they would have to continue their work without the manipulatives. This is not an uncommon occurrence in schools. The dominant paradigm for conventional teaching prescribes that all students have access to a particular resource at the same time. All students work with manipulatives; all students work on computers to construct a journal article; all students look at an onion skin under a microscope. This approach to resource utilization can prove to be costly and ineffective. Instead, consider having a smaller number of resources available in the classroom for a longer period of time. Five sets of manipulatives could remain in the classroom for the year, shared by students who sign up for particular time slots. One or two microscopes could be used by students through the year rather than by everyone for one particular lesson.

A limited resource may be set up in its own physical area, such as in the case of a microscope, ant farm, sculpting wheel, listening center, and so forth. Other limited resources may be housed in containers and stored on a shelf, as in the case of math manipulatives, art supplies for a particular project, robotics kits, educational games, jump ropes, small percussion instruments, and the like. In both cases, however, students will sign-up for an available time slot to make use of this limited resource. Decide what limited resources your students will need and where in your room you will allocate space for them.

Use the Walls

Consider how you will make deliberate and purposeful use of your classroom walls. Create a *quality work board* to offer inspiration for producing high-quality work. Designate a *help board* for students to sign-up for your help when you are available. Provide areas for students to post their own work. Display various references around the room so that students gain valuable information at a glance. This might include a color wheel, regular polygons, the alphabet, a word wall, common words in a world language, parts of speech, the periodic chart, and more. If you share a room, consider a trifold presentation board that students can set up at the beginning of class and store away at the end of class.

Rather than thinking of your walls as something to decorate, consider how they can serve as a valuable resource for your students in the learning process. Creative use of the walls can add a lot of instructional space to the classroom.

How Big the Screen?

Shifting paradigms requires thoughtful reflection on the "why" of one's actions. The invention of the interactive whiteboard triggered a purchasing frenzy across schools. The interactive whiteboards were designated to be placed in the front of the classroom by the same administrators who were promoting a move from lecture-based instruction to student-centered instruction. This physical setup, however, perpetuates the dominant paradigm of whole-class instruction with everyone looking at the screen in the front of the room. This phenomenon demonstrates how difficult it is to shift paradigms. Alternatively, these devices could be installed in a corner of the room for student *collaboration* and *small-group mini-lessons*.

I was working with a group of teachers who had been allocated a specified amount of money to purchase resources for their classrooms. They came to me to say that they wanted to purchase large-screen televisions that could also serve as computer monitors. I asked them to think about their use in the classroom. One of the goals of the *Learner-Active, Technology-Infused Classroom* is to always use the talents of the teacher to the fullest. If the entire classroom is watching a video segment, the teacher is sitting idle, not sharing valuable expertise, talents, and knowledge with students. As we continued to discuss the *why* behind this, the teachers realized that they were falling into the trap of the conventional paradigm. Instead, they purchased smaller units and designated them as limited-resource areas. If students were to watch a particular video segment, they would sign up to watch with a couple of peers and answer a set of prediscussion questions, to be later addressed with the entire class.

Any time you are inclined to set up an area of the classroom or purchase a resource that the entire class can use at the same time, stop and ask yourself why. You may find that as you apply the paradigm shifts of the *Learner-Active, Technology-Infused Classroom*, you arrive at a very different decision.

Media-Based Collaboration

Classroom media tables are one of the more recent additions to furniture catalogs. They look like a conference table cut in half across the width so that the flat end is against a wall with a large-screen display on it and the students sit around the rounded edge. Students can then display their computer screen on the large-screen display to share their ideas and collaborate.

Most large-screen televisions and displays allow you to "cast" your computer onto them. They also allow for videoconferencing with others in remote locations. One or two of these added to a classroom can promote greater media-based collaboration.

Hospitals began using remote presence devices years ago to allow doctors to visit patients, and more recently to allow hospitalized students to attend school. I use the Beam by Suitable Technologies to visit one of the schools with which we partner. From my computer, I can drive the Beam around the school; I can see with 180-degree peripheral vision as if I were standing there in person. I think similar devices should be used to allow students in *Learner-Active, Technology-Infused Classrooms* to partner with one another across schools, states, and countries.

Comfortable, Fun, Dual-Purpose Furniture

Where do you like to sit to read a good book? Give your students some options. Adirondack chairs, butterfly chairs, and beanbag chairs are less expensive options. Have you seen the bookshelf walls with round cutouts with cushions for students to literally curl up with a good book? Have you heard of the cardboard furniture (very compressed and heavy cardboard) that you can build or have students build? Innovative furniture abounds, particularly when you look at office and library furniture options. Seek out innovative seating for classrooms and you'll find great inspiration for rethinking furniture in your classroom.

As I discuss in my book *Building Executive Function: The Missing Link to Student Achievement* (Sulla, 2018), recent research has shown that standing desks can improve executive functioning. Plus, as students are growing, sometimes standing instead of sitting eliminates fidgeting. You can provide stand-up workspace through high-top tables and stools or through individual standing desks. Exercise is another executive function builder, and you can purchase desks today that have bicycle pedals so students can be moving while reading or working. For students, this can help to focus them on their work while moving.

Search the Web and look for innovative furniture ideas.

The Teacher's Desk

Consider how much teacher space is designated in the classroom. In some classrooms, the teacher has a desk, side table, and a couple of file cabinets all positioned across the front of the room, away from the board, thereby designating about seven to ten feet of the front of the room for the teacher's use. In the *Learner-Active, Technology-Infused Classroom*, when students are in the room, teachers are never seated at their desks or working apart from students. Let me say that again: in the *Learner-Active, Technology-Infused Classroom*, when students are in the room, teachers are never seated at their desks or working apart from students. This is very important, as teachers need to spend their time facilitating learning and instructing. So all of that "teacher space" goes unused.

I've had teachers decide to remove their desks from the classroom to provide for more space, indicating that when students aren't in the room, they can use any table or desk to accomplish their work. All they need are some file cabinets and/or bookcases for their belongings, and those can fit in a corner of a room or against a wall. I've had teachers ask for smaller desks and/or push their desks against a side wall to open up more space in the room.

In one co-teaching classroom, the teachers asked for two teachers' desks so that both teachers would be seen as being equally important. Within a short period of time, they both asked to have their desks removed, realizing they took up too much space.

Consider how much space is designated in your classroom for the teacher. Take time to rethink furniture choices and positions.

Put Students in Charge

As students become acclimated to the *Learner-Active, Technology-Infused Classroom*, particularly when they are in a school in which they attend such classrooms in successive years, engage them in rethinking classroom furniture or in designating how existing furniture should be arranged. Student voice is powerful in designing their own classroom. (You can let them know what you need to make your work easier.) A unit on measurement could involve groups of students designing a new arrangement for the classroom such that each group sees their plan in action for one month of the year.

A group of fourth-grade students were enjoying flexible seating, based on their teacher's resourcefulness. When students in other classrooms indicated a desire for flexible seating, the class wrote for an educational foundation grant and ended up securing the funds for other classrooms to have flexible seating as well. These students were tremendously proud of what they made happen (efficacy is powerful), and their classroom didn't even receive any of the funding, as they already had flexible seating!

RECAP

The physical classroom space supports your philosophy of teaching and learning. As you design your *Learner-Active, Technology-Infused Classroom*, consider how you can rethink the use of physical space to create an environment that is aligned with your philosophy. This chapter outlined several areas for you to consider. Use these summary points as you reflect:

- ◆ Collaborative work space;
- ◆ Individual work space;
- ◆ Discourse centers;

- Computer areas;
- Resource and folder area;
- Small-group mini-lesson area;
- Meeting area;
- Limited-resource area;
- Use of the walls as instructional resources;
- Media-based collaborative spaces;
- Comfortable, fun, dual-purpose furniture;
- Teacher's desk;
- Student Voice in Classroom Design.

REFERENCE

Sulla, N. (2018). *Building executive function: The missing link to student achievement*. New York, NY: Routledge.

8

Principles and Paradigm Shifts

The *Learner-Active, Technology-Infused Classroom* embodies four major paradigm shifts and ten principles. Throughout this book, you've explored all of these. Review the *ALU* and classroom plan you're designing to see what structures and strategies you might want to add to foster the ten principles and what paradigm shifts you need to hold dear as you rethink your daily life as an educator focusing on increasing student engagement, empowerment, and efficacy.

Principle 1: Higher-Order, Open-Ended Thinking

Higher-order thinking relies on, and thus builds, executive function skills. Seeing multiple sides to a situation, changing perspective, thinking about multiple concepts simultaneously, making inferences and predictions, applying former approaches to new situations, and being creative are just some of the executive function skills that are activated when you offer students higher-order challenges to tackle. While it is true that one must master the lower levels of Bloom's taxonomy before achieving the higher, attempting to build higher-order skills creates a *felt need* for the lower-order skills.

Asking students to start a campaign to help feed the hungry sparks dozens of questions and ideas focusing on the higher-order application of lower-order skills to solve a problem. Challenging students to write a letter to convince their favorite author to write a next book about their town involves myriad skills for reading, analyzing, and writing. Armed with a motivating challenge, students will work to accomplish the lower-order skills in order to be able to handle the higher-order skills. Deciding where to build an airport requires skills of map reading, graph reading, research, and more. Designing a butterfly garden involves mastery of many ELA, math, and science skills.

I've been in many classrooms in which teachers focus heavily on building basic skills absent a greater context through lessons, demonstrations, guided practice, and independent practice. Students are, at worst, bored and tuned out, and, at best, compliant. Neither state promotes long-term retention of learning. Students, however, will work tirelessly to solve a motivating problem, opening the door for building the basic skills in the context of something larger. The *Learner-Active, Technology-Infused Classroom* is a higher-order thinking playground! Students are engaged in higher levels of understanding and application of content in order to address the *problem-based task*. They have a variety of ways of learning; and they utilize higher-order skills in their decision making regarding when, how, and with whom they will learn.

What Higher-Order, Open-Ended Thinking Looks Like in the Classroom

- ◆ Rather than merely presenting back information that they learned, students seek out information while working to offer solutions to solve open-ended problems;

- ◆ Teachers construct problems in which the solutions reside in the "unknown," forcing students to grapple with content that drives them back to what is "known";

- ◆ Students are given carefully crafted higher-order problems to solve that drive them to learn lower-order skills;

- ◆ Teachers design instructional activities that provide students with a challenge level slightly higher than their ability level, continuing to build toward higher and higher levels of cognitive function;

- ◆ Teachers function as instructional facilitators, asking questions that cause students to think at the higher levels of Bloom's Taxonomy;

- ◆ Students participate in a wide range of strategic learning activities that foster content attainment and reach for synthesis and evaluation;

- ◆ Students manage how they will spend their time, making numerous decisions involving increasingly higher-order thinking;

- ◆ Students themselves propose suggestions for enhancing the *problem-based task* or become problem finders themselves, developing their own *problem-based tasks* to pursue.

Principle 2: High Academic Standards

Students can accomplish amazing things when faced with high expectations and instructional supports: the two go hand in hand. Conversely, raising academic rigor absent instructional support will only result in more failure. Teachers must overcome the

> **"Students can accomplish amazing things when faced with high expectations and instructional supports: the two go hand in hand."**

tendency to teach to the level of the lowest-performing students and resist the temptation to think students aren't ready or able to achieve at high levels. Instead, they must teach to a high level and help all students reach that level through appropriate resources, accessible tools, and differentiated opportunities to learn. That is the true meaning of educational equity.

Teachers often design their *analytic rubrics* so that most students can meet the Practitioner column without too much effort and many can reach the Expert column. Here's a fun challenge for you. Take your *analytic rubric*, cut out the Novice column, shift the remaining columns to the left, and write a new Expert column. This will ensure that you are presenting academic challenges to all students.

Look at your wall hangings and make sure that you are posting materials to the bulletin boards that offer higher expectations rather than content your students should already know. Post resources that students can glance at while working that support their success. This may sound obvious, but take a look at your classroom walls and ask yourself, "If students get stuck learning this skill or concept, what is posted on the wall that will help them?" A first-grade teacher told her students to go beyond using small words like *good* and *great*; they created a word wall of more descriptive words. While a student was sharing this with me, looking for a better word, I told her she was the quintessential word finder. Of course, she then said, "What does that mean?" The next thing I know, she found the teacher to ask her if she could add *quintessential* to the word wall. I recently walked into a beginning French class. I sat across from a student and, in French, said hello, to which she responded in French. I then, continuing in French, asked her how she was. She responded, in French, so-so. I then asked her why and she told me, in English, that was as far as she could go on her own at this point; she then pointed to the wall behind me that had beginning conversation phrases. Empower students to find what they need in the moment!

When facilitating, ask probing questions to prompt higher-order thinking. Share information that raises expectations. Challenge students with suggestions. Ask "What if?" questions.

Finally, your own word choice in the classroom can be used to achieve *high academic standards*. Use terms that are related to your field, even at the youngest levels. Most state standards now refer to these as academic vocabulary and domain-specific vocabulary. Choose your words carefully. Think about the number of times you use "do" during the course of a conversation and, instead, use "conduct," "complete," "accomplish," and the like.

Avoid teaching the vocabulary word and, instead, give students a *felt need* to know the word. Use a word in context that is new to your students, and then define it in the same sentence. For example, "I appreciate your veracity . . . your truthfulness." The student just learned a new word. Cognitively, at the point you say "veracity," the student will most likely wonder what the word means, creating a level of cognitive dissonance. By then hearing the definition, the student will most likely remember it.

What High Academic Standards Look Like in the Classroom

- The expert column of an *analytic rubric* pushes students to tackle extended content and greater higher-order thinking related to the content;

- The classroom walls are filled with resources to support students and push their thinking;

- The teacher introduces vocabulary words, defining them in the sentence, while speaking;

- The teacher uses sophisticated sentence structure and grammar as modeling for students;

- When facilitating, the teacher asks questions that probe thinking, offer new information, and present challenges.

Principle 3: Learning From a Felt Need

Years ago, I was teaching a high school computer science class in programming. It was a time when text-based, computerized adventure games were popular—before computer graphics! On the first day of class, I had my students play these computer games and write about their experiences. At the end of the period, I told them that during the semester, they were going to design original programs. First, they had to map out their ideas for their games; then they would begin to write the programs. When my students needed to display text on the screen, I taught them how by offering a *how-to sheet* or a *small-group mini-lesson*. When they needed to refer to the player by name, I likewise taught them how to store variables. When a few were ready to keep track of the items the player picked up during the game, I taught them to use arrays (multivariable structures.) I then established them as *peer experts* as an option for their classmates. I carefully constructed the *problem-based task* so that students would need to use all of the concepts and skills in the curriculum. They learned through a *felt need*.

It can be easier just to present content to students; however, it is unlikely that they will remember it past the test, if that far. When students experience a *felt need* to learn, and they are then provided with just-in-time instruction, they retain that learning.

What Learning From a Felt Need Looks Like in the Classroom

♦ Students develop or are presented with *problem-based tasks* at the start of a unit of study that drive the need to learn concepts and skills;

♦ Students develop or read the *analytic rubric* at the start of a unit, identifying what they will need to learn in order to address the problem. From there, the teachers design instructional opportunities;

♦ Teachers offer *small-group mini-lessons* based on students' articulated needs;

♦ Students can explain why they are doing whatever activity they are doing and connect it to a greater instructional goal;

♦ Students access learning resources as they need them from a *resource area* and online sources;

♦ Students seek out additional resources in order to explore their own interests further.

Principle 4: Global Citizenship

In his book, *The World Is Flat*, Thomas Friedman (2006) presents ten major events that have led to the increasing globalization of our society. It was just the beginning of a rapidly advancing focus on preparing students to be global citizens, realizing we are all part of one world: one small interdependent world. Technology has played a significant role in leveling the playing field economically across the globe. In a flat world, someone using a product in South America may be helped by someone in India. The distance between people around the world is greatly reduced by the ability to video conference, email, and send instant messages at a cost no different from talking to one's neighbor.

People are becoming increasingly aware of others around the world, helped, in part by social media and websites. Events in one part of the world affect the entire world economically, environmentally, and politically. We can no longer refer to ourselves as just citizens of our towns or countries: we are rapidly becoming world citizens.

The *Learner-Active, Technology-Infused Classroom* provides students with many opportunities for building their skills as *global citizens*. Make direct connections to other countries in your classroom activities. Students can engage in online activities with students in other parts of the world.

Build students' overall awareness of other countries. Students studying government structures can identify similar governments in countries around the world. Students can trace inventions to other countries; and they can look at today's manufacturing cycle in terms of other countries around the world.

Build students' cultural acceptance of others around the world. You can begin with your students' national heritage and explore cultural customs and beliefs that exist today in those countries. In their lifetimes, students may visit and/or work in other countries. Technology will allow them to work virtually with people from around the world.

Build students' higher-order skills of analyzing cause-and-effect relationships among countries. As your students work to solve problems, have them consider what impact, if any, their solutions will have on other parts of the world.

What Global Citizenship Looks Like in the Classroom

♦ Students gather information through the Internet on issues and events from around the world;

♦ Students engage in *Authentic Learning Units* (*ALUs*) that require a knowledge of and consideration for countries around the world;

♦ Students follow news from around the world and relate it to their own studies;

♦ Students engage with outside experts and students around the world through technology, showing evidence of their understanding of cultural differences;

♦ Teachers provide learning opportunities for students to interact with members of the larger community in which they live;

♦ Students participate in service projects that have an impact on their school, town, state, country, and the world.

Principle 5: Technology Infusion

The *Merriam-Webster* online dictionary definition of the word *integrate* is "to form, coordinate or blend into a functioning or unified whole"; the definition of the word *infuse* is "to cause to be permeated with something . . . that alters usually for the better." For far too long, the use of technology in the classroom has begun with the technology itself, assuming that if we take the goal of studying spreadsheets and the goal of studying immigration patterns, we can blend the two into one project with two goals. This is integration.

When technology permeates the classroom setting, students who are studying immigration naturally turn to the Internet to search for information, use spreadsheets to generate graphs, use videoconferencing to interview immigrants, use multimedia to present a position statement, and more. Technology is not the goal; immigration is. Technology is merely a ubiquitous partner in the learning process. This is the goal of technology infusion.

Computer technology should be seamlessly infused into the classroom curriculum, with perhaps key benchmarks at certain grade levels. Computing devices need to be as readily available as pencils; and with smaller and less expensive computing devices, this is now a real possibility. While many popular uses of computers are automational, allowing students to accomplish that which they could without a computer, though with more difficulty, the power of technology lies in allowing us to accomplish that which without a computer is impossible or too complicated: transformational technology use. Gathering real-time data from around the world, engaging in simulations, programming robots, engaging in "what if?" analysis given a set of numeric data, collaborating with those in remote locations, and more are just some of the ways technology enhances the learning environment through transformational use.

Learning how to use technology should be a "just-in-time" experience. Teaching students the A to Z of using a particular application fails to honor brain research and the need to build sense and meaning to maximize retention. As students use various applications, *how-to sheets* and video resources can provide them with specific skill instruction to meet their needs. It is not important to learn how to center a title if you are not using titles in your paper. At the point you need to learn to center a title, it is important that you know where to look to find the information. These days, much of that information can be found on the Internet.

Technology should be seamlessly infused into the learning environment, with students accessing hardware and software as needed to pursue the greater goals of completing their *problem-based tasks*. When used effectively, technology becomes a powerful partner in the learning process and particularly for differentiating instruction. Even the youngest students can use digital tablets to scan QR codes and access instructional videos, videotape themselves, and upload images and videos to a site for teachers to access. A television ad for a tablet PC has the student using the device to communicate with friends, capture photos of interesting scenes around her, look up information, create, and more. An adult sees her lying on the lawn working on the device and says, "What are you doing on your computer?" Her response is, "What's a computer?" That's infusion!

What Technology Infusion Looks Like in the Classroom

♦ Students seek out technology when they need it in the course of pursuing other learning goals;

♦ Technology is readily available all of the time in the classroom;

♦ Teachers use technology to deliver lessons and have students engage in *learning activities*;

♦ Teachers use technology to communicate and collaborate with students;

♦ Teachers use technology to gather and analyze student achievement data and communicate with parents;

♦ Technology is utilized to provide multiple means of representation (*Universal Design for Learning*) for students at various learning readiness levels.

Principle 6: Individual Learning Path

Clearly, there are not enough hours in a day to set up an *individual learning path* for every student and monitor each student's progress. This is why *individual learning path* and *student responsibility for learning* go hand in hand. If you provide students, even the youngest, with tools for assessing their own learning style preferences, and you offer various learning options, they will learn to make appropriate choices, with you providing guidance on those choices.

A teacher had students begin the year by completing an online assessment of their learning styles, which provided a graph of their preferences. They then designed business cards to hand out to their teachers and *home group* members so others would get to know them. More importantly, the students themselves became aware of how some preferred listening to someone offer directions while others preferred seeing a written set of directions and diagram.

Some teachers use a version of the "Learning Styles and Readiness Grid" (see Appendix I, but consider different headings for student use) as a choice sheet from which students select *learning activities* based on their preferences and abilities. It's not unusual for primary-level teachers to offers students book selections with different levels of difficulty from which students choose, with the teacher's feedback.

Assessment should not be merely a tool of the teacher; students should self-assess to become aware of their cognitive strengths and weaknesses. They can use a *learning dashboard* (Chapter 5) to monitor their progress.

As the teacher and student determine where the student needs to build greater skills, together they can lay out a plan for success. When students are treated as partners in their own instructional plan, they make many decisions independent of the teacher.

A fourth-grade math teacher and I developed structures to allow students to develop their own *individual learning paths*. She would give students a math pretest consisting of five questions from each key skill in the unit. Students then self-scored the tests and analyzed their results. If they answered all five questions on a skill correctly, they completed a challenge activity that presented them with a higher-cognitive-level problem using that skill. If they answered three to four questions correctly, they completed two to three activities that focused on practicing the skill. If they answered one or two questions on a skill correctly, they completed *learning activities* related to building the skill, including required computer activities, podcasts, *peer expert* sessions, or *small-group mini-lessons*. If they did not answer any questions correctly, they began with introductory skill-building activities. This may sound like a lot of work—and it is up front—but consider how this approach allows students to follow an *individual learning path*. Once the pretests and activities are in place, the teacher is free to facilitate, advise, and offer targeted, direct instruction. The following year, materials may need to be reviewed and modified, but with far less effort than the initial year. The initial outlay of effort on the part of the teacher to design structures to build an *individual learning path* pays off in higher student achievement, more meaningful interactions with students, and decreased effort in lesson design over the long term.

What Individual Learning Paths Look Like in the Classroom

- Teachers and students utilize assessment data to craft individual student plans to address the standards, identifying specific activities or creating individualized expectations for students;

- Students follow personal *activity lists* that address their learning styles and cognitive levels;

- Students self-assess content mastery and skill level, sharing their analysis with the teacher to mutually agree upon a learning path;

- Teachers and students identify or create varied *learning activities* for building content and skill mastery such that students can engage in those that are most well suited for them;

- Students make decisions about how they will learn a skill or build content mastery.

Principle 7: Student Responsibility for Learning

Consider three compelling reasons for building *student responsibility for learning*. First, it will make your work easier in that students will make informed decisions about how to master curricular goals. Second, students will not always have you around to guide them as they learn throughout their lives. Third, doing so builds executive function. Conventional wisdom places teachers in an authority role in which they tell students what to do, when to do it, and how to do it, with the belief that students would fail without that level of direction. In the *Learner-Active, Technology-Infused Classroom*, the emphasis is on building students' skills in self-assessment and decision making in the learning process such that they can truly become lifelong learners.

Children are inquisitive from birth. From the time they can talk, they start asking questions and explore everything within their reach. The quest for learning is innate, and children learn a tremendous amount from their peers. A young skateboarder sees an interesting move and begins to put a plan into place to learn that move. It may include watching others in person, on television, and on videos posted on the Internet. It may include creating a practice course and making it increasingly harder. It may include endless hours of practice. Your students know how to take charge of their learning, but schools teach them early on simply to listen to the teachers and do as they are told, thus squelching this natural pursuit of learning in favor of compliance.

If you asked me to teach you the parts of speech, I could sit down and describe each one and offer examples, but that would merely be telling you and expecting you to memorize, not fostering a learning environment. Alternatively, I could design a set of activities that would allow you to engage with sentences and explore the interrelationships that exist among the words in the context of a bigger writing challenge for you, thus building in you a *felt need* for and a knowledge of the parts of speech that would last a lifetime. The former is easier; the latter requires great forethought and planning. However, in the case of the former, I will be presenting that lesson over and over again with student after student, year after year. In the case of the latter, I will design it once and empower a great number of students to take responsibility for learning, with only minor revisions across the years. The up-front investment required for designing the *Learner-Active, Technology-Infused Classroom*, which depends heavily on the principle of *student responsibility for learning*, will pay off considerably in student achievement and a greater sense of efficacy for you, the teacher.

What Student Responsibility for Learning Looks Like in the Classroom

♦ Students schedule their own time in the classroom based on the teacher's articulated expectations, choices of a diverse range of learning activities, including those they propose, and availability of a variety of resources;

♦ Students use *analytic rubrics*, checklists, and other structures to self-assess and set goals, with the guidance of the teacher;

♦ Students access a *resource area*, *help boards*, *quality work boards*, and *peer expert boards* in their quest for learning;

♦ Students reflect on their progress and practices and make adjustments to become more effective and productive learners, both as members of *home groups* and as individuals.

Principle 8: Connected Learning

Students are motivated by real-world events, fueled by accessibility via the Internet. Brain research demonstrates that it is important to connect learning to students' lives; the reality-based shift in society provides additional evidence of the importance of *connected learning*.

Problem-based tasks provide the real-world authenticity for learning; the next step is to make deliberate connections to students' lives. Language arts teachers have students write stories about themselves. A social studies unit on the pilgrims begins with the recent sale of one-way tickets to colonize Mars; would you take the flight? Health teachers have students study their own nutrition and that of meals in the school cafeteria. In designing *problem-based tasks*, consider the activities or requirements that could be used to connect the learning to students' lives.

Connected learning also means connecting learning across the disciplines. Given the departmentalized nature of school, students do not always see how one subject's skills and concepts relate to the next. Fractions are used in cooking; the Greeks invented geometry; informational text is present in every subject area; art is filled with the use of math skills; and so forth.

What Connected Learning Looks Like in the Classroom

♦ Students engage in *problem-based tasks* based on real-world scenarios;

- Students engage in activities that ask students to reflect on the content based on their own lives and experiences;

- Students articulate how content from other subject areas helped them in completing the *problem-based task*;

- Teachers present connections to other subject areas in their *benchmark lessons, small-group mini-lessons*, and other instructional materials;

- Teachers use the Expert column of *analytic rubrics* to encourage students to explore further related content of interest.

Principle 9: Collaboration

Cooperative learning describes a group working together and typically dividing up tasks to complete a particular assignment. The word *cooperate* intimates "putting up with one another" for the common good. For example, if the class wants to get to lunch on time, everyone should cooperate and get on the line and be quiet. *Collaborate*, on the other hand, intimates that some new knowledge is going to be developed based on the "two-heads-are-better-than-one" principle. *Collaboration* results in an end product that is enhanced by the input of more than one person; thus, collaborative activities are open-ended and focused on higher-order thinking.

> "*Collaboration* results in an end product that is enhanced by the input of more than one person; thus, collaborative activities are open-ended and focused on higher-order thinking."

Problem-based tasks offer students rich opportunities to collaborate. Devising a plan to convince an author to write a book about your town, creating a plan to improve recycling in the school, deciding on where to build an airport, developing ideas for cleaning up a local river, developing a campaign to engage people in exercising their voting rights, proposing a plan and budget for a family vacation, writing an original song to promote school unity, and the like are all powerful venues for *collaboration*.

Consequently, it is important to carefully structure collaborative work. Students should work together to brainstorm, critique ideas, share relevant information, develop questions, and evaluate their work. They should work independently to research topics, build content mastery, and develop ideas to bring to the larger group. As you design your activity lists, be sure to build in a meaningful distinction between individual work and group work.

It can be useful to have students develop a set of "team norms" of expected rules of engagement, such as: one person speaks at a time, all members are encouraged to participate, and avoid monopolizing the conversation. Additionally, students need to be able to handle "roadblocks" that veer the discussion off topic. Construct a "roadblock management chart" by dividing a piece of paper into four quadrants. Label them:

♦ Off topic—save for a later discussion;

♦ We need more information that is not available right now—save until information is available;

♦ We do not have the authority to make this decision;

♦ We need other people to make this decision.

When students find themselves stuck in an unresolved conversation, they should stop and write down the current discussion points in one of the four quadrants. This allows them to capture the information and frees them to move on.

Students may also need collaborative brainstorming tools, such as Edward de Bono's ever-popular "six hats" (1996) or "PMI" (1992). The six hats method has the students look at a problem or proposed solution from six perspectives. The yellow hat is optimistic, black hat is skeptical, red hat expresses emotion, green hat is creative, blue hat is into the organization of the process, and white hat focuses on objective facts. This method allows you to honor all perspectives, such as: "Put on your yellow hat for a minute and tell me what is great about this idea. Put on your black hat and tell me what could go wrong or why it won't work. Put on your green hat to see if you can come up with another idea."

PMI stands for Plus, Minus, and Interesting facts or questions. Students use a three-column sheet to analyze a possible solution or idea. In a short, designated amount of time, they write down two positive points, two negative points, and then two related, interesting ideas or questions. Following personal reflection, each group member has an opportunity to share and be heard. Students in the group begin to see emerging trends and innovative ideas.

Both of these tools, and others, help students build their skills in critical thinking and problem solving, which are important skills for collaboration. Consider introducing a new tool every couple of weeks to build your students' repertoire of collaborative work tools.

You'll want to establish a process for handling conflicts among team members as well. The first step should be to have the students sit down and talk about their differences to see if they can work it out. If that doesn't work, you might suggest the use of a peer mediator. Next, you might have the students sit down with you. Avoid allowing students to complain about one another to you without the other present. They are in a learning mode, so you do need to ensure that the collaborative relationships are productive and enhancing each student's individual progress. In your facilitation, you will get a sense if one student is not working to the effort of the rest of the team, if one student is being too bossy, and so forth. It is clearly better for you to assess the ability of the group members to work well collaboratively than it is for them to approach you and complain about one another. Ultimately, you want them to take responsibility for building collaborative relationships.

What Collaboration Looks Like in the Classroom

♦ Two to four students meet with a specific goal that is part of a greater problem-solving effort. For example, when deciding where to build the next airport, an early group effort would be to brainstorm everything the students need to know to begin to make a decision;

♦ Students are challenged, in groups, to solve open-ended problems requiring them to apply curricular content, through which they build mastery in that content;

♦ Students use various structures, including protocols and norms, to ensure that all students have the opportunity to participate and that all group interactions are positive;

♦ Students take individual responsibility to contribute expertise and information to the group;

♦ Students take the responsibility for each member of the group being successful in both content mastery and group interactions;

♦ Students use Internet-based tools to work collaboratively both inside and outside the classroom;

♦ Students use Internet-based tools to work collaboratively with students in other classrooms and geographically distant locations.

Principle 10: High Social Capital

The term *social capital* dates as far back as 1916 (Hanifan) to an article on rural schooling pointing out that social networks bring a benefit to their members. A family is a social network, as is a local community, work community, and, these days, online social communities. In more recent years, James Coleman (1988) popularized the term, suggesting that social networks, specifically local communities, had a direct correlation to the production of their members and the achievement of students in schools.

High social capital can be described as the relationships that are forged in a community between its adults and its young people. In communities that are characterized by *high social capital*, parents often know the names of other children in the neighborhood; they'll offer children they know a ride; they'll cheer for children at sporting events and congratulate individuals on their successes; they'll call one another to share what they saw, particularly if anything they see is suspicious. Children who grow up in communities with *high social capital* tend to do well in school. In communities that are characterized by low social capital, children move through the neighborhood seemingly unnoticed; often no one at home asks about them or their schooling; sometimes children are left home alone for long periods of time without anyone checking in on them; parents in the community do not necessarily know the other children nor engage with them. Children who grow up in communities with low social capital tend to struggle in school. Furthermore, children from communities with low social capital who attend private or parochial schools that foster *high social capital* tend to improve their academic performance.

Strong, caring relationships between adults and children contribute to improved student performance. These relationships are a characteristic of the *Learner-Active, Technology-Infused Classroom*. In conventional schooling, in which teachers spent much of their time in the front of the room dispensing information, there are few opportunities to build relationships between adults and children. A student might enjoy a positive comment on a paper from a teacher, or the teacher might ask the student to linger after school to talk about accomplishments, and occasionally a teacher would be seen at a school event engaging in conversation with a student.

In the *Learner-Active, Technology-Infused Classroom*, teachers build strong relationships with students throughout the day. They increase social capital through the venue of the *small-group mini-lessons* during which they are sitting with and talking to a small number of students, sharing information, asking questions, and encouraging students to succeed. Teachers have numerous one-on-one conversations with students throughout the course of the day. As teachers move throughout the classroom, the "never hover" rule causes teachers to pull up a chair and sit with students face to face, engaging in productive and motivating conversations about content.

In classrooms with more than one adult, such as the co-teaching classroom, and in classrooms that regularly involve parents and community members, students enjoy considerable interaction with adults who care about them. This builds *high social capital*, which yields results in increased student achievement.

What High Social Capital Looks Like in the Classroom

- ♦ Teachers spend class time largely sitting with students discussing their work, goals, and accomplishments;

- Multiple adults work in the classroom with students, thus providing greater adult–student interaction;

- Teachers and students design *problem-based tasks* and instructional activities that require students to engage with their parents, family members, and other adults in their lives;

- Parents and community members are regular participants in the learning process, either in person or through virtual connections;

- Teachers and students develop online or print newsletters for the community that celebrate the successes of the students.

Paradigm: Teaching From a Felt Need

As you move forward in implementing your *Learner-Active, Technology-Infused Classroom*, continuously ask yourself if you're responding to students' *felt need* to learn. At the unit level, that means either presenting students with a compelling problem that will motivate them or, ultimately, having students identify problems they want to solve while you determine how their problems can build required curricular skills. Even at the skill level, however, how will you connect learning to meaningful purposes? Within your *ALU*, work to ensure that all learning stems from students feeling a need for the information. This includes encouraging them to decide how their solutions to problems could be even better, leading to new learning.

Paradigm: Teacher as Ferry Versus Teacher as Bridge Builder

As you design, reflect on, and redesign your *Learner-Active, Technology-Infused Classroom*, keep in the forefront of your mind the goal of becoming a bridge builder who empowers students. Compliance is no longer enough! Think through the smallest events in your classroom: what students do when they enter, how they hand in papers, how they get materials, how they get help, how they make suggestions, and so forth. How can you build the structures to put them in charge of their own learning?

Paradigm: Don't Grade the Learning Process

While there is a tendency in schools to grade anything students hand in, remember that in the *Learner-Active, Technology-Infused Classroom*, you are using a *problem-based task* to build a felt need for learning and to launch a unit of study. Students should not be able to accomplish this without you at this point in their studies. Throughout the unit, you will be guiding them, offering feedback and suggestions, celebrating their successes. By the time their solution is ready to be presented, it should be in the *Practitioner* column of the *analytic rubric* because of your involvement; that's your job. Remember, to grade it would merely be grading yourself. Rather than grading the learning experience, offer a testing situation transfer task (Chapter 3) to grade individual content mastery.

Paradigm: Trigger Awareness

When you stand in front of your class, use all of your inspiration, talents, knowledge, expertise, experience, and tricks of the trade to trigger students' awareness of what they need to learn. Then, mic drop! Walk away! The true learning will take place when students engage in learning activities, not from you. If you feel the urge to teach the whole class because you want to ensure that they get it, forget it! Brain research will tell you that approach is futile, as not all of your students are ready to learn. Instead, identify a set of *learning activities*, including *small-group mini-lessons* for targeted audiences, to ensure that all students learn. Inspire, then lead students to learn through their own engagement with content.

RECAP

Consider your classroom, the unit you are designing, and the overall activities, structures, and strategies that take place in your classroom. Continually reflect on how you can foster these ten principles in your classroom:

♦ Higher-order, open-ended problem solving;

♦ High academic standards;

♦ Learning from a felt need;

♦ Global citizenship;

♦ Technology infusion;

♦ Individual learning path;

♦ Student responsibility for learning;

♦ Connected learning;

♦ Collaboration;

♦ High social capital.

Continually reflect on how you can reflect the four key paradigm shifts:

- ◆ Teaching from a felt need;
- ◆ Teacher as ferry versus teacher as bridge builder;
- ◆ Don't grade the learning;
- ◆ Trigger awareness.

REFERENCES

Coleman, J. S. (1988). Social capital in the creation of human capital. *American Journal of Sociology, Supplement 94*, S95–S120.

de Bono, E. (1992). *Serious creativity*. New York, NY: Harper Business.

de Bono, E. (1996). *Six thinking hats* (2nd ed.). Boston, MA: Back Bay Books.

Friedman T. (2006). *The world is flat*. London: Penguin.

Hanifan, L. J. (1916). The rural school community center. *Annals of the American Academy of Political and Social Science 67*, 130–138.

9

Special Considerations

The *Learner-Active, Technology-Infused Classroom* is a framework for putting students in charge of their own learning. It holds much promise for increasing student engagement, empowerment, and efficacy leading to stronger student achievement. Given that it is a framework for instruction, it is flexible enough to accommodate most of the instructional approaches that schools are pursuing, such as co-teaching classrooms, STEM and STEAM, Universal Design for Learning (UDL), Response to Intervention (RTI), and more. It allows you to address the needs of all students in one fully differentiated classroom environment, including students with disabilities, English language learners, gifted learners, and those who struggle with learning content. This chapter will address a number of the various ways that the *Learner-Active, Technology-Infused Classroom* can meet the needs of your classroom, school, or district. It's important to remember that the *Learner-Active, Technology-Infused Classroom* is not a strategy that you use some of the time; it's an umbrella, of sorts, that pulls together all of the programs, resources, and approaches you wish to incorporate into your classroom.

> "the *Learner-Active, Technology-Infused Classroom* is not a strategy that you use some of the time; it's an umbrella, of sorts, that pulls together all of the programs, resources, and approaches you wish to incorporate into your classroom."

No matter what your instructional need, you can emphasize different aspects of the *Learner-Active, Technology-Infused Classroom* to address it. You can incorporate customized language to promote a specific approach. For example, if you are implementing Accountable Talk (University of Pittsburgh), your discussion protocols would include language related to the types of questions and statements they will make, such as affirm, agree, disagree, clarify, and so forth.

No matter what your overarching goal, given that your *Learner-Active, Technology-Infused Classroom* is a departure from conventional classrooms, take care to introduce students to the various structures and strategies so that they meet with success from day one. This is accomplished through a *priming plan*. Beyond that, customize your classroom structures and language to meet your needs: just stay true to the paradigm shifts and the "why" behind each structure as you do.

The Priming Plan

In many cases, students in a *Learner-Active, Technology-Infused Classroom* will experience a variety of new structures and have different responsibilities from the classrooms from which they came. In order to avoid having students begin the year or course with confusion and frustration, it's important to begin with a *priming plan*. This is a one- to two-week unit that engages students in a variety of activities aimed at three overarching goals:

♦ Introducing students to all of the structures of the *Learner-Active, Technology-Infused Classroom*;

♦ Priming students for academic success through hope, confidence, and optimism;

♦ Gathering assessment data related to academics and social interaction to make decisions for the first *Authentic Learning Unit (ALU)*.

You will design a variety of activities such that, throughout the *priming plan*, students will be engaged individually, in small groups, and in pairs both with and without your direct involvement. Given that you want to observe student interactions with others, change *home groups* daily and have every activity focusing on different ways in which to learn with and without others. That means you will not use a typical *ALU*, since an *ALU* is meant to be collaborative in nature and span a period of several weeks. You will introduce students to the structures of *problem-based tasks* and *analytic rubrics*, but one that can be addressed in a few days.

Your role in the *Learner-Active, Technology-Infused Classroom* is to act as a bridge builder to empower your students, not as a ferry moving them along. However, in the beginning, you need to start out somewhat like a ferry to offer enough overt direction and gradually release the control to your students over the course of the *priming plan*. After the *priming plan*, you'll launch your first ALU.

Walking Through the Door

As you envision your students walking into your classroom space for the first time, how will you immediately engage and empower them? A popular approach is to engage them in a scavenger hunt of sorts to locate structures and learn the meaning of different places in the classroom.

Imagine students walking into the room and having you hand them a puzzle piece. Their job is to find the other two or three people that make up the puzzle. When the group assembles the puzzle, it offers them directions. A fourth-grade teacher used cardinal directions to reinforce that learning; one puzzle, for example, offered the direction, "from the door, walk twenty steps northwest to the reading corner." Once in the reading corner, students followed directions there. In this case, it was for one student to read aloud the purpose of the reading corner and the expectations (quiet reading only, books put away at the end of the visit). The directions then had students engage in a short activity. In this case, it was to find a book of interest that each had not yet read. Each student was to write down the book title, author, and illustrator and, based on just the cover, write what they think the book might be about. They then read for five minutes and wrote an opinion statement about the book at this point and whether they felt they would want to finish it. They then were invited to look through other books in the reading corner. After fifteen minutes, they followed another set of directions to find another area. Students moved around the room, experiencing all of the different areas. They read about the purpose and usage of the *help board*. Then they put their names on the *help board* with a topic they would each like to learn about. They then engaged in a short activity on becoming resourceful. When they arrived at the *small-group mini-lesson* area, they met with the teacher, who shared more on their role in the classroom and answered questions. After the first two rotations, the teacher interrupted the rotations to offer a *benchmark lesson* and explain its purpose and the expectations for students.

It is always great to see students taking charge of what they are doing from the minute they walk in the classroom. In this case, students had to read and follow directions, engage individually and in groups, with and without the teacher, as they learned about the classroom. They rotated, however, for specific periods of time. While this is appropriate for the opening of school, the idea of rotational centers must give way to students managing their own time, deciding when and for how long to engage in which activities.

You could offer fifth graders math problems to solve in which they must arrive at an answer and find a group based on common answers. You could offer students cities and a map and have them find their group based on a common state or country. It's fun to watch the students try to figure out who is in their group. For third graders and up, be careful to structure it so that they must find their group before finding their location. Otherwise, students will just go to a location and wait for others to arrive; that's mere compliance. Get them engaged in problem solving from the start: who else has this number? How will I find the students who have word cards with the same number of syllables? Who else has synonyms for the word I was given? Who else has a matching puzzle piece?

For primary students, you might hand them a colored card as they walk in the room and have them find the other students with that color and go to an area of the room marked by that color. You could give them puzzle pieces that make up a letter of the alphabet, leading to a marked area of the room. Once in their areas, you can let students simply engage in whatever is in that area, perhaps blocks, puzzles, games, and the like. You could also use a digital device in some so that students could play the video of you talking about the area. After about ten minutes, you would pull the group together and start to talk about the classroom and how they will work in the classroom. Obviously, you will need to guide kindergarten students more carefully.

Older students might be able to fill out a scavenger hunt, looking for information about various areas of the room. For example:

- I would find a ruler in the _____.

- I can find the list of *small-group mini-lessons* _____.

- When I schedule my time, I must include a start and _____ time.

- I should plan out my day with others in my _____.

The key is to put students in a position of being in charge of their own actions as soon as they walk through the door. That means coming up with a way to have them find a group, a set of activities or locations, and clear directions they can follow on their own or, in the case of primary students, understand by nature of the activity.

Priming Plan Tasks

Unlike in an *ALU*, the *priming plan* tasks should be short. For kindergarten and first grade, you might offer a task that takes just a day or two, focused on the school experience. Here are some examples:

- All of your other classmates need to learn about who you are. You are going to make "A Poster of You." Students would write or have the teacher write their names, cut and paste things they like to eat or do, and include any of a number of other criteria.

- It's the start of the school year. Let's jump in! What parts will be easy? What parts will be hard? What do you want to learn? What will it take to jump? You are going to write your book of hopes for the school year. What do you want to learn? How will you keep on working until you get there? Students will create a picture book with or without words and sentences, depending on ability, of things they want to learn and what they will do to push through when the going gets tough. This is a great introduction for building grit and the character needed to succeed in school. You can pair this with reading the book, *Jabari Jumps*

(Cornwall, 2017) to them. It's a book about a boy learning to jump off a diving board.

♦ If animals could talk! What if animals could really talk? What would they say about school? You are going to adopt a pet. You will pick any animal you want. You will then share a story of your pet's day in school. Students will explore different types of animals, pick one, and either write or just share about what that pet would like and not like about the classroom. An elephant might find it too small. An ant might worry about being stepped on and feel that the chairs are too high. A bear might find that the chairs aren't big enough. You could go in a lot of directions here.

From second grade on, you can develop tasks that similarly focus on school and students' experiences or on the community.

♦ Let's have the best school year ever! As you learn more about our goals in ___ grade, your job is to create a guide for you and for me to ensure you have the best school year ever. Students will write about their goals for school, assess themselves on a Great Student Rubric, take a learning styles inventory, and more.

♦ We are a classroom of great students; and we are part of a greater community. How can we contribute to a better community within the school and outside? Students then brainstorm problems they can tackle and create lists of ideas for addressing them. This could culminate in a poster, skit, multimedia presentation, or anything else you like.

♦ The Game of Classroom! This is especially good for students who have learned in *Learner-Active, Technology-Infused Classrooms* in the past and have some level of knowledge of the structures. Students get to know the classroom and you as a teacher and develop a board game that others can play. Given the complexity of this, you might have students develop the games in pairs and allocate time for them to work on it throughout the *priming plan* while using other time to have them working with others. The games should require students to have to know the ins and outs of this *Learner-Active, Technology-Infused Classroom*.

Try to identify *problem-based tasks* that may involve some learning but focus more on knowledge students already have. The *problem-based task* in an *ALU* is meant to be used to launch a unit through which students are learning new content; that's why they span several weeks. However, if your students already knew all of the content, that same *ALU* would probably take a day or two; that's the intent here. You're seeking to find out what skills and content they possess, who they are as learners, and how they interact with others while teaching them to utilize the structures of your *Learner-Active, Technology-Infused Classroom.*

Priming Plan Activities

Unlike the activities that are part of an *ALU,* which are meant to promote learning new content, during the *priming plan,* the activities will focus more on strengthening foundational skills and learning how to use the classroom structures. Offer short assessments of their content knowledge. You might use a facilitation grid of some key prerequisite skills you expect them to have. You might offer some preassessments to see if some students have already mastered some of the content of the next unit.

Offer *benchmark lessons* on content needed for the *problem-based tasks,* how to succeed in the classroom, and to set the stage for the *ALU* that will start soon. At the start of the year, particularly if students are used to teachers presenting content first, conduct four or more short *benchmark lessons* across the day. As the *priming plan* progresses, transition students to fewer each day, ensuring they understand that the *benchmark lesson* will offer them an idea of what they need to learn to succeed in finding a solution for their *problem-based tasks.* Offer benchmark lessons on the purpose and use of the *two-pocket folder, analytic rubric, activity list, schedule,* and more.

The *learning activities* and other resources should include *how-to sheets, direction sheets,* and *protocols.* Have students engage in small-group discussions following a *protocol.* Have them follow *direction sheets* as a group to engage in an activity. Have them retrieve skill-based *how-to sheets* from the resource table. The sooner students learn to independently follow printed instructions, the better the classroom will run.

Create activities that will ensure students understand all of the structures of your *Learner-Active, Technology-Infused Classroom.* Take time to offer assessments and to gather facilitation data so you have a strong sense of what each student will need to succeed on your first *ALU.*

Some teachers write their students a letter for each to open and read, telling the student about themselves and asking that they write a letter about themselves in return. This can serve as a writing assessment.

Great Student Rubric

Introduce students to rubrics in the *priming plan* by using a *Great Student Rubric* in which you offer clearly articulated expectations for student behavior and work habits. See Appendix J for sample *Great Student Rubrics.* Develop one that works for you and your students. Have students assess themselves, set goals, and reflect on their progress. Strong work habits and behavior lay a strong foundation for academic achievement. Your *Great*

Student Rubric can address key executive function skills as well. Depending on the level of familiarity your students have with the *Learner-Active, Technology-Infused Classroom*, you can have them offer suggestions for designing the *Great Student Rubric*.

Sociograms

Observe how students work with one another. Who are the natural leaders? Who are inclined to take over? Who are inclined to depend too heavily on others? Which students seem to work well together? Which do not? After the first week of school, you can create a sociogram by asking students to write down three other students in the class with whom they like to work, explaining that you may not always be able to have them working together, but you will try for at least some of the time. Then put a set of circles on a page with one student's name per circle. Draw arrows from each student to the ones they said they would like as work partners. Once all the lines are drawn, analyze your sociogram. Some students will have a lot of arrows pointing at them, designating them as stars. You can use your stars wisely to teach them to model productive behaviors and proper use of structures. Some students will have few to no arrows pointing at them, designating them as isolates. You'll want to keep an eye on these students to ensure they are well placed in groups in which they can thrive. Two students who choose one another are said to have made a mutual choice. Three or more students who all mutually choose one another are known as a clique. The insights you glean from a sociogram can be useful as you start creating *home groups* for the first *ALU*.

Response to Intervention (RTI) and Multi-Tiered System of Supports (MTSS)

The RTI framework is a powerful approach to instruction that avoids labeling students by ability or disability and instead speaks to the need for different types of instructional interventions. Educators begin with "Tier I" instruction for all students, using high-quality, differentiated strategies and formative assessment to gauge student progress. If some students begin to fall behind in content mastery, educators are asked to apply "Tier II" intervention methods, involving small-group instruction. The goal is to position students to succeed through Tier I instruction. If students receiving Tier II interventions are still failing to master content, educators are asked to provide them with "Tier III" interventions, involving one-on-one instruction, often with a specialized teacher. The *Learner-Active, Technology-Infused Classroom* provides the perfect venue for offering Tiers I, II, and III instruction, potentially, all in the same physical classroom. With students managing their own time in a fully differentiated instructional environment, it's easy for teachers to provide Tier II *small-group mini-lessons* and provide students who are struggling with specific content more targeted, ability-based *learning activities*. A coteacher can join the classroom, working with small groups or individual students, maximizing productivity in this classroom that is characterized by minimal whole-group instruction. The *Learner-Active, Technology-Infused Classroom* is a model RTI classroom.

A multi-tiered system of supports (MTSS) includes RTI but expands beyond its academic focus to include social and emotional supports. It involves continual progress monitoring through formative assessments. *Home groups*, *Great Student Rubrics*, and *peer experts* are just a few structures of the *Learner-Active, Technology-Infused Classroom* that can provide social supports. Given the differentiated learning environment and heavy reliance on teacher facilitation, the *Learner-Active, Technology-Infused Classroom* provides the perfect venue for supporting students in social and emotional learning as well as academic achievement. Varied formative assessments and *content facilitation grids* provide for continual progress monitoring.

If you are attempting to embrace an MTSS or RTI approach to instruction, this book will help you design an effective classroom aligned with a multi-tiered system of supports.

The Co-Teaching, Inclusive Classroom

An inclusive classroom is one in which students with and without disabilities learn together. The differentiated nature of the *Learner-Active, Technology-Infused Classroom* makes it the perfect venue for an inclusive setting. Students will be working on different activities, often oblivious to what anyone else is working on. Teachers can offer all students the support they need to excel.

To address the needs of a diverse class of learners, some of which are identified as having learning disabilities, typically two certified teachers, at least one with special education certification, join together to coteach the group of students. In a conventional classroom setting that focuses on the teacher first presenting content, followed by students practicing toward mastery, having two teachers in a classroom can present some challenges. Often the sharing of teaching falls into one of three categories: one teacher presents content while the other quietly kneels or sits next to a student offering cues, such as pointing to the place on a paper; the teachers split the group and both teach to a subset group; or one teacher teaches and the other grades papers or prepares for a future lesson. None of these is optimal, however, as the structure of a teacher-centered environment does not easily lend itself to co-teaching.

The *Learner-Active, Technology-Infused Classroom* is a student-driven learning environment that offers teachers new possibilities for joining together to promote student achievement. It is the optimal framework for co-teaching.

There are four distinctly different ways in which coteachers engage in the *Learner-Active, Technology-Infused Classroom*:

- **Group and Guide:** While one teacher is offering a *small-group mini-lesson*, the other is facilitating the rest of the class, guiding them academically and in their processes. Both teachers take turns offering *small-group mini-lessons* so that one is not always the instructor in this setting.

- **Dual-Focus Facilitation:** When students are working on various activities they've scheduled, both teachers move around the classroom, facilitating learning. While both teachers will assist students as needed, they each have a specific focus for their facilitation and utilize a *facilitation grid* tailored to that focus. For example, one may be looking to glean data related to student mastery of the unit content, while the other may be focusing on executive function skills. The teachers would carry both *facilitation grids* to capture formative assessment data as it emerges; however, their questions would be geared to their facilitation focus.

- **Balanced Benchmark Lesson:** During a benchmark lesson, rather than having one teacher present while the other watches, both teachers play a role. This requires some level of planning and coordination, but strategically, the teachers can play off one another. One might ask questions while the other responds. One might offer a statement or explanation followed by the other then contributing, which causes students to have to attend and shift focus from one to the other, thus building executive function. The two teachers might act out a skit. Two fifth-grade teachers were launching a travel unit and came dressed up as tourists, acting out a skit to present the *problem-based task* statement to the students.

- **Individualized Inspiration:** One teacher holds individual conferences with students while the other facilitates learning. In a *Learner-Active, Technology-Infused Classroom* with one teacher, it is difficult to offer one-on-one conferences, as it takes the teacher away from the rest of the class. With two teachers, one can home in on individual students to review their progress and inspire them to tackle new challenges. Teachers can share this responsibility, with one meeting with part of the class and the other meeting with the rest. These conferences can also be offered to a subset of students who are at a point at which the conference makes sense.

It is important to create a culture of equal adults in the co-teaching classroom. Both names should be on the door. Students should see themselves as having two teachers, not a regular education teacher and a special education teacher. I am not a fan of the big teacher desk in a classroom, as it takes up a lot of precious space. While teachers may need space for their belongings and materials, during class, they are with students, and when students are out of the room, they can use any table space in the classroom to accomplish their work. So two desks would definitely not be my preference; however, equality is important in creating a co-teaching culture. Both teachers should have space for materials in the classroom. If there is going to be a desk, it should be shared, or the teachers should each have a small desk.

STEM/STEAM

Computer automation has shifted the job market away from the rote, factory jobs of the last three centuries to a focus on design. At this point, people are needed to solve problems and design product solutions; computer-automated factories build those products. Consider the rise of the 3-D printer that allows students to create models that they otherwise would have had to build by hand. Are we developing a future workforce of design-oriented people? Add to that the need for more workers in the areas of science, technology, engineering, and math. Job positions lie vacant for months waiting for qualified individuals.

STEM (science, technology, engineering, and math) and STEAM (arts added) education has emerged as a priority in schools. Additional letters have entered into the name as well. For the purpose of this section, I will use the term *STEM*, acknowledging that the additional foci are addressed here as well. As with most innovations, schools are challenged by the idea of infusing the concept into the current instructional plan. Instead, they add a course, specialized teacher, or program. You will often hear of STEM days, the STEM lab, the STEM teacher, and so forth. The problem, still, is that students can learn to program objects, build prototypes, and land flight simulator jets without making connections to or tapping into their passion for STEM careers. Until we view STEM as a part of a rich, bold tapestry of every student's daily experience, we will fall short of preparing students for STEM careers for the following reason.

What is most obvious about STEM in schools is what I will refer to as the "stuff": 3-D printers, robot kits, programmable objects, computer simulations, 3-D goggles. These are all very exciting and, for students, a wonderful departure from their typical daily instructional resources. STEM resources can be expensive, and in a conventional setting in which every student needs a pair of 3-D goggles or a robot kit, budget constraints can limit access to a wide variety of materials. Given the *Learner-Active, Technology-Infused Classroom* is a place where not all students are working on the same activity at the same time, you can purchase fewer of each STEM item and, thus, a wider variety of items. Students will then sign-up for *limited resources* so that the class can get the most out of the resources available.

It is incumbent upon educators to attach the STEM "stuff" to a greater purpose, which, in the *Learner-Active, Technology-Infused Classroom*, is a *problem-based task*. In the case of STEM, that would be a real-world problem to solve that requires the STEM "stuff" to solve. Students can design solutions to the challenges faced by disabled persons in everyday life. Given the heightened concern about the reduction in the population of our natural pollinators, bees and bats, they can seek to design an automated pollinator drone. University students, organizations, and even K–12 students are engaging in designing and printing prosthetic hands for those in need. One organization of volunteers, enablingthefuture.org, as of the writing of this book, allows you to obtain a hand, build a hand, or volunteer to help in building hands for others. And then there are the more personal daily challenges students face. One of our client teachers had her young students design and print devices that would prevent their round crayons and pencils from rolling off their desks. How will our plants get enough water over the school vacation? Can you design an app for your tablet or phone to improve people's daily lives that doesn't yet exist? Given a real-world problem to solve, students engage even more deeply in learning how to use the "stuff" of STEM. However, even that's not enough to prepare students for STEM careers.

The *Learner-Active, Technology-Infused Classroom* is a perfect venue for STEM. Students engage in a *problem-based task*, and they can sign-up for the use of limited resources. What makes someone passionate about STEM and pursuing a related career? It's the way a person's mind works, the way they think about the world around them, the way they see connections among the disciplines and possibilities for solutions. They possess what I call the mindsets of STEM. I believe if we are truly to prepare students to pursue a STEM career, it is our moral imperative to ensure they possess the mindsets of the scientist, technologist, engineer, and mathematician (see Figure 9.1). Otherwise, all we've given them are great experiences with fun STEM "stuff." In order to transfer their learning to the world around them, seeing the world through a STEM lens requires that students possess the mindsets of STEM. While watching students look through 3-D goggles and print on 3-D printers is exciting, hearing them make connections and speak in ways that demonstrate their true understanding of STEM is even more exciting!

Accomplishing this simply requires tapping into some powerful ideas that are already available to you. The Next Generation Science Standards

Figure 9.1. The Moral Imperative of STEM

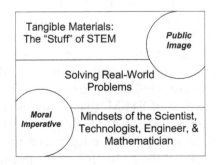

(www.nextgenscience.org) offer a set of crosscutting concepts that transcend the disciplines: patterns; cause and effect; scale, proportion, and quantity; systems and systems models; energy and matter (flows, cycles, and conservation); structure and function; stability and change. Several of those concepts are easily identifiable in other content. Making those concepts visible to students across the subjects builds in them the mindset of a scientist. The Common Core offers math practice standards, which, similarly, cross all subject areas. A technologist considers all the ways in which technology can help in solving problems, including information retrieval, communication, collaboration, simulation, modeling, design, and presentation. An engineer uses a design process, which can be applied across all subject areas. See Appendix K for a chart illustrating these mindsets.

In the problem-based learning environment of the *Learner-Active, Technology-Infused Classroom*, students can engage in real-world problem solving using an engineering design process and STEM technologies while building the mindsets of a scientist, technologist, engineer, and mathematician.

Design Process

Throughout school, students learn the scientific method: a series of six steps for uncovering a scientific truth. Scientific method seeks to explain what exists. A well-conducted experiment will prove that certain plants thrive in sunlight, gravity pulls objects to the Earth, oil and water do not mix, and so forth.

When solving an open-ended, authentic problem, there is no one right answer or known truth. The solution to the global water crisis does not yet exist. Inventions and innovations are, by nature, that which does not yet exist. While various experiments and the use of the scientific method are necessary in solving open-ended problems, the overarching approach should be guided by a design process. A design process seeks to create that which does not exist. IDE Corp.'s (www.idecorp.com) design process is depicted in Figure 9.2 and explained in what follows.

Figure 9.2. IDE Corp.'s Design Process

(c) 2016, IDE Corp. - reprinted with permission

- ◆ Formulate—Think through the problem and ensure that you understand it fully. Ask yourself:
  - – What is the reality?
  - – How does this situation affect others?
  - – What is the ideal situation?
  - – What must it be like for those affected by this problem?
  - – What would happen if the problem was not solved?
- ◆ Explore—Delving into the problem more deeply, search for existing information, conduct experiments, and gather as much knowledge as you can about the various aspects of the problem. This is where subject-area content learning takes place. Ask yourself:
  - – What do you know?
  - – What do you need to know?
  - – How will you learn that?
  - – What are some reliable sources you can use to gather your information?
  - – Who would be affected by solving or ignoring the problem?
- ◆ Ideate—Generate as many possible solutions as you can, being careful not to judge any. Just let your creativity flow. Ask yourself:
  - – What are some solutions to the problem?
  - – Do you need to explore further before you can create a solution?

- Sift—Consider all the ideas generated to see which, if any, would work. Ask yourself:
  - Which ideas could work?
  - Which ideas are feasible?
  - What are the possible unintended consequences of each idea?
  - What else could go wrong?
  - Do you need to explore and/or ideate further? Do you need more ideas?

- Simulate—Once you have an idea you think will work, give it wings! Create a prototype, mock-up, sample, model, or anything else that will allow you to test it to build your confidence that it is a viable solution. Ask yourself:
  - How might you create a prototype or mock-up that you can test out?
  - How can you test your solution?
  - What did you learn from this prototype that will help you with the next one?
  - Were you able to test your solution?
  - Should you return to sift or ideate further solutions?

- Advocate—No idea will change the world if it isn't implemented or shared. The final step of the design process is to promote your idea: share it with an appropriate audience. Ask yourself:
  - Who needs to know this; who is your audience?
  - Who can help you put your ideas into action?
  - How will you share your ideas (a video, website, model, etc.)?
  - Where will/can your ideas end up?

While the design process is linear in that you must move through the steps in order, at any point, you can return to a prior step. Once you simulate your chosen idea, you may find it doesn't work. At that point you would return to either sift through other ideas, ideate some more, or explore the topic further.

Given that in the *Learner-Active, Technology-Infused Classroom*, students are always working to solve real-world problems, offer them a design process to guide their work. Whether they're developing a prototype for a space vehicle for Mars, a poem, or a plan for running a food drive, students can use a design process to guide their process. The discipline of the process and the individual, purposeful steps will help build executive function and increase likelihood of success.

Equity-Focused Instruction

Not all students come to school with the same background, skills, learning styles, or prerequisite knowledge. Educational equity involves providing students with the supports that they individually need to succeed. Instructional lessons delivered to the entire class do not necessarily take into account the differences among students, and if they do, the presenter is hard pressed to meet the needs of all students from the front of the room.

A classroom provides students with **resources** (such as audio recordings, learning centers, texts, and videos), **tools for learning** (such as calculators, computers, manipulatives, and rulers), and **opportunities for instruction** (such as *learning activities*, *peer expert* assistance, teachers' facilitation, and teachers' lessons). Equality means offering all students the same resources, tools, and opportunities; equity means offering each student the resources, tools, and opportunities that student needs to succeed. While one student might need an auditory explanation of a concept, another might need a visual to accompany any description. While one student might easily follow a *how-to sheet* to learn a skill, another student who lacks strong executive function might need additional visuals and chunking of content. While one student may access a *learning activity* on a skill listed on the *analytic rubric*, another might be missing a prerequisite skill and first need instruction in that skill. While one student might learn a skill after one instructional lesson, another might need two or three. While one student might engage immediately with a *learning activity*, another might need support in feeling emotionally safe to engage.

The level of differentiation and individual activity inherent in the *Learner-Active, Technology-Infused Classroom* allows each student to engage in the *learning activities* needed and progress at a pace that will maximize success. With teacher facilitation being the predominant mode of student–teacher interaction, individual students are more able to receive the instructional guidance and support they need. Given students learn to schedule their own time—determining what, how, and when they will learn—they are empowered to select the resources, tools, and opportunities to learn that would most benefit them. For those who lack the experience or executive function to make such choices, a teacher's *small-group mini-lesson* guides them through the process to design their schedules.

Regardless of students' abilities or background, all students deserve the right to learn through compelling problems, seeking solutions that require higher-order thinking. All too often, students who lack executive function or grade-level skills are relegated to endless practice of lower-order skills, which can be boring and demoralizing. Beginning the study of a unit with a problem to solve allows all students to set their sights on finding a solution; equity means providing all students with the supports they need to achieve at high levels. The "bar" is the same, whether inside the classroom or outside the classroom; equity means providing each student with the differentiated supports needed to achieve. Using problem-based learning, students can also engage in solving problems related to equity issues in their community and the world at large.

The *Learner-Active, Technology-Infused Classroom*, with its emphasis on problem-based learning and student voice and choice, facilitated by a masterful teacher, is the quintessential educational equity environment.

Universal Design for Learning (UDL)

UDL was developed by David Rose, a Harvard School of Education lecturer and the chief education officer at the Center for Applied Special Technology (cast.org). It is "a framework to improve and optimize teaching and learning for all people based on scientific insights into how humans learn" (cast.org). At the core is a philosophical commitment to access for all. A great metaphor I've heard for understanding that is the difference between a retrofitted building and the Guggenheim museum. Years ago, buildings were constructed with the assumption that all people were ambulatory, thus many included stairs. The Americans With Disabilities Act of 1990 ushered in a time when buildings were then retrofitted with ramps, as an afterthought, in order to provide those with disabilities access. Frank Lloyd Wright's design of the Guggenheim Museum, whether intentional or not, provided access for all in its design. One navigates the museum via a spiral ramp, which has a grade of three degrees. Thus, the Guggenheim, built in 1959, was constructed with access for all in mind. Classroom curriculum, throughout history, has been designed with the academically able in mind. When students are deemed to have academic disabilities, teachers make modifications and accommodations (instructional retrofitting). What would it look like if classroom curriculum were designed with access for all in mind?

If you are thinking the *Learner-Active, Technology-Infused Classroom*, you're right! The intent of its instructional design is to provide all students with the instructional resources, tools, and instructional opportunities they need to succeed. As you design your *activity list*, you take into account learners of all learning styles and cognitive levels and offer appropriate *learning activities*.

The UDL framework addresses affective networks (the why of learning, or engagement), recognition networks (the what of learning, or representation), and strategic networks (the how of learning, or action and expression.)

The UDL guidelines for addressing these three networks include, as just a sampling, providing options for recruiting interest (choice and autonomy; relevance, value, and authenticity; and minimized threats and distractions); providing options for perception (customizing the display of information, alternatives for auditory information, alternatives for visual information); and providing options for executive functions (goal setting, planning and strategy development, and progress monitoring). As you review the full list of guidelines at cast.org, you will see that the *Learner-Active, Technology-Infused Classroom* is the ultimate UDL learning environment.

English Language Learners

Students who do not speak the native language of the classroom environment need additional supports to maximize their achievement. They benefit from visual cues; scaffolding allowing them to transition, at times using their native language, such as in journal writing; supports for understanding culturally unique expressions, which might include videos or pictures explaining terms such as "drive up the wall" or "piece of cake"; and engaging in small-group work where they are continually hearing the language and may be willing to speak in a more risk-free environment. Three obvious advantages of the *Learner-Active, Technology-Infused Classroom* for ELLs is that the level of individualized learning and differentiation allows students to receive the instructional supports each needs; the classroom is a social environment that exposes students to a significant amount of spoken language, including that of peers; and the framework lends itself to a teacher trained to support ELLs engaging with students in the classroom through one-on-one facilitation and *small-group mini-lessons* as well as partnering with the teacher to design customized *analytic rubrics*, *activity lists*, *learning activities*, and the like. Learning is social, and students learn well from one another. There is not a learning environment more socially oriented than the *Learner-Active, Technology-Infused Classroom*. ELLs will thrive in a well-run, *Learner-Active, Technology-Infused Classroom*.

The Flipped Classroom

Some equate the *Learner-Active, Technology-Infused Classroom* with the flipped classroom, but they are, in fact, different approaches. The flipped classroom seeks to reverse the actions of the conventional classroom in which teachers deliver content through classroom lectures and students engage further and practice at home. In the flipped classroom, students watch video lectures, collaborate with others through digital venues, and research information at home; they then engage in discussions and other activities to deepen their understanding of content in the classroom.

In the *Learner-Active, Technology-Infused Classroom*, all *learning activities* take place in the classroom, where assistance from the teacher is readily available. However, aligned with a key goal of the flipped classroom, students do not sit and listen to teachers' lectures, and content is not presented primarily by the teacher. Rather, the teacher develops a comprehensive, differentiated collection of *learning activities* that offer alternative ways for students to grapple with content, with teacher-directed lessons being one of the options.

Both models utilize technology, though the *Learner-Active, Technology-Infused Classroom* relies more on the use of technology in the classroom than outside of the classroom. Both models give students more responsibility for their own learning, with the flipped classroom focusing on student responsibility at home to complete key activities and the *Learner-Active, Technology-Infused Classroom* focusing on students managing all of their activities, in class and at home. The key paradigm shifts involving "felt need" (beginning a unit with an authentic problem-based task) and "Teacher as Bridge Builder" (allowing students to manage their individual learning path) are also unique to the *Learner-Active, Technology-Infused Classroom*.

The Virtual *Learner-Active, Technology-Infused Classroom*

The *Learner-Active, Technology-Infused Classroom* can easily be implemented as a virtual classroom. *Benchmark lessons* would be offered through either live video conference sessions or pre-recorded videos. *Small-group mini-lessons* would be offered through live video conference sessions. In more conventional virtual learning environments, students digitally submit assignments and await teacher feedback. In the *Learner-Active, Technology-Infused Classroom*, teachers actively facilitate learning as students are engaged in *learning activities*, meaning they would review work in progress and, in a cloud-based environment, offer comments directly in student documents. It is important, therefore, to select an online environment that allows for that level of virtual teacher facilitation.

Gifted Learners

While many students in school may be intelligent and high achievers, few are truly gifted. The former are easily served in the *Learner-Active, Technology-Infused Classroom*; truly gifted people (approximately one percent of the population) can be well served in the *Learner-Active, Technology-Infused Classroom* if teachers recognize the attributes and needs of gifted learners. While gifted learners possess many unique attributes, such as a love of problem solving, strong vocabulary, and abstract thinking, most of their attributes are addressed in the overall structures and strategies inherent in the *Learner-Active, Technology-Infused Classroom*. Here we will consider those that require a specific understanding on the part of the teacher:

♦ A propensity to daydream—One of the attributes of gifted people is creativity, which is not always nurtured in school but fits well with the problem-based nature of the *Learner-Active, Technology-Infused Classroom*. One of the habits of highly creative people is daydreaming (Kaufman & Gregoire, 2015), which does not tend to align well with teachers' expectations for learners. It is important to allow gifted students the time to wander in their thoughts.

♦ An interest in doing things differently—Your gifted learners will be the ones to recommend alternative *ALUs, learning activities*, classroom structures, and the like. As long as you are comfortable and their ideas are in line with the underlying paradigms and principles of the *Learner-Active, Technology-Infused Classroom*, let them! If you are not able or willing to allow them to pursue an idea, be honest as to why not.

♦ High levels of frustration—Your gifted learners may exhibit frustration and a temper when having difficulty meeting performance standards. While the *facilitation roadmap* would indicate that in cases of extreme frustration, you should provide direct instruction, this may not be the case with gifted learners. Noticing when the gifted learner is reaching a level of frustration and intervening is an important first step. Talk the student through the situation, offering them perspective and helping them develop a plan for working through the difficult situation.

♦ Wide interests—Gifted learners can appear to be distracted by ideas and unfocused in their work at times. That is because their minds are taking in everything, making connections, and exploring, most likely far beyond the content you've set before them. In most cases, the gifted learner will be able to meet your expectations and keep running with multiple ideas and interests. However, in the case that the giftedness prevents the student from focusing on the basic content-related requirements, use a graphic organizer that has those requirements in one area, with other areas for the student to capture ideas and questions to which to return after addressing the requirements.

These are just a few attributes to consider. If you have gifted learners in your classroom, seek out a more complete list of attributes and consider how they will be addressed in the *Learner-Active, Technology-Infused Classroom*.

Executive Function

The *Learner-Active, Technology-Infused Classroom* is a veritable executive function playground. As outlined in *Building Executive Function: The Missing Link to Student Achievement* (Sulla, 2018), executive function skills are necessary for key life skills: conscious control, engagement, collaboration, empowerment, efficacy, and leadership. These key life skills are aligned with the intended outcomes of the *Learner-Active, Technology-Infused Classroom*.

Students build significant executive function through the structures of the *Learner-Active, Technology-Infused Classroom*. Consider that when students manage a *two-pocket folder*, they must store and manipulate visual information, identify same and different, follow multiple steps, hold on to information while considering other information, categorize information, shift focus from one event to another, catch and correct errors, think about multiple concepts simultaneously, set goals, manage time, work toward a goal, organize actions and thoughts, consider future consequences in light of current action, attend to an activity, focus, concentrate, think before acting, initiate a task, persist in a task, monitor performance, and reflect on goals. That's twenty-one executive function skills exercised in just one of the structures of the *Learner-Active, Technology-Infused Classroom*. Similar lists could be generated for all of the structures. Putting students in charge of their own learning builds tremendous executive function.

While one might argue that students need executive function in order to function successfully in a *Learner-Active, Technology-Infused Classroom*, in fact, this classroom model builds executive function every day. Returning to the structure of the *two-pocket folder*, if students are weak in executive function, they would attend a *small-group mini-lesson* in which the teacher would walk them through daily folder management. The teacher would provide checklists or *how-to sheets* that they could learn to use to gradually take responsibility for their *two-pocket folders* on their own, as they build the necessary executive function skills.

The problem-based nature of the *Learner-Active, Technology-Infused Classroom* builds the executive function skills of defining a problem, analyzing, creating mental images, generating possible solutions, anticipating, predicting outcomes, evaluating, being creative, applying former approaches to new situations, changing perspective, seeing multiple sides to a situation, being open to others' points of view, and more.

A masterful teacher with a strong working knowledge of executive function can support students in building executive function through the various structures and strategies of the *Learner-Active, Technology-Infused Classroom*.

Mapping Other Instructional Approaches to the *Learner-Active, Technology-Infused Classroom*

The *Learner-Active, Technology-Infused Classroom* is a framework for putting students in charge of their own learning, focusing on engagement, empowerment, and efficacy. Most instructional approaches aimed at specific content mastery fit within this framework. If you are looking to stay true to the *Learner-Active, Technology-Infused Classroom*, before adopting curricular programs and approaches, consider the extent to which they align to two of the key paradigm shifts:

- *Felt Need*—The *Learner-Active, Technology-Infused Classroom* uses a *problem-based task* to launch a unit of study, focusing on the application aspect of content mastery at the start of the unit. Does the curricular program or approach in question allow for the development of a problem-based task to serve as the core of the unit?

- *Teacher as Bridge Builder*—The *Learner-Active, Technology-Infused Classroom* allows students significant choice and voice, with the teacher creating the venue through which that should happen. It is students who decide how they will learn, with the teacher's guidance. It is students who decide when they will tackle various *learning activities*, *practice activities*, and application of content in designing the final product or performance. Any program or instructional approach, for example, that requires all students to study the content at a particular time of the day would significantly conflict with student voice and choice in the classroom. While some programs may presume all students will be engaged in studying the subject area at the same time (since the *Learner-Active, Technology-Infused Classroom* is unique in the concept of allowing students to study different subject areas at times that make sense to them), that does not necessarily mean that you could not apply the principles and strategies of a particular program or approach within the framework of the *Learner-Active, Technology-Infused Classroom*.

The *Learner-Active, Technology-Infused School*

Once all of the teachers in a school are running *Learner-Active, Technology-Infused Classrooms*, you have a *Learner-Active, Technology-Infused School*! It's important to realize that as students are progressing through the grade levels, entirely immersed in this framework, they need to have the structures becoming more complex as they go. Just as standards increase in complexity from year to year, so should the structures of the *Learner-Active, Technology-Infused Classroom*.

For example, ultimately the *analytic rubric* should drive students' action. As they see, for example, that their advertisement must include the use of idioms, they will have a *felt need* to learn about idioms and will pursue that learning. In the early grades and when first introduced to the *Learner-Active, Technology-Infused Classroom*, the *activity list* offers students choice, required, and optional activities for learning idioms. At some point, assuming adequate technology is available, the *activity list* can be eliminated and replaced by a hyperlinked rubric. On the *analytic rubric*, the term "idiom" would be hyperlinked to a page that contains choice, required, and optional activities. Students would recognize from the *analytic rubric* the need to learn about idioms rather than being prompted by the *activity list* and pursue that learning. At higher levels, most likely high school, students will be given fewer *learning activities* and instead build their resourcefulness to pursue learning absent of a clear structure. But for the purposes of this book, if students are learning in *Learner-Active, Technology-Infused Classrooms* from kindergarten, by fourth or fifth grade, you can move to reduce the dependency on the *activity list*.

As students progress through the grades, problems should become less defined so that students have more voice in specifically what they would like to pursue related to the problem. Eventually, students can become problem finders most of the time. After students have spent years addressing problems presented by the teacher, even though some may be open to student ideas, they will understand the nature of open-ended, authentic problems and be able to identify them on their own. Again, by fourth or fifth grade, you should be able to allow students to explore a content area to identify current problems they would like to solve. As students are more able to work effectively in the *Learner-Active, Technology-Infused Classroom*, you may feel comfortable having different groups of students pursuing different problems.

Rubrics, too, will become more open to student voice. You might offer several rows and have students design additional rows based on their interests. For example, in *Designer Pizza* (Appendix A), some students might decide they also want to calculate the menus in terms of percentages of pies, converting their fractions to percentages; some might want to create fractional options of other menu items; and so forth. Assuming the ideas are in line with content, as opposed to being peripheral and thus taking time away from the subject-area focus, let students have increased voice in their rubrics.

Students can play a greater role in self-assessment and reflection as the years progress. If students become familiar with the use of the *learning dashboard* in the early grades, they can build toward simply taking curricular standards and designing their own *learning dashboards*, thinking more deeply about what they need to accomplish. They will be better able to assess their progress and report to you on that, along with their future learning plans.

They will be better able to answer more metacognitive questions about their learning process. As the years progress, students should be challenged to think at much higher levels in the *Learner-Active, Technology-Infused Classroom*, given they've mastered the structures through which they learn.

In terms of the physical classroom, as the years progress, students should be given much more voice in the classroom setup; after all, it is their learning environment. Imagine having students walk into a room in which all of the furniture is stored in one area or in the hallway and the walls are blank. Given they know the way a *Learner-Active, Technology-Infused Classroom* runs, they could be responsible for working in groups to design aspects of the physical classroom and have teams discuss and reach consensus about setup.

Where you have multiple classrooms available, you could designate certain rooms for specific activities, allowing students to move freely among the classrooms and teachers to serve as a resource team to a greater number of students. You can have students take greater responsibility for the school outside of their classrooms, adding their voice to how the media center and cafeteria are used, hallways are decorated, and outside areas are landscaped and used.

You can create multiage classrooms in which students learn with those who are older and/or younger than them in the same classroom. Here's a radical thought: you can have students select their teachers based on their understanding of their learning needs, personalities, and interests.

Overall, you want to move toward greater student voice and less dependence on teacher-defined structures. Whereas choice is a matter of working from a set of possibilities created by the teacher, voice is a matter of designing those possibilities. As the years progress, teachers can put more of their effort into being critical resources and thought partners for students.

"Whereas choice is a matter of working from a set of possibilities created by the teacher, voice is a matter of designing those possibilities."

The *Learner-Active, Technology-Infused Classroom* Rubric

As you design your *Learner-Active, Technology-Infused Classroom*, you'll be happy to know there's a rubric to guide you. The journey to rethinking your classroom to break the mold and pave a new road for your students to change the world can be both exhilarating and daunting. Reading the book is a great first step. As for implementation, just start! It's a journey of one *ALU* at a time, one structure after another building to create a new special place called your classroom.

If you are not working directly with IDE Corp. consultants, you still have several ongoing resources to guide you, including my blog, YouTube channel, Twitter feed, Twitter chat, and other books—you can find links to each at nancysulla.com. You can also reference some *ALU* ideas and instructional planning tools, including the *LATIC Rubric*, as part of the free content available at www.ideportal.com.

In your first year of implementing a *Learner-Active, Technology-Infused Classroom*, do not even attempt to assess yourself with a rubric. Use this as a horizon line. In your second year, you can begin to self-assess and set goals from it. Figure 9.3 offers two rows from the area "Engaging the Learner" that address *how-to sheets* and *how-to videos* and *small-group mini-lessons*. Note that this rubric is different from the ones you'll be using with your students. It has three columns:

- Emerging is the place you'll flourish in for approximately three years, so be good with that! You could have an entire rubric around that one column. However, for our purposes, it's giving you the end goal. This is the column that explains everything you, as the teacher, will design, put in place, and execute. This column represents what you will do to create your *Learner-Active, Technology-Infused Classroom*. However, the goal of all that you do is to empower students to take charge of their own learning and move toward efficacy.

- Column two describes what students will do as a result of all of your effort in column one. If you've designed an effective *Learner-Active, Technology-Infused Classroom*, the students will visibly take charge of their own learning. So essentially, your students earn you the second-column score. They can only succeed, however, if you've put in place all the structures and strategies in the first column. In your third year of implementation, take a good look at this second column to see where your students are taking charge of their own learning. Where they may not be, return to the first column to see how you might modify your implementation. Ultimately, the goal is to build efficacious students who can partner with you to co-create the learning environment.

- Column three describes how students and teachers will create classroom structures and strategies together. This is your year five target, so you can begin looking at this column in year four. The reason you don't want to attempt to accomplish this in year one is that you and your students have to gain complete familiarity with and internalize the paradigm shifts of the *Learner-Active, Technology-Infused Classroom* first in order for third-column implementation to be accurate and successful.

Figure 9.3. The *Learner-Active, Technology-Infused Classroom* Rubric

		Emerging	Practitioner	Reflective Practitioner
Engaging the Learner	**How-To Sheets and Videos**	the teacher(s): ☐ designs how-to sheets, podcasts, and screencasts on concepts and skills students will need in order to address the problem-based task (learning activities) ☐ provides directions that are detailed, easy-to-follow, and designed to ensure success ☐ includes graphics and screenshots to enhance learning	the students: ☐ seek out and use how-to resources to learn skills and concepts as needed ☐ identify and locate additional "how to" resources as needed both in and out of the classroom ☐ design how-to sheets and videos once they've mastered a skill	meets all of the criteria in the *practitioner* column plus: ☐ students demonstrate a deeper understanding of what makes a quality how-to podcast, screencast and vodcast by incorporating wait time/pauses and voice inflection to capture the listener's attention ☐ teachers and students contribute to a collection of how-to resources that ensure all students can learn prerequisite, requisite, and advanced content through a variety of modalities
	Small-Group, Mini-Lessons	the teacher(s): ☐ designs narrowly targeted skill acquisition small-group, mini-lessons that last 5 – 15 minutes ☐ establishes a sign-up procedure with a maximum of 6 students and overflow slots ☐ makes students aware of small-group, mini-lessons in advance so that they can sign up and/or be "invited" to them ☐ allows for small-group, mini-lessons to be offered by various adults who work in the classroom	the students: ☐ identify their need to attend a small-group, mini-lesson(s) ☐ use a "checkout" quiz or other assessment in order to attend an advanced-content (challenge) small-group, mini-lesson ☐ seek out opportunities for skill practice following a small-group, mini-lesson	meets all of the criteria in the *practitioner* column plus ☐ generate requests for small-group, mini-lessons ☐ serve as appropriately vetted peer experts who offer some small-group, mini-lessons ☐ teacher and student develop guidelines for outside experts to offer small-group, mini-lessons

portion of LATIC Rubric from www.ideportal.com, copyright 2017, IDE Corp. — www.idecorp.com

Brain surgeons have, as their goal, performing successful brain surgery; however, they do not attempt this in their first year of residency. They may, in fact, engage in five years of residency toward becoming masterful at brain surgery. So consider this rubric your five-year residency program for designing your own amazing, world-changing, *Learner-Active, Technology-Infused Classroom*. Read, design, implement, read again, reflect, redesign, and enjoy every minute of it. The destination is rewarding; but the journey is life changing.

RECAP

Get your students off to a good start with a *priming plan*. Develop a series of activities for the first week or two of school, including those that:

+ Introduce students to the structures of your classroom;

+ Prime students for success, building hope, confidence, and optimism;

+ Gather assessment data.

The *Learner-Active, Technology-Infused Classroom* is a framework that can serve as the backdrop for most other programs, including:

+ RTI/MTSS;

+ The co-teaching/inclusive classroom;

+ STEM/STEAM;

+ Design process;

+ Equity-focused instruction;

+ Universal Design for Learning (UDL);

+ English language learners;

+ The flipped classroom;

+ The virtual *Learner-Active, Technology-Infused Classroom*;

+ Gifted learners;

+ Executive function;

+ Other instructional approaches that can be mapped to the key paradigm shifts.

Once enough teachers are implementing the *Learner-Active, Technology-Infused Classroom*, you can begin to address the unique nature of a *Learner-Active, Technology-Infused School*. This means developmentally modifying structures across the years to match the growing understanding of the model by your students.

Over the course of the next five years, keep reflecting and revising, using the LATIC Rubric available at www.ideportal.com. Keep in mind that the columns indicate:

- ♦ What you will do;

- ♦ What your students will do when they are empowered;

- ♦ What you and your students will co-create as they build efficacy.

REFERENCES

Cornwall, G. (2017). *Jabari jumps*. Somerville, MA: Candlewick Press.

Kaufman, S. B., & Gregoire, C. (2015). *Wired to create: Unraveling the mysteries of the creative mind*. New York, NY: Penguin.

Sulla, N. (2018). *Building executive function: The missing link to student achievement*. New York, NY: Routledge.

Appendix A
Designer Pizza

Many pizza shops today offer a variety of pizzas by the slice. So, for example, you could purchase a slice of pepperoni pizza and a slice of Hawaiian pizza. Typically, however, round pizzas are cut into eight slices. What if you wanted a larger piece of everything pizza and smaller pieces of cheese pizza and buffalo chicken pizza? Maybe pizza shops should consider more customization of pizza purchases!

Develop a quality plan you could present to a local pizza shop or chain to innovate pizza purchases. Offer a variety of types of pizza slices of various sizes based on some initial market research to determine popular pizza preferences.

Design "Meal Options" of slice combinations, for example: one-eighth slice buffalo chicken, one-fifth slice pepperoni, and one-twelfth slices of cheese pizza.

Once you develop your plan, work as a team to select meal options to combine into one plan. Identify your target pizza shop and determine their full-size pie prices to calculate menu costs. Start designing your menus!

Designer Pizza *Rubric*

	Novice	Apprentice	Practitioner	Expert
Market Research: Survey	◆ survey offers at least six different types of pizzas ◆ survey designed to gather top three choices per respondent	◆ survey offers at least nine different types of pizzas ◆ survey designed to gather top three choices per respondent ◆ survey conducted to gather data from at least ten people	◆ survey offers at least twelve different types of pizzas ◆ survey designed to gather top three choices per respondent ◆ survey conducted to gather data from at least twenty people	all of *Practitioner* plus includes one additional survey question whose data can be graphed
Market Research: Bar Graph of Survey Results	includes survey results with data labels	◆ includes survey results with: ◆ data labels ◆ key of different colors for different pizza types ◆ an analysis statement of the most and least popular pizza types	◆ includes survey results with: ◆ data labels ◆ key of different colors for different pizza types ◆ number of votes per slice ◆ data ordered from most to least popular ◆ at least five analysis statements from the data	all of *Practitioner* plus includes percentages for each pizza type

(Appendix A continues on next page.)

	Novice	Apprentice	Practitioner	Expert
Pizza Slice Options	◆ based on data, offers three+ types of pizzas, each with a specified slice size ◆ offers three different slice sizes: fifths, quarters, and thirds	◆ based on data, offers five+ types of pizzas, each with a specified slice size ◆ offers at least four different slice sizes, including fifths, quarters, and thirds	◆ based on data, offers eight+ types of pizzas, each with a specified slice size ◆ offers at least six different slice sizes, including fifths, quarters, and thirds ◆ lists slice offerings from smallest to largest	all of *Practitioner* plus includes at least two different size options per pizza type
Menu Offerings	◆ offers at least three meal options with two or more slices each ◆ includes total size of each menu offering ◆ includes "Pizza Designer's Log" with accurate calculations of meal size, showing all work	◆ offers at least eight meal options, at least four of which offer three or more slice combinations ◆ includes total size of each menu offering, properly reduced to lowest terms ◆ includes "Pizza Designer's Log" with accurate calculations of meal size, showing all work	◆ offers at least twelve meal options, at least eight of which offer three or more slice combinations ◆ includes total size of each menu offering, properly reduced to lowest terms ◆ includes "Pizza Designer's Log" with accurate calculations of meal size and price, showing all work	all of *Practitioner* plus either ◆ some menu items that offer five+ slice combinations that total exactly one pie or ◆ caloric intake for at least three of the meals
Test Marketing	◆ tests the plan by accurately calculating the cost of orders from three classmates who select three slices to make up a custom meal ◆ includes all work in "Pizza Designer's Log"	◆ tests the plan by accurately calculating the cost of orders from six classmates who select from three to four slices to make up a custom meal ◆ includes all work in "Pizza Designer's Log"	◆ tests the plan by accurately calculating the cost of orders from ten classmates who select from three to five slices to make up a custom meal ◆ includes all work in "Pizza Designer's Log"	all of *Practitioner* plus includes cost savings for at least three classmates had they had to purchase each desired slice as an eighth of a pie

How-To Sheets	Learning Centers	How-To Videos/Podcasts
◆ Designing a survey ◆ Conducting a survey ◆ Tallying survey results ◆ Creating a bar graph ◆ Finding the least common denominator ◆ Reducing fractions to lowest terms	◆ Ordering fractions ◆ Adding fractions ◆ Reducing fractions to lowest terms ◆ Exploring pizza menu items	◆ Adding fractions ◆ Subtracting fractions ◆ Ordering fractions ◆ Reducing fractions to lowest terms ◆ Creating bar graphs ◆ Dividing with money ◆ Multiplying with money
Benchmark Lessons ◆ Why market research? ◆ What bar graphs tell us ◆ Fractions: parts of a whole ◆ Ordering fractions ◆ Adding and subtracting fractions ◆ Calculating cost	**Designer Pizza** **Scaffold for Learning**	**Small-Group Mini-Lessons** ◆ Creating a survey ◆ Creating bar graphs ◆ Adding fractions ◆ Subtracting fractions ◆ Reducing fractions to lowest terms ◆ Ordering fractions ◆ Calculating percentages
Interactive Websites ◆ Shodor: fraction sorter ◆ Math is fun: interactive fractions ◆ Visual fractions: fraction designer	**Peer Tutoring** ◆ Adding and subtracting fractions ◆ Simplifying fractions ◆ Creating a bar graph	**Technology Uses** ◆ Designing survey: medium ◆ Generating bar graph ◆ IXL ◆ Spreadsheet as cost calculator
Homework ◆ Conduct survey ◆ Generate bar graphs of household items ◆ Practice: add and subtract fractions ◆ Practice: simplify fractions	**Individual Tasks** ◆ Design and conduct survey ◆ Generate bar graph ◆ Learning activities for fraction computation ◆ Create pizza menu	**Group Tasks** ◆ Reviewing group members' surveys ◆ Analyzing group data ◆ Checking group members' calculations ◆ Combining group menus for a pitch to a pizza shop

Designer Pizza *Content Facilitation Grid*

M mastered PE peer expert R needs reinforcement HW needs homework ML needs small-group mini-lesson Student Name	Identifies fractional parts of 1/2, 1/3, and 1/4	Compares fractions using < , > or =	Identifies numerator and denominator	Adds fractions with like denominators	Subtracts fractions with like denominators	Identifies the least common denominator between two or more fractions	Adds fractions with unlike denominators	Subtracts fractions with unlike denominators	Orders fractions from least to greatest	Subtracts fractions from a whole number	Reduces a fraction to lowest terms	Reduces an improper fraction to a mixed number

Designer Pizza *Facilitation Questions*

Comprehension Questions
What is the least common denominator? What must be true in order to add or subtract fractions?

Application Questions
How do you find the least common denominator between two fractions? Three? How does _____ fraction relate to the whole? Why is a bar graph the best way to represent this data? Is there another graphical representation you could have used instead of a bar graph?

Connection Questions
How does adding and subtracting fractions relate to something outside of school? Outside of designing a pizza, where else would you order fractions? Why is surveying people prior to designing the menu important?

Synthesis Questions
How would the fraction change if you doubled the order? Tripled it? How could people split the cost among them? If you would have doubled the number of people surveyed, would the data be relatively the same?

Metacognitive Questions
What was the most difficult part of this task for you? Is there another way that you could have solved that question? Explain your thought process in arriving at that solution.

Appendix B
A Butterfly Garden

Have you ever seen butterflies in person or on video? Have you ever been to a butterfly garden? Butterflies are beautiful to look at, adding wonderful color to our world. They are also helpful to the plants and animals around them, and they help pollinate plants that produce food for us. Butterflies, however, demand some very special host plants in order to live during the different stages of their life cycle; and those plants are on the decline. With increasing habitat loss, butterflies are finding fewer and fewer places with the plants they need to thrive. This is resulting in the quasi-extinction of butterflies. The good news is, you can help!

Explore butterflies and the various plants that will attract butterflies native to our area. Design a butterfly garden that someone in the community could plant and that we could plant at the school to attract butterflies and help them thrive. Spread the word and educate others about the threat to the butterfly population.

A Butterfly Garden *Rubric*

Design Process Journal *(each group member submits a journal to support the garden plan)*				
	Novice	**Apprentice**	**Practitioner**	**Expert**
Formulate	states the problem to be solved and why it is important to solve it	describes the problem to be solved, why it is important to solve it, and known causes	describes: ❏ the problem ❏ known causes ❏ how other living beings are affected ❏ what will happen if we do not solve it	all of *Practitioner* plus: includes facts and statistics to show how the problem has worsened over time
Explore	includes relevant information from reading one nonfiction book on butterflies	includes: ❏ at least two questions to be answered through reading ❏ relevant information from reading at least two nonfiction books and at least one fiction book on butterflies	includes: ❏ at least five questions to be answered through reading ❏ relevant information from reading at least three nonfiction books on butterflies ❏ relevant information from reading at least two fiction books on butterflies ❏ information on and sketch of the life cycle of butterflies ❏ list of plants that attract butterflies, noting which grow in the local climate	all of *Practitioner* plus: includes a table to use while reading to write down ❏ questions that come to mind to answer and then ❏ the answers, once found
Ideate	includes at least one idea to use in designing the garden	includes a list of at least three different ideas to use in designing the garden	includes: ❏ at least three different ideas to use in designing the garden with why the idea will be good for attracting butterflies ❏ at least three different ways to convince people to build a butterfly garden	all of *Practitioner* plus: includes sketches of ideas for gardens

(Appendix B continues on next page.)

Design Process Journal *(each group member submits a journal to support the garden plan)*				
	Novice	**Apprentice**	**Practitioner**	**Expert**
Sift	a table (designed by the group) with each group member's ideas and the group's thoughts on which could work	includes: ❑ a table (designed by the group) with each group member's ideas and the group's thoughts on which could work ❑ notes from group discussion on favorite idea for each of the two categories	includes: ❑ a table (designed by the group) with each group member's ideas and ❑ how feasible each is ❑ what could go wrong ❑ notes from group discussion on favorite idea for each of the two categories with pros and cons for each ❑ signature of all group members indicating the decision was reached through consensus	all of *Practitioner* plus: includes a list of at least two experts who might be able to offer an opinion on the garden plan
Simulate	includes sketch of drawing of garden with all plants labeled	includes: ❑ sketch of drawing of garden with all plants labeled ❑ plants listed with average height for each	includes: ❑ sketch of drawing of garden with all plants labeled ❑ plants listed with average height and sun requirement for each ❑ notes on why each plant was chosen along with evidence supporting it	all of *Practitioner* plus: timeline for plant growth from seed to when butterflies will be drawn to the garden
Advocate	includes list of people with whom to share the garden plan	includes description of chosen audience type and list of people (of this audience type) with whom to share the garden plan	includes: ❑ description of chosen audience type to receive the garden plan ❑ list of at least three people with whom to share the garden plan ❑ at least one organization that might fund or build a butterfly garden	all of *Practitioner* plus: records short video file with thoughts from the designers to send as well

| Evidence of Revisiting Steps | includes notes indicating a return to a previous step | ☐ labels notes for each step in the design process
☐ includes arrows in the notes to indicate the need to return to a former step and why | ☐ labels notes for each step in the design process
☐ includes arrows in the notes to indicate the design process path with arrows to show return to a former step with explanation as to why | all of *Practitioner* plus: includes reflection on how the process went and what could have been done differently at any of the steps to make it go more smoothly |

Garden Plan *(the group submits one plan signed by all group members to acknowledge this is their best work):*

	Novice	Apprentice	Practitioner	Expert
Introduction	explanation of why someone should build a butterfly garden	one to two paragraphs that build a case for building a butterfly garden, using facts and statistics	☐ one to two paragraphs that build a case for building a butterfly garden, using facts and statistics ☐ organizational structure with supporting reasons	all of *Practitioner* plus: message is clearly tailored for the intended audience through various techniques
Butterfly Life Cycle	includes stages of the butterfly life cycle	includes stages that clearly show the butterfly at each stage and arrows from one stage to the next	includes all stages of the life cycle with: ☐ accurate image of butterfly in each stage ☐ arrows from one stage to the next ☐ accurate and neat labels ☐ approximate length of time for each stage	all of *Practitioner* plus: includes life cycle of one of the plants with a paragraph about similarities and differences
Garden Size	scale drawing (using grid) of garden layout	☐ scale drawing (using grid) of garden layout ☐ accurate dimensions for all sides	☐ scale drawing (using grid) of garden layout ☐ accurate dimensions for all sides ☐ accurately calculated perimeter ☐ accurately calculated area	all of *Practitioner* plus: includes garden that is an irregular polygon

(Appendix B continues on next page.)

Garden Plan *(the group submits one plan signed by all group members to acknowledge this is their best work):*

	Novice	Apprentice	Practitioner	Expert
Garden Plants	list of garden plants to purchase and plant	❑ list of a variety of garden plants to purchase and plant that complement one another ❑ plants included on drawing, labeled neatly	❑ list of a variety of garden plants to purchase and plant that complement one another ❑ plants included on drawing, labeled neatly ❑ written description of plants and where in the garden to plant each, along with planting directions (i.e., depth of planting, distance from other plants, etc.)	all of *Practitioner* plus: includes elements other than plants
Garden Cost	budget with approximate unit pricing for each plant, soil, fencing, and any other garden needs	accurate calculations for all materials and plants needed	❑ budget with approximate unit pricing for each plant, soil, fencing, and any other garden needs ❑ accurate calculations for all materials and plants needed ❑ accurate subtotal, state tax, and total	all of *Practitioner* plus: includes actual pricing and store or online site from which to purchase all that is needed to get started
Addressing the Audience	statement addressing the specific audience for whom the garden plan is intended	some evidence of wording, images, brochure decoration, etc. to address the specific audience for whom the garden plan is intended	evidence of wording, images, brochure decoration, etc. throughout to address the specific audience for whom the garden plan is intended	all of *Practitioner* plus specific statements aimed at connecting the intended audience's interests and lives to the garden design

Appendix C
Using Numbers and
Words to Feed Others

Sadly, some families don't have enough to eat every day. There are places that help to give them food. These places are called food pantries. Food pantries give food to people when they don't have enough food at home. People and companies donate food throughout the year.

This month it is our turn to help stock a local food pantry. For the next few weeks, we will be collecting food to share. This will include canned fruits and vegetables, dairy, snacks, and more. We will need to let our family and friends know what foods we need. To make sure we have enough variety, we will keep a count of what has already been brought in and decide what types of food we still want to collect. Let's show our community we care.

Using Numbers and Words to Feed Others
Rubric for the Food Collection Letter

	I am Working on It!	I Did It!	I Did It And . . .
Food List	I wrote a list of foods we can collect.	I wrote a list of at least ten different foods we can collect ❑ I did it! I chose foods that will not spoil over the next month. ❑ I did it!	I made sure my foods are healthy.
Food List Categories	I put each of the foods I listed in the correct food plate category.	I put each of the foods I listed in the correct food plate category. ❑ I did it! I used my list to create a sample meal using the food plate. ❑ I did it!	I identified foods that fell into more than one category on the food plate.
My Opinion	I wrote a sentence about why people should donate to help us collect the foods on our food list.	I wrote at least two sentences about why people should donate to help us collect the foods on our food list. ❑ I did it!	I explained why the different types of food are important.
Pictures for My Letter	I drew a picture of the food items.	I drew pictures of at least three food items with numbers of what we hope to collect. ❑ I did it!	I drew a picture of the food plate with at least one food item in each category and numbers of what we hope to collect.

Using Numbers and Words to Feed Others
Rubric for the Food Collection Tallying

	I am Working on It!	I Did It!	I Did It And . . .
Counting and Recording Donations	Each day, I count up to 100 foods when they are in rows and write down the total number.	Each day, I count up to 100 foods when they are in rows or when they are scattered and write down the total number. ☐ I did it!	Each day, I count up to 100 foods in rows or scattered and tell how many more we need to make our goal.
Comparing Donations to Food List	Each week, I count and record the number of foods collected for two food categories.	Each week, I count and record the number of foods collected for each food category. ☐ I did it!	Each week, I count and record the number of foods collected for each food category and write down how many more we collected for each.
Weekly Progress Report	Each week, I write one statement about how many items we collected for one or more categories.	Each week, I write at least three comparison statements about how many items we collected in various categories. ☐ I did it!	Each week, I write comparison statements for items collected and order them from least to most.

Appendix D
Can a Frog, Turtle, and Fish Help Us?

Funny Frog, Terrific Turtle, and Fast Fish live in a pond. They spend their time playing, eating, breathing, moving, sleeping, and more. Human beings live their lives in much the same way, but in a different place than a pond. Could Funny Frog, Terrific Turtle, and Fast Fish help us in our lives?

Human beings need to protect themselves from the weather. Some have to watch out for hurricanes, tornadoes, mudslides, hail, and very hot sunshine. They like to travel places in cars, trains, planes, and buses. They need to lift and carry things, run and jump, and more. So how might Funny Frog, Terrific Turtle, and Fast Fish help?

Explore and observe what Funny Frog, Terrific Turtle, and Fast Fish use their body parts to survive. Then design an invention to help human beings in some way that is based upon the body parts and abilities of a frog, turtle, and/or fish.

Can a Frog, Turtle, and Fish Help Us? *Body Parts Rubric*

	I am Working on It!	I Did It!	I Did It And . . .
Frog Drawing	I named at least four frog body parts.	I labeled at least four frog body parts. ❑ I did it! I wrote how they help the frog. ❑ I did it!	I made a chart of how each part is like or not like a human body part.
Turtle Drawing	I named at least four turtle body parts.	I labeled at least four turtle body parts. ❑ I did it! I wrote how they help the turtle. ❑ I did it!	I made a chart of how each part is like or not like a human body part.
Fish Drawing	I named at least four fish body parts.	I labeled at least four fish body parts. ❑ I did it! I wrote how they help the fish. ❑ I did it!	I made a chart of how each part is like or not like a human body part.

Can a Frog, Turtle, and Fish Help Us? *Invention Rubric*

	I am Working on It!	I Did It!	I Did It And . . .
Idea Chart	I made a chart of animal body parts.	I made a chart of at least ten animal body parts. ❑ I did it! I wrote about how they could help a human. ❑ I did it!	I included animals other than a frog, turtle, and fish on my chart.
Invention Drawing	I drew my invention to help humans.	I drew my invention to help humans. ❑ I did it! I wrote about how it came from what I learned about the body parts of animals. ❑ I did it!	I explained to the teacher why my invention is the best ever using at least three reasons.

Appendix E
Oh, The Places We Can Go!—Version A

What different places have you visited in our state? Have you visited other states? Have you visited other countries? Who determined the location of your last vacation?

What if you were in charge of planning your next family vacation? Where would you go and why?

This is your chance to plan a dream vacation from start to finish. There are so many aspects to consider, such as form of travel, where to stay, activities, and food expenses. Be thorough, because you never know if your dream vacation could become a reality!

Share your ideas with others! Create a brochure or presentation about your dream vacation to present to your family and others who might want to go. You might even want to send it to that location's Chamber of Commerce!

Rubric for The Places We Can Go! Part 1

	I Am Just Getting Started	I Am Working On It	I Did It!	I Did It And . . .
Brainstorming Notes	❑ I listed two possible places to visit. ❑ I explained my selection. ❑ I listed at least one book or website I used to gather notes.	❑ I listed three possible places to visit, including in other states. ❑ I explained my selection based on the interests of my family members. ❑ I listed at least two books or websites I used to gather notes.	❑ I listed four possible places, including in other states and other countries. ❑ I listed the pros and cons of each. ❑ I explained the selection based on the interests of my family members. ❑ I listed at least four relevant books and valid websites I used to gather notes.	I identified two similar locations and compared them with my selection. I included an explanation of my selection.
Map of Area	I created an original map with: ❑ a title ❑ the general outline of the area ❑ the location of the hotel	I created an original map with: ❑ a title ❑ compass rose ❑ landscape of area with landmarks (train station, landmark, museum, etc.) ❑ location of hotel	I created an original map with: ❑ a title ❑ compass rose ❑ landscape of the area with landmarks ❑ at least five labeled points of interest ❑ map key	I included one or more insets with details of an area that contains a point of interest.

Rubric for The Places We Can Go! Part 2

	Novice	Apprentice	Practitioner	Expert
Itinerary	I wrote an itinerary of the vacation, including: ❏ the location (city, state, country) ❏ distance from my home ❏ length of travel time	I wrote an itinerary of the vacation, including: ❏ the location (city, state, country) ❏ distance from my home ❏ times and dates for arrival and departure ❏ at least two activities with specified dates	I wrote an itinerary of the vacation with written descriptions, including: ❏ precise location ❏ distance from my home using the most precise standard unit ❏ relation, in terms of direction, to my home ❏ dates and times, to the nearest five minutes, for arrival and departure to hotel ❏ list of at least one activity per day with schedule for each day	I included at least two restaurants each for breakfast, lunch, and dinner, with the distance from the hotel, using the most precise measurement, and why I chose them.
Budget	I itemized costs for transportation and the hotel for entire duration of the vacation.	I itemized costs for the entire duration of the vacation, including: ❏ transportation ❏ hotel ❏ meals	I itemized costs and calculated the total cost for the family for the duration of the vacation, including: ❏ transportation ❏ hotel ❏ meals ❏ activities on the itinerary	I provided alternative activities for at least two activities and included cost comparisons.

Rubric for The Places We Can Go! Part 3

	Novice	Apprentice	Practitioner	Expert
Presentation of Information	❏ I stated an opinion as to why this vacation is worth taking. ❏ I included the map, itinerary, and budget. ❏ I explained some of the activities and the prices.	❏ I stated an opinion as to why this vacation is worth taking. ❏ I included the map, itinerary, and budget in a way that makes sense to the reader or viewer.	❏ I stated an opinion as to why this vacation is worth taking. ❏ I included several reasons for taking the vacation, using linking words to make connections between ideas. ❏ I included the map, itinerary, and budget in a way that makes sense to the reader or viewer, including an introduction for each. ❏ I explained the daily list of activities and prices, utilizing a chart, graph, or visual aid. ❏ I included a concluding statement. ❏ I included images of points of interest.	I included personal statements from my family members regarding selection (written or videotaped).

Appendix F
Oh, The Places We Can Go!—Version B

What different places have you visited in our state? Have you visited other states? Have you visited other countries? Who determined the location of your last vacation?

What if you were in charge of planning your next family vacation? Where would you go and why?

This is your chance to plan a dream vacation from start to finish. There are so many aspects to consider, such as form of travel, where to stay, activities, and food expenses. Be thorough, because you never know if your dream vacation could become a reality!

Share your ideas with others! Create a brochure or presentation about your dream vacation to present to your family and others who might want to go. You might even want to send it to that location's Chamber of Commerce!

Rubric for The Places We Can Go!

	Novice	Apprentice	Practitioner	Expert
Brainstorming Notes	includes ❑ two possible places ❑ explanation of selection ❑ at least one book or website used to gather notes	includes ❑ three possible places, including in other states ❑ explanation of selection based on the interests of all family members ❑ at least two books or websites used to gather notes	includes ❑ four possible places, including in other states and other countries ❑ pros and cons of each ❑ explanation of selection based on the interests of all family members ❑ at least four books or websites used to gather notes	all of *Practitioner* plus two similar locations with notes that compare and contrast them with the selection, including an explanation of selection
Original Map of Area	includes: ❑ a title ❑ the general outline of the area ❑ the location of hotel	includes: ❑ title ❑ compass rose ❑ landscape of area with landmarks (train station, landmark, museum, etc.) ❑ location of hotel	includes: ❑ title ❑ compass rose ❑ landscape of the area with landmarks ❑ at least five labeled points of interest ❑ map key	all of *Practitioner* plus includes one or more insets with details of an area that contains a point of interest
Itinerary	includes: ❑ location (city, state, country) ❑ distance from home ❑ length of travel time	includes: ❑ location (city, state, country) ❑ distance from home ❑ times and dates for arrival and departure ❑ at least two activities with specified dates	includes: ❑ precise location ❑ distance from my home using the most precise standard measurement ❑ relation, in terms of direction, to my home ❑ dates and times, to the nearest five minutes, for arrival and departure to hotel ❑ list of at least one activity per day with schedule for each day	all of *Practitioner* plus at least two restaurants each for breakfast, lunch, and dinner, with the distance from the hotel, using the most precise standard measurement, and why I chose them

(Appendix F continues on next page.)

	Novice	Apprentice	Practitioner	Expert
Budget	Itemizes costs for transportation and hotel for entire duration of vacation	Itemizes costs for entire duration of vacation, including: ❏ transportation to and from the destination ❏ hotel ❏ meals (three per day)	Itemizes costs and calculates total cost for the family for the duration of vacation, including: ❏ transportation to and from the destination and for each day ❏ hotel ❏ meals (three per day plus snacks) ❏ activities on the itinerary	All of *Practitioner* plus provides alternative activities for at least two activities that include cost comparisons
Presentation of Information	❏ states an opinion as to where to go on vacation ❏ includes the map, itinerary, and budget ❏ explains some of the activities and the prices	❏ states an opinion as to where to go and why this vacation is worth taking ❏ includes the map, itinerary, and budget in a way that makes sense to the reader or viewer	❏ states an opinion as to where to go and why this vacation is worth taking ❏ includes several reasons for taking the vacation, using linking words to make connections between ideas ❏ includes the map, itinerary, and budget in a way that makes sense to the reader or viewer, including an introduction for each ❏ explains the daily list of activities and prices, utilizing a chart, graph, or visual aid ❏ includes a concluding statement ❏ includes images of points of interest	all of *Practitioner* plus includes personal statements from family members regarding selection (written or videotaped)

Appendix G
A Place for Robots

Have you ever watched a movie or a cartoon in which robots can complete tasks in the place of humans? In the animated movie *WALL-E*, robots help humans after the Earth is considered no longer habitable. Some robots go and take care of the humans on a floating space station, while others stay on Earth and clean up the leftover debris. Another group travels back and forth between Earth and the space station looking for signs of life, which would mean that the humans can go back to Earth.

In the real world, NASA (National Aeronautics and Space Administration) has done a great deal of work with robotics. Robotics is the branch of technology that deals with the design, construction, operation, and application of robots. One of NASA's biggest uses of robots is in space exploration. NASA uses robots to travel to and explore places that aren't safe for humans, such as Saturn and Mars.

NASA is preparing for another space exploration mission to Europa Clipper, Saturn's icy moon. It is a high priority to explore due to a salty underground ocean found under the moon's crust. This excursion is planned to take place in the 2020s; it will take NASA several years to develop and create the equipment. Once NASA has access to data from Europa Clipper, it needs to determine if the moon can sustain life. What makes a planet sustainable?

NASA is still designing the robotic tools necessary for this particular mission. Every mission uses different robots for different purposes. How will robots help us determine if Europa Clipper is a habitable moon? Why do companies use robots instead of humans for similar missions? What would it take to design a robot that can collect, preserve, and return evidence of one of the three necessities to sustain life? What would the process of this design and creation look like?

Your challenge will be to create a working model for this mission that can be shared with the education department at NASA, including an argument for why your design is essential to the mission.

A Place for Robots *Rubric*

	Novice	Apprentice	Practitioner	Expert
Design Process Journal: Initial Research (Explore)	includes the purpose of robots and examples of their use in space exploration	includes: ❑ summary of the various uses and purpose of robots ❑ key ideas and details from research ❑ citations for multiple sources	includes: ❑ evidence from informational texts to analyze, reflect, and research space exploration and robotics ❑ relevant information from experiences, print, and digital sources ❑ summary of information in notes ❑ multiple, valid, cited sources to build knowledge about investigation of space exploration and the use of robotics in space	all of *Practitioner* plus, includes an interview with an expert in the field of space exploration or robotics
Design Process Journal: Use of Design Process	documents some of the steps in the Design Process to attempt to create a robotic model	❑ documents all of the steps in the Design Process to create a robotic model ❑ includes both process and reflection notes ❑ states one way to improve design from initial idea	❑ documents, in detail, all steps of the Design Process ❑ provides evidence of reflection and rounding back to earlier stages in the Design Process to improve model ❑ includes relevant information from experiences to provide organized, detailed description of the Design Process in action	all of *Practitioner* plus, provides analysis of errors, and addresses any constraints to the Design Process

	Novice	Apprentice	Practitioner	Expert
Robotic Working Model	reflects design as specified in the Design Journal	❏ functions as specified in the Design Journal ❏ moves based on remote control or programming	❏ functions as specified in the Design Journal ❏ moves based on programming ❏ responds appropriately to obstacles ❏ navigates rough terrain ❏ collects a sample of evidence and preserves the sample for return to Earth	all of *Practitioner* plus: can collect and preserve multiple samples of evidence for sustaining life
Final Proposal	❏ introduction of concepts of robotics used in space exploration ❏ some facts and details ❏ a list of resources used at the end of the proposal	❏ introduction of concepts of robotics used in space exploration as hook ❏ findings presented using the Design Process system view framework ❏ research embedded throughout proposal ❏ sources cited at the end of proposal ❏ opinion is supported with facts and detail to strengthen the argument for the design	❏ introduction with claim supported by research and a logical sequence ❏ integrates information from several texts on robotics or space exploration ❏ cites sources throughout the proposal ❏ includes evidence and direct quotes from multiple credible, timely sources ❏ references using Design Process, showing journey through several attempts at model design ❏ includes words, phrases, and clauses to create cohesion and clarify relationships between claim and evidence ❏ includes concluding statement that supports argument and addresses their audience	all of *Practitioner* plus: includes an online tool, e.g., website to advocate solution beyond the classroom

Appendix H
Rubric to Assess a Benchmark Lesson

	Novice	Apprentice	Practitioner	Expert
Topic	selects a concept (not skill) that is meaningful to the students	selects a concept (not skill) that is key to understanding the content of the unit and is meaningful to the students	selects a concept (not skill) that is key to understanding the content of the unit, is meaningful to the students, and is based upon need as determined by assessment data from the classroom and/or standardized test	all of *Practitioner* plus chooses a title that is provocative, related to the concept/topic
Opening	states the objective of the benchmark up front	explains why the content to be covered is important for the students to know	❏ begins with a reflective question to focus students on the need for the content ❏ uses students' responses, a news story, a metaphor, or some other technique to build a *felt need* for the concept	all of *Practitioner* plus uses a multi-sensory approach to building the *felt need* (e.g., print, sound, visuals, etc.)
Content	a significant amount of content related to the topic, covered quickly	❏ hones content to that which can be reasonably "digested" in 10 minutes ❏ includes at least three clear points	❏ narrowly focused content that can be reasonably "digested" in 10 minutes ❏ a number of clear points made regarding the concept ❏ connects the content to the *ALU* to build a *felt need* to learn related skills ❏ logical presentation sequence that builds to content mastery	all of *Practitioner* plus includes facts, statistics, charts, graphs, video, sound, etc., to illustrate points

	Novice	Apprentice	Practitioner	Expert
Delivery	includes two to three of the six criteria under *Practitioner*	includes four to five of the six criteria under *Practitioner*	❏ repeats key points ❏ speaks clearly, articulates, and uses appropriate volume for the venue ❏ uses pauses to allow the students' brains to process a point ❏ uses appropriately sophisticated vocabulary ❏ does not read from notes or screen; rather, speaks as if knowing the content ❏ makes eye contact with audience	all of *Practitioner* plus uses tone, speed, and volume as tools; uses appropriate metaphors, anecdotes, and/or analogies to make points
Logistics	10–15 minutes in length	❏ 10–15 minutes ❏ all necessary visuals or materials set up in advance	❏ 10–15 minutes ❏ all necessary visuals or materials set up in advance ❏ stands or moves around the room to engage the audience and ensure visibility for all	all of *Practitioner* plus creates a physical room arrangement and ambiance to position the audience for optimal learning
Closing	summarizes key points	❏ summarizes key points ❏ closes with a clear, final statement	❏ reiterates how the related skills will help students in solving the *ALU* problem ❏ summarizes key points ❏ closes with a metaphor, quote, or other technique to punctuate the content	all of *Practitioner* plus ends with a thought-provoking question to promote continued thinking about the content

Appendix I
Learning Styles and
Readiness Grid

When you stand before your class to teach a skill, you can be sure that students are not in the same place cognitively or in terms of learning styles. Consequently, instruction will only be moderately effective. Differentiated instruction involves using varied *learning activities* to meet the needs of all learners. Select a skill you might teach. Consider the student who lacks the prerequisite knowledge to learn the skill, the student who is cognitively ready to learn the skill, and the student who already knows the skill you're about to teach. Then, for each category of student, consider three possible levels of learning style. Brainstorm nine different ways a student could address the same skill, preferably independent of the teacher. You may never have nine different activities going on at the same time for a skill, but you might choose, say, three. These would become choice activities on your *activity list*.

	Distal Zone A student who will be challenged to learn this skill or lacks the prerequisite skills	Proximal Zone A student who is ready to learn this or is on grade level	Current Knowledge A student who is ready to move beyond this or is above grade level
Visual			
Auditory			
Tactile/Kinesthetic			

Appendix J
The "Great Student" Rubric

Version 1

	Novice	Apprentice	Practitioner	Expert *All of Practitioner plus*
Individual Responsibility	comes to class ready to learn: ♦ brings completed homework ♦ has materials and necessary tools ♦ with prompting, starts tasks	♦ starts tasks without prompting from teacher ♦ uses the *help board* rather than interrupting the teacher ♦ completes activities for group work	♦ completes all work to be handed in on time ♦ follows through on all group responsibilities when in need of help: ♦ rereads directions ♦ reviews notes ♦ quietly asks others for help ♦ adds name to *help board* ♦ if unable to continue without help, moves on to something else productive	when finished early, works to improve upon the work to be handed in or works on challenge/ optional activities

(Appendix J continues on next page.)

	Novice	Apprentice	Practitioner	Expert *All of Practitioner plus*
Folder Organization	brings any current and prior work needed for class each day	work is organized to easily access work in progress and completed work	◆ stores current schedule and activity list, direction sheets, current unfinished work, and completed work for the unit in ways that allow easy access ◆ stores papers from previous units at home	able to explain organization strategy and changes made over time
Focus	◆ with prompting from teacher or peer, starts tasks ◆ if off task, with prompting from teacher or peer, resumes task	◆ recognizes loss of focus and gets back on task without teacher or peer prompting ◆ when working individually, chooses a seat to minimize distractions	◆ stays on task throughout an activity ◆ switches from one activity to the next with minimal "down time" ◆ refrains from distracting others ◆ reserves off-task conversations for out-of-class time	can explain the strategies for: ◆ effectively staying focused during school and homework
Participation	participates in group lessons and activities	◆ comes to group lessons and activities prepared ◆ asks and answers questions to clarify content or directions ◆ offers ideas	◆ actively listens to others and relates comments to their contributions ◆ uses text to back up opinions ◆ asks higher-order, content-related questions	◆ offers praise and constructive criticism to peers ◆ accepts and utilizes constructive criticism

Version 2

This *Great Student Rubric* was inspired by Paul Tough's book, *How Children Succeed*.

	Novice *begin reflecting here*	Apprentice	Practitioner *read here first*	Expert *all of Practitioner plus*
Grit and Optimism	◆ sets individual, clear goals for each class ◆ identifies skills and topics that are a struggle and believes growth is possible	◆ perseveres with even difficult tasks ◆ when struggling, identifies reasons behind failure and tries new strategies	◆ consistently hands in quality work on time ◆ persists through challenges to achieve quality work ◆ analyzes failures and setbacks and develops strategy for breaking through	◆ articulates strategies to develop grit ◆ explains how optimism affects success in class
Self-Control	◆ does everything possible to get to school each day ◆ reserves off-task conversations for lunchtime ◆ brings prior work necessary for class each day ◆ meets pacing guide for each class	◆ gets to work right away without reminders ◆ maintains appropriate volume in class ◆ identifies at least two strategies to stay focused in class ◆ resists distraction ◆ uses directions to increase success	◆ uses rubric to help guide learning throughout the unit ◆ accurately self-checks work in class ◆ uses directions and notes to help answer questions before asking others ◆ refrains from distracting others ◆ refrains from interrupting others when speaking	◆ explains organizational strategies and changes made over time ◆ explains the strategies used for effectively managing time in school and at home

(Appendix J continues on next page.)

	Novice *begin reflecting here*	Apprentice	Practitioner *read here first*	Expert *all of Practitioner plus*
Collaboration: Gratitude and Social Intelligence	◆ identifies a clear role during partner or small-group work ◆ is polite to peers (including *please* and *thank you*) ◆ is polite to teacher (including *please* and *thank you*) ◆ keeps temper in check	◆ adapts to different social situations ◆ allows others to speak without interruption (actively listens) ◆ follows through on partner or small-group responsibilities ◆ helps group meet goals ◆ works to resolve differences with others	◆ able to find solutions to conflicting opinions with others ◆ shows appreciation ◆ puts forth effort to make a difference for others in class ◆ makes suggestions to group to work more effectively	assists group members in reaching consensus and resolving conflict
Curiosity and Zest	identifies topics in class that are interesting/ exciting to explore	demonstrates enthusiasm for learning and applying content	◆ asks questions to aid in learning more effectively ◆ approaches new situations with excitement and energy	makes real-world connections (can be cross-subject) to content from class without prompting

Tough, P. (2012). *How children succeed: Grit, curiosity, and the hidden power of character*. New York: Houghton Mifflin Harcourt.

Version 3: For primary students

	Learning	Practicing	Got It!
I'm Ready to Learn	◆ I need reminders to bring work, books, pencils, or other tools. ◆ I get to work when told.	◆ I come to class with all tools needed to learn. ◆ I get my work done right away without being told.	all of Practicing plus checks the board for any changes or information from the teacher before getting to work
I'm Responsible	◆ I complete most work on time. ◆ I find a safe place to store my papers and other items so I don't lose them.	◆ I complete all my work on time. ◆ I meet all deadlines.	all of Practicing plus when finished early, works to improve the work before handing in
I Pay Attention	◆ I usually stay on task. ◆ I can quickly get back on task with a reminder from teacher or classmates.	◆ I stay on task. ◆ I quickly get back on task when distracted. ◆ I keep off-task conversations for lunch or free time.	all of Practicing plus takes steps to stay focused including moving to a better workspace to reduce distractions
I Can Work With Others	◆ I can carry out my role with reminders. ◆ I try to share my materials and space.	◆ I work with my team to decide on roles and jobs. ◆ I can carry out my role effectively. ◆ I share material and space.	all of Practicing plus makes sure that all group members have opportunities at all roles, materials, and classroom spaces
I Manage My Time	◆ I can plan my schedule with help. ◆ I try to stick with my schedule. ◆ I can explain why some activities took more or less time.	◆ I can plan my schedule without help. ◆ I can complete activities within the time limits. ◆ I can adjust my plan as needed while still meeting expectations.	all of Practicing plus I can explain my strategies for planning and scheduling to others

Appendix K
Creating a Culture of
#STEMLATIC

INSTRUCTIONAL BALANCE:	Scientific Method ❑ Seeks to explain what exists	Engineering Design Process ❑ Seeks to design that which does not exist

	Scientist	Technologist	Engineer	Mathematician
STEM MINDSETS	*NGSS Cross-Cutting Concepts* ❑ Patterns ❑ Cause and Effect ❑ Scale, Proportion, and Quantity ❑ Systems and System Models ❑ Energy and Matter: Flows, Cycles, and Conservation ❑ Structure and Function ❑ Stability and Change	❑ Information Retrieval ❑ Communication ❑ Collaboration ❑ Simulation ❑ Modeling ❑ Design ❑ Presentation	*Design Process* ❑ Formulate ❑ Explore ❑ Ideate ❑ Sift ❑ Simulate ❑ Advocate	*Math Practice Standards* ❑ Make sense of problems and persevere in solving them ❑ Reason abstractly and quantitatively ❑ Construct viable arguments; critique others' reasoning ❑ Model with mathematics ❑ Use appropriate tools strategically ❑ Attend to precision ❑ Look for and make use of structure ❑ Look for and express regularity in repeated reasoning

	Engagement (not compliance)	Student Responsibility for Learning	Academic Rigor
LATIC	❑ Felt Need ❑ Problem-Based Learning ❑ Audience ❑ Belonging—Collaboration ❑ Executive Function (access)	❑ Self-Assessment ❑ Goal Setting ❑ Scheduling Time ❑ Resource Sign-Up ❑ Peer Experts	❑ Higher-Order Thinking ❑ Content Application ❑ Strong Rubric ❑ "Reach" Expert Column ❑ Teacher Facilitation

Index

Note: Page numbers in italics indicate figures.

Bach, Cyndie 3
benchmark lessons: analytic rubrics and 55; concepts and 82, 95, 112; conducting 90–94, 123; co-teaching and 213; example of 92; learning map and 85; opting out of 94–95; primacy-recency effect 91; priming plan and 210; problem-based tasks and 90; recording 99; rubrics for 94, 258–259; scaffold for learning and 30, 89, 94; whole-class 90–94, 116
Bloom, Benjamin 159
Bloom's Taxonomy 160, 187
Book of Learning and Forgetting, The (Smith) 28
brainstorming: analytic rubrics and 53, 54, 72, 249, 253; collaborative learning and 107, 110, 178, 198–200; home groups and 122; learning activities and 115–116; problem-based tasks and 32–34, 41–42; real-world problems and 36–37, 209; scaffold for learning and 88; skill building 260; teachers and 175; tools for 199
breakpoint formative assessment 165, 165, 166–167
Building Executive Function (Sulla) 173, 224
"Butterfly Garden": activity lists 130, 131, 132; analytic rubric for 52, 239–242; application of knowledge in 132; context for 29; life cycle unit 29, 238

"Can a Frog, Turtle, and Fish Help Us?": analytic rubrics and 48, 68, 247; inventions and 47, 246
cause-and-effect relationships 71, 192
choice activities 129–130
Choice Theory (Glasser) 119
classic learning 28
classroom design: collaborative work space in 178–179; computer areas 180; desks in 175–179, 184; discourse centers in 180; dual-purpose furniture in 184; flexible seating in 176–177, 185; "hoteling" in 179; individual work space in 179; interactive whiteboards in 183; limited-resource area 182; media-based collaboration 183–184; meeting areas 181; personal-space structures in 175–176; quality work board 182; resource and folder area 180–181; sign-up sheets in 179; small-group mini-lesson area 181; student input 227; student responsibility for 185; teacher's desk in 181, 184–185; walls in 182, 189–190

clover tables 178–179
cognitive levels 68–69
Coleman, James 152–153, 200
collaborative learning: brainstorming and 107, 110, 178, 198–200; in the classroom 200; computer technology and 107; conflicts in 199–200; consensus and 107; media-based 183–184; problem-based tasks 37, 42, 107, 198; roadblocks in 198–199; structure of 198; team norms of engagement in 198
collaborative work space 178
communities: problem-based tasks and 34, 209, 220; social capital and 152–153, 200–201; student interaction with 192, 202
compliance model 8
comprehension questions 162–163
comprehensive formative assessments 165, 165, 167
computer technology: classroom design for 180; classroom use of 194; collaborative learning and 107; digital generation and 14–15; efficacy and 5–6; global citizenship and 191–192; infusion of 192–193; integration of 192–193; introduction of 3; just-in-time-learning 193; learning activities and 116, 194; mindsets for 216; multiple means of representation in 194; podcasts and 97–98; problem-based tasks and 193; QR codes 98; quality work and 140; screencasts and 97–98; skills in 82; teacher facilitation and 29; videos and 97–98; virtual classrooms 222
concepts: benchmark lessons and 82, 90, 93–95, 112, 121; comprehensive assessments and 167; connected learning and 197; content facilitation grid 159, 169–170; cross-disciplinary 216; executive function skills and 187, 224; graphic organizer for 42, 43; how-to sheets 111; learning activities and 80; peer experts and 138; problem-based tasks and 34–35, 79, 190; skill building and 113; small-group mini-lessons and 30
Conceptual Blockbusting (Adams) 38
connected learning: in the classroom 197–198; concepts and 197; problem-based tasks and 197–198
connection questions 163
consensus 107

content: application questions 163; assessing time spent on 42–44; authentic contexts for 38–39; comprehension questions 162–163; connection questions 163; extended 68–69; facilitation questions and 162–163; graphic organizer for 42–43, *43*; homework and 110; meaning and 38–39; metacognition questions 164; open-ended problems and 44; reinforcing 110; synthesis questions 163–164

content facilitation grid: concepts and skills in 159, 169–170; example of *171*, 236; formative assessment data and 154, 159; structure of 159; student progress and 170, 173; weekly 170

contrived equilibrium 19–20

Control Theory (Glasser) 119

cooperative learning 198

co-teaching classrooms: benchmark lessons and 213; classroom design 185; dual-focus facilitation 213; equality in 214; group and guiding in 213; high social capital and 201; inclusive 18, 212; individualized inspiration in 213–214; instructional design and 205; Response to Intervention (RTI) and 212

Creating a Food Chain: differentiation grid *113*; differentiation grid for proximal and distal zones *114*, *115*

creative thinking 31

critical thinking 31, 199

Csikszentmihalyi, Mihaly 82, *82*

cultural acceptance 192

curricular standards: Authentic Learning Unit (ALU) design and 34, 42; content and 42

Daches, Alysse 3

De Bono, Edward 199

"Designer Pizza": analytic rubrics for 64, 226, 233–235; content facilitation grid 236; facilitation questions 237; felt need and 29, 35–36; fractions unit 29, 35–36, 64–65, 226, 232–233; learning map *85*, *112*; as problem-based task 29, 65; skills in 35–36; surveys and 84; transfer task and 76

design process: advocating in 218; analytic rubrics and 49, *52*; depiction of *217*; exploring in 217; formulating 217; guiding instruction with 218–219; ideating in 217; scientific method in 216; sifting in

218; simulating in 218; STEM/STEAM education 43, 216

desks 175–179, 184

differentiated learning activities: benchmark lessons 89–94; learning styles in 86, *86*, 87; participatory structures in 87–89; practice activities and 87; student engagement and 78–80, 83, 87; zone of proximal development (ZPD) and 113, *113*, 114, *114*, 115, *115*

differentiation grids *113*, *114*, 115, *115*

digital generation: characteristics of 14; effects of technology on 14–15; how-to podcasts, screencasts and video 100

digital resource area 138

discourse centers 180

dual-focus facilitation 213

dynamic disequilibrium 19

education: compliance model 8; efficacy model 8–9; global citizenship and 7, 192–193; purpose and 5; reality pedagogy 9; *see also* learning

educational equity: high academic standards in 189, 219–220; learning activities and 219; opportunities for instruction and 219; resources for 219; tools for learning and 219

efficacy model: empowerment and 9, 150; facilitation of learning and 173–174; purpose and 5, 22–23; student engagement and 8–9; technology and 5–6

Emdin, Christopher 9

empowerment: efficacy model and 9, 150; executive function skills and 124, 136; student responsibility for learning and 118–119, 124, 136

English language learners: home groups for 122; individualized learning and 221; instructional design and 205; social environments for 221

equity-focused instruction *see* educational equity

executive function skills: categorizing information 71; cause-and-effect relationships 71; empowerment and 124, 129, 136; facilitation grid for *172*; higher-order thinking and 187; kindergarten 126; learning dashboard and 140–141; life skills and *172*, 173, 224; multiple points of view and 71; predicting outcomes 71; student

hands-on learning styles 86

Heifetz, Ron 8

help boards: classroom space for 182; peer experts and 108; students and 12, 118, 139; teachers and 139; time spent on 139

high academic standards: analytic rubrics and 69, 189–190; in the classroom 190; classroom wall materials and 189–190; educational equity and 189; word choice and 189–190

higher cognitive levels 68–69

higher-order, open-ended thinking: in the classroom 188; collaborative learning and 107, 178; evaluation and 160; executive function skills and 187; facilitation of learning and 152, 162, 188–189; learning activities and 109; problem-based tasks and 188; synthesis and 160

high social capital: academic performance and 201; advantages of 201; in the classroom 201–202; communities and 200–201; *see also* social capital

holistic rubrics 58, 76

home groups: belonging and 121–122; brainstorming and 122; brainstorming in 122; size and composition of 122; sociograms and 211; student selection of 123; table journals and 141

homework: cognitive benefits of 108; design of 109; final presentations and 110; peripheral content as 109; practice activities and 109; purpose for 109–110; reinforcing content in 110

"hoteling" 179

how-to podcasts: audio scripts for 98; auditory learning styles and 99; skill building and 97–98, 100

how-to screencasts: auditory learning styles and 99; images for *99*; skill building and 97–98, 100; voice-over in 98

how-to sheets: just-in-time-learning and 97; learning centers and 105; resource area 118; skill building and 96–97, *97*, 98, 113; visual learning styles and 99

how-to videos: learning activities and 79; skill building and 97–98, 100; small-group mini-lessons and 99–100

IDE Corp. 2, 36, 56, 86, 120, *217*, 228

IEP goals 140

inclusive classrooms 18, 212

independent learning: analytic rubrics and 136–137; how-to sheets and 96; learning centers and 104

individualized inspiration 213–214

individual learning activities 107, 116

individual learning paths: activity lists and 195; in the classroom 195; learning activities and 194–195; learning dashboard 195; student responsibility for learning and 194–195

individual work space 179

instructional design: academic rigor and 12–13; adaptive change and 19–20; analytic rubrics 12; critical goals for 9–13, *13*; framework for 17–20; paradigm shift in 28, *28*, 29; problem-based learning and 33; small-group mini-lessons 12; strategies for 22; student engagement and 10–11; student responsibility for learning 11–12

interactive websites and applications *see* Internet

interactive whiteboards 183

Internet 129; choice activities and 129; interactive websites and applications 80, 104, 106, 129; learning activities and 80, 104; real-world problems and 37; teacher facilitation and 29

just-in-time-learning 97, 193

kindergarten: activity lists 127, *127*, 128; analytic rubrics 59, 65, 123; home groups in 121–122; learning activities 95–96; priming plan task 208–209; scheduling in 126–129; time management and 17; unit length for 33, 35

kinesthetic/tactile learning style 113, 260

LATIC *see* Learner-Active Technology-Infused Classrooms

Learner-Active, Technology-Infused Classrooms: adaptive change and 19–20; authentic tasks and 39; classroom design in 175–176; co-teaching and 211–214; critical goals for 9–10, *13*; design process 216–219; efficacy and 5, 9, 150; empowerment and 150; English language learners and 205, 221; equity-focused instruction 219–220; executive function skills and 224; facilitation of learning in 154–155, 161, 173; framework for teaching and learning in 17–20, 26, 205, 230; gifted learners and 222–223; instructional approaches and 225; interdependence in 153; Multi-Tier System of Supports (MTSS) and 212; priming plan 205–211, 230; principles and paradigm shifts in 187–204; problem-based learning and 16, 25–26, 29, 31–33; Response to Intervention (RTI) and 211–212; rubrics and 227–228, 229, 230; social capital and 201; STEM/ STEAM education 18, 205, 214–216, 266; student engagement and 8–9; student responsibility for learning 120–121; systems map of 146, 147; three pillars of 26, 26; time management and 17, 124–125; Universal Design for Learning (UDL) and 205, 220–221; virtual 222

Learner-Active, Technology-Infused Schools 225–226, 231

learning: classic 28; felt need and 27–28, 33, 45; instructional path for 89; official 28; state of flow and 82; see also education; problem-based learning

learning activities: brainstorming 115–116; cognitive readiness and 80; collaborative 107; components of 80; computer-based 116, 194; defining 95; directions in 96; feedback in 96; global citizenship and 192; grading 202–203; how-to sheets 96; individual 107, 116; Internet and 104; learning centers as 104–105; learning map and 83–85, 110–111; level of 80; non-teacher intensive 21; scaffold for learning 112; skill building 95–96; structure for 21–22, 22; student engagement and 79; task management grid 168–169; teacher facilitation and 109; teacher-intensive 21; time management and 21; zone of proximal development (ZPD) and 80–82; see also differentiated learning activities

learning centers: categories in 104–105; defining 104; design of 105–106; how-to sheets and 105; as independent activities 104–105; sign-up sheets for 106, 143–144

learning dashboard: example of 141; executive function skills and 140–141; IEP goals 140; individual progress and 140–141; self-assessment and 195, 227; student-designed 227

learning map: analytic rubrics and 111; benchmark lessons and 85; concepts and skills in 84–85, 111–112; design of 83; example of 111, 112; how-to sheets 111; learning activities in 110–111; peer experts and 84–85; scaffold for learning and 111

learning styles: auditory 86, 99, 260; differentiated learning activities and 86, 86, 87; felt need and 87; hands-on 86; kinesthetic/tactile 113, 260; readiness grid 260; visual 86, 96, 99, 260

Learning Styles and Readiness Grid 115, 194

leveling up approach: facilitation questions and 159; learning challenges and 157; skill building and 82–83

lifelong learning 119, 196

life skills: changing plans as 103, 144; executive function skills and 173, 224

limited-resource area 182

limited-resource sign-up sheets: benchmark lessons for 144; classroom resources and 141, 143; classroom space and 179; example of 143; learning centers and 106, 143–144; student scheduling and 141, 143–144; time management and 128

Linksy, Marty 8

low social capital 201; see also social capital

math practice standards 216

McTighe, J. 76

meaning: content and 13, 24, 38–39; context and 38; felt need and 29; homework and 108–109; information and 11–12, 38; skill building for 95

media-based collaboration 183–184

meeting areas 181

metacognition questions 164

metacognitive leaps 68–69

multiage classrooms 227

Multi-Tier System of Supports (MTSS) 18, 212

Next Generation Science Standards 215

non-teacher intensive activities 21

note-taking skills 93

official learning 28

"Oh, The Places We Can Go!": analytic rubrics and 53–54, 71, 72–73, 74–75, 250–251, 253–254; problem-based tasks 248, 252 open-ended problems: collaborative learning and 107; creative thinking and 31–32; curricular content in 44; felt need and 40; grappling with content in 32, 40, 42; student engagement and 31–32, 40–41

participatory structures: scaffold for learning and 87–89, 110, 129; small-group mini-lessons 93

peer expert board 108, 138

peer experts: defining 107; effectiveness of 107–108; help boards and 108; learning activities and 79; learning map and 84–85; scaffold for learning and 30; small-group mini-lessons and 104, 108; student responsibility for learning and 138

"Place for Robots": analytic rubric for 256–257; robotics design 43, 255–256; targeted content in 43

Planning a Playground 66, 70

PMI (Plus, Minus, and Interesting) 199

podcasts see how-to podcasts

points of view 71

practice activities: defining 96; as homework 109; student engagement and 87, 89; task management grid 168–169

predicting outcomes 71

Prensky, Marc 82

primacy-recency effect 91

priming plan: activities for 210; benchmark lessons in 210; Great Student Rubric in 210–211; initial engagement 206–208, 230; introduction of 205–206; problem-based tasks 209–210; sociograms 211; student responsibility for learning and 207–208; task in 208–210

problem-based learning: activity lists 30; analytic rubrics and 29; defining 25n1; felt need and 25, 29–30, 35, 190–191, 225; scaffold for learning 30; small-group mini-lessons in 30; student engagement and 24–25; teacher facilitation and 29–30

problem-based tasks: analytic rubrics and 57; application of 36; authenticity and relevance in 38–39; benchmark lessons 90; brainstorming and 32–34, 41–42; collaboration and 37, 42, 198; computer technology and 193; concepts and skills in 116; connected learning and 197–198; curricular standards in 35; felt need

and 30, 37, 76, 79; final product in 63; generating ideas in 110; higher-order thinking and 107, 188; learning map and 112; motivation and 123; open-ended 31–32, 40–41, 107; priming plan 209–210; real-world situations in 32, 37; resource area and 124; small-groups and 32; student-designed 226; student responsibility for 15–16, 31–32; teacher-designed 25–26; teacher facilitation and 138

problem-based task statement 34, 44–45, 121, 124

problem solving 199

project-based learning 25n1

pull-out programs 134

QR codes 98

quality work board: classroom space for 182; digital examples of 140; high-quality work on 139–140

readiness grid 260

reality pedagogy 9

real-world problems: brainstorming 36–37, 209; content and 44; design process for 218; ideas for 37; learning activities 39; problem-based tasks and 32, 215; student engagement and 160, 197, 215–216

reflection: collaborative learning and 199; self-assessment and 165, 226; shifting paradigms and 183; student focus and 91, 123–124; student progress and 133–134; table journals and 119, 133–134, 141, 148; teachers and 20, 22–23

reflective practitioners 20

relevance 38–39

required activities 130

resource area: analytic rubrics and 124; digital 138, 181; how-to sheets 118; organization of 137–138; sign-up sheets for 106; student responsibility for learning and 137–138, 180–181; task statements in 124

Response to Intervention (RTI) 18, 205, 211–212

roadblock management chart 199

Rose, David 220

RTI see Response to Intervention (RTI)

rubrics: as assessment 57–58, 76; benchmark lessons and 258–259; Great Student Rubrics 210–211, 261–265; holistic 58, 76;

LATIC 227–228; student-designed 226; as technical change 8; *see also* analytic rubrics

scaffold for learning: activity lists 30, 125–126; benchmark lessons 30, 89, 94; brainstorming and 88; components of 88, *88*, 89; interactive websites and applications 106; learning activities and 84, 112, 116; learning map and 111; participatory structures 110; practice activities and 89; skill building 95

scheduling: benchmark lessons on 128; cognitive levels and 136; empowerment and 136; instruction in 133; kindergarten 126–129; limited resource sign-up sheets and 141, 143–144; pull-out programs and 134; *see also* time management

schools: LATIC 225–226, 231; past practices in 7–8; society and 6; *see also* education

scientific method 216

screencasts *see* how-to screencasts

second grade: home groups in 122; priming plan task 209; problem-based tasks in 209; rubrics and 55, 124; scheduling in 125–126; task statements in 124; unit length for 33, 35

self-assessment: analytic rubrics and 125, 136; learning dashboard 195; reflection and *165*, 226; small-group mini-lessons and 144–145; students and 103, 120, 125, 194–195, 226–227

sign-up sheets: learning centers 106; small-group mini-lessons 144–145, *145*, 145; *see also* limited resource sign-up sheets

six hats method 199

skill building: brainstorming 260; differentiated learning activities 113–114; felt need and 97; how-to podcasts 97–100; how-to screencasts 97–100; how-to sheets 96–99, 113; how-to videos 97–98, 100; leveling up approach to 82–83; scaffold for learning and 95; small-group mini-lessons and 84, 100–101; zone of proximal development (ZPD) and 83, 112–113

small-group mini-lessons: academically-focused 100–101; classroom space for 181; co-teaching and 213; direct instruction and 145; gifted learners and 103; how-to sheets and 97; how-to videos and 99–100; instructional design and 12, 79; note-taking skills 93; peer experts and 104, 108; problem-based learning and 30;

scheduling 102–104; self-assessment and 103, 144–145; sign-up sheets for 144–145, *145*, 145; skills and 84, 100–103; social capital and 201; structure of 101–103; student engagement and 25; time slots for 102

small learning communities (SLC) 153

Smith, Frank 28

social capital: advantages of 153; community relationships and 152–153; small-group mini-lessons and 201; social networks and 200; teachers and 152, 181; *see also* high social capital

social networks 200

society 6, 191

sociograms 211

Sousa, D. 12

special education students 132

#STEMLATIC 266

STEM/STEAM education: computer technology and 214; content and 43; creating a culture of 266; design process in 43, 216; instructional design and 18, 205; integration of 214–215; learning centers and 105, 180; mindsets for 215, *216*; moral imperative of 215, *216*; problem-based tasks and 215; workforce needs 214–215

student-directed formative assessments 165, *165*, 167

student engagement: differentiated learning activities and 78–80, 83, 87; efficacy model and 8–9; first day 206–208; instructional design and 10–11; open-ended problems and 31–32, 40–41; problem-based learning and 24–25; real-world problems and 160, 197, 215–216; scavenger hunts 206, 208; state of flow and 82

student responsibility for learning: administrative functions and 136; analytic rubrics and 136–137; in the classroom 197; decision-making and 196; empowerment and 118–119, 124, 136, 196; executive function skills and 136, 196, 224; help boards 138–139; individual learning paths and 194–195; instructional design and 11–12; lifelong learning and 196; limited resource sign-up sheets and 143–144; peer experts and 138; problem-based tasks and 16; reflection and 133–134; resource area 137–138; scheduling 135–136; school progression of 226; self-assessment and 144–145, 196; skill building and 119–120; structures for 124, 146, 148; teacher facilitation and 120–121; time management and 16–17, 21–22, 124–126, 133; trigger awareness paradigm in 203

students: achievement by 135; collaborative learning and 107; connected learning and 197; empowerment and 202, 206–207, 226–227; home groups and 121–123; learning dashboard 226–227; problem design and 226; reflection and 226; rubric design and 226; self-assessment and 103, 120, 125, 194–195, 226–227; skill building and 6; *see also* peer experts

student work folders: analytic rubrics and 135; benchmark lessons for 134; digital 121, 134; executive function skills and 224; holistic assessment and 135; management of 224; organization of 134; resource area for 180–181; two-pocket 121, 134, 224

Sulla, N. 173, 224

summative assessment 164–165

synthesis questions 163–164

table journals: digital 141; example of *142*; home group effectiveness and 141; reflection and 119, 133–134, 141, 148

tables 178–179

Tapscott, Don 14

task management grid 168, *169*, 168–169

task-rubric partnership 57, *57*, 58

task statements *see* problem-based task statement

teacher-intensive activities 21

teachers: as bridge builders 95, 104, 120, 202–203, 206, 222, 225; conference sign-up sheets 144; empowerment and 202; empowerment paradigm 202; as facilitator 26, 29–30, 120–121, 138–139, 202, 206; felt need paradigm 202; as GPS 149–150; grading paradigm 202–203; help boards and 139; journaling and 19–20, 22, 121; LATIC rubric and 227–228, *229*, 230; reflection and 20, 22–23; social capital and 201; trigger awareness paradigm 203

teacher's desk 181, 184–185

technical change 8

technology *see* computer technology

temperature gauge formative assessments 165, *165*, 166

third grade: analytic rubrics for 49, 55; creation of lesson plans in 108; home groups in 122; priming plan task 209; scheduling 118, 125; student engagement 207; student work folders 135; unit length for 33, 35

time management: activity lists and 125–126, 133; felt need and 126; student responsibility for 16–17, 21–22, 124–126, 133

transfer task 76, 203

"Tree of Whys" 36–37, *37*

UDL *see* Universal Design for Learning (UDL)

unintended consequences 71

Universal Design for Learning (UDL): computer technology and 194; framework of 220; guidelines for 220–221; instructional design and 205, 220

"Using Numbers and Words to Feed Others": analytic rubrics and 49, 64, 123–124, 244–245; learning map 83–84, *84*, *111*; mixing content in 35; problem-based tasks 35, 243

video gaming 82–83

video recording 100; *see also* how-to videos

virtual classrooms 222

visual learning styles 86, 96, 99, 260

vocabulary 189–190

Vygotsky, Lev 80, 82, 112

websites and applications *see* Internet

whole-class lessons: benchmark lessons 90–94, 116; class sets of materials for 105; concepts and 82; ineffectiveness of 80, 87

Wiggins, W. 76

World is Flat, The (Friedman) 191

Wright, Frank Lloyd 220

zone of proximal development (ZPD): body of knowledge and 80–81; components of *81*; differentiated learning activities 83, *113*, 114, *114*, 115, *115*; skill building 112–113